W9-BPL-190

*f***P**

LET'S FIX IT!

Overcoming the Crisis in Manufacturing

RICHARD J. SCHONBERGER

THE FREE PRESS

NEW YORK LONDON TORONTO SYDNEY SINGAPORE

*f*P

THE FREE PRESS
A Division of Simon & Schuster, Inc.
1230 Avenue of the Americas
New York, NY 10020

THE FREE PRESS and colophon are trademarks of Simon & Schuster, Inc.

For information regarding special discounts for bulk purchases,
please contact Simon & Schuster Special Sales:
1-800-456-6798 or business@simonandschuster.com

Designed by Lisa Chovnick

Manufactured in the United States of America

10   9   8   7   6   5   4   3   2   1

Library of Congress Cataloging-in-Publication Data
Schonberger, Richard.
Let's fix it! : overcoming the crisis in manufacturing / Richard J. Schonberger.
p. cm.
Includes bibliographical references (p.) and index.
1. Industrial management.   2. Manufacturing industries—Management.   I. Title.
HD31 .S3384 2001
670'.68—dc21   2001050117

ISBN 0-7432-1551-6

CONTENTS

Forget about stock market prices. By the time this book gets into your hands, share prices may be way up, way down, or in between. Neither stock prices nor their recent direction will tell you anything about industrial competitiveness. That is a matter that requires digging much more deeply.

We've done the digging. Actually, we've probed and plumbed with research encompassing the past half century. And, with companion research, we've plunged forward with projections into the next ten or twenty years.

Alarm bells should be ringing. The analysis shows that many of the renowned exemplars of continuous improvement aren't improving anymore, lean thinking and six sigma notwithstanding. As Kermit the Frog didn't quite say, it isn't easy staying lean.

If this were 1970, we shouldn't be concerned. Back then, global markets were largely closed. Economic and political barriers were the norm, getting in the way of finding new markets. More to the point, the barriers insulated manufacturers from competition other than local/regional. No more. The new world economy opens the door to competitive assaults from anywhere, the more so as we move forward toward 2010, 2020, and 2030. John Chambers, CEO of Cisco Systems, describes the new era as one in which "everything gets cheaper forever. The ability to [compare] prices from 1,000 [competitors] rather than three will drive down prices."[1] Call it, if you will, hypercompetition. For prestigious manufacturers to be showing up as smug and complacent in such a time should be, for them and their stakeholders, unsettling.

In this book we suggest the following reasons for the blunting of competitive edges in such a time:

- Complacency—a societal, industrial, and national tendency.

- Stock-hyping deals that divert attention from "the basics" of world-class excellence.

- New, job-hopping managers; no trial-by-fire experience.

- Retention of old, nonprofitable customers and SKUs.

- Retention of command and control.

■ Legacies of bad equipment, systems, and job designs.

■ Disjointed and narrowly focused world-class implementations.

Chapter 1 gives complacency a full treatment, and elaborates briefly on the other six factors. Further commentary and examples follow in other chapters.

The challenge in doing the research and writing this book is the subject matter: the ill-defined field of management. Moreover, it is management of manufacturing companies, which are overwhelming, interwoven mixtures of things to be managed. The endless succession of management fads testifies to the field's instability. It begs for grounding not only in verifiable, cross-checked facts, but also in inferences drawn from wide-ranging sights, sounds, snippets, tendencies, examples, and short- and long-term trends. The latter—the trends—support a fair amount of the content of this book. That is to say, this book is about trends in industrial renewal.

The aims of the book are ambitious. The book's messages will not fully convince the spectrum of its potential readership: executives, team leaders, investors, the business press, economists, professors and students, and natural-born skeptics. The book's foundation, though, is research—three streams of it. It's time for research. In the business world, research typically lags development of new ideas and applications.

The current business knowledge renaissance dates back to about 1980, when the West discovered the Toyota system and total quality. Since then, Big Business Books have appeared with numbing regularity on best-seller lists, alongside potboilers by Danielle Steel. Mainly, they have been war-story books. They have named names, telling what, where, when, and how companies, especially manufacturers, were able to rise up from basket-case fates to renewed industrial prominence. Tom Peters's books set the tone. My own four preceding books on simplicity and what it means to be a world-class manufacturing company were of the same genre.

That such books are based on stories and anecdotes is not to deny the validity of their content. What was in my own books was correct, still valid, and in no need of retraction. (Except that in the first one, *Japanese Manufacturing Techniques: Nine Hidden Lessons in Simplicity*,[2] the word *worker* appeared frequently. The word has long since been abolished from my vocabulary, since it implies a two-class system of thinker-managers and doer-worker-bees—not at all world class.) The same goes, I think, for similar-themed early and mid-1980s books by Robert Hall, Roy Harmon, and Kyoshi Suzaki. Since we were early-stage learners, relying on limited observation, the longevity of our messages is a bit surprising.

Straight war-story books don't attract much attention anymore, nor should they (especially those that wrap their points around the nameless, such as "a well-known Fortune 500 diversified manufacturer"). It is not that inferences drawn from the case studies of Hewlett-Packard and Milliken and Company (or unnamed X, Inc.) cry out for "proof." Since their success stories are so much infused with a formula of low-cost simplicity and customer-focused common sense, we believe. (On the other hand are claims of superior performance tied to complex, high-cost automated equipment, inscrutable information technologies, or fuzzy notions about leadership and swinging on ropes together in the wilderness. These are the kinds of claims that beg the question "Where's the hard evidence?")

This book, as with its predecessors, names names most of the time, and says what, where, when, and how. It continues, as well, in advocating the by now well-tested prescriptions, but with many additions. The interrelated concepts and techniques going by words like "lean" and "world class" have been fused together. They form a cohesive system of assessment and application. The underpinnings are emergent principles. They stand the tests of time and sense. They are nourished, not replaced, by the best ideas from each new management movement—from reengineering to six sigma, and from activity-based costing to balanced scorecards. World-class principles-based management is all about coping with hypercompetitiveness. The upcoming chapters explain, with collected data, why they must be the standard of excellence in the twenty-first century.

1

Complacency

The law of entropy has it that all things tend to run down. Only by importing negentropy—applied information—can we stave off this fate. Beavers possess the know-how (information) to keep water from swiftly taking its entropic course—downhill. Man continually innovates and uses the resulting information to make water climb uphill, keeping crops irrigated and toilets flushing on the uppermost floors of skyscrapers.

Nations and companies run down, too. Their declines follow from not innovating, not applying new information to combat entropy. In social systems such failings often take the form of *complacency.*

Through much of the twentieth century the United States was the world's manufacturing colossus. By the 1970s decline was apparent and the cover-story topic of any number of business publications. Telling research shows that the downslide actually began in the 1950s. Later, by applying new ideas (some borrowed, others homegrown), U.S. industry renewed itself and regained its global industrial supremacy. The United Kingdom, then continental Europe, followed suit.

The same patterns of ascendancy and decline—and the need for renewal—take place in every country and region. We've seen it in Japan, with its own extended period of economic malaise. Japan had sloughed off the devastation of World War II to emerge dominant in world markets for automobiles, machine tools, and a cornucopia of consumer electronics. The principal driving force was innovations in industrial management that originated mainly in the Toyota family of companies. The Toyota system—just-in-time and related concepts of rooting out wastes and delays—was fully developed by 1970. Those innovations pumped the Japanese economy for another two decades as other companies installed their own versions of Toyota concepts. By the nineties, however, the competitive engine had run out of gas (life-giving new knowledge).

Manufacturers in other countries got a late start. Simplistic explanations of Japan's success (community of the rice fields, quality control circles) had diverted attention. Finally, in the early 1980s, Toyota's get-lean success formula was out in the open. What happened next is remarkable: Western industry (mainly in the United States, at first) avidly learned and applied—and then began to innovate itself. By the late 1980s the United States had taken the baton. It became the globe's fount of new ideas on how to manage a manufacturing enterprise.

Chapter 2 summarizes the most important Japanese innovations, pre-1980s, and the equally notable contributions of the West, late 1980s and 1990s. The body of this chapter probes the complacency problem, especially for manufacturing companies. Main topics are the rising importance of good management, how to size up competitive strength, and why manufacturing leaders fade.

MANAGEMENT: THE DIFFERENTIATOR

When it comes to countries, competitiveness may be measured by economic numbers such as gross domestic product. More to the point, for this book's purpose, is competitiveness for a business—most specifically a manufacturer. Earnings and market share are inadequate. They tell where the company was, not where it is going. All too often a company has its best year ever and two or three years later is in a death spiral.

Digital Equipment Corp. (DEC) comes to mind. In 1987 the company's

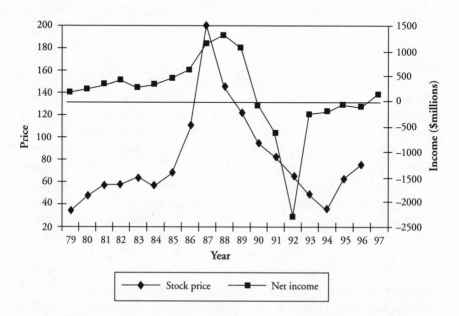

Exhibit 1.1. Common Stock Price and Net Income at Digital Equipment Corp.

common stock price hit its all-time high, and cocksure executives leased the *QE II* ocean liner for the three thousand–odd guests invited to its spare-no-expense DECWORLD extravaganza. Exhibit 1.1 shows, one year later, DEC's spectacular rise in earnings suddenly reversing itself and its common stock price falling as far and fast as it had risen. In 1998 DEC was gone, absorbed by Compaq Computer.

Some companies luck out. They stumble upon a technology that gives an instant competitive edge, covering up what may be serious management flaws. Superior companies will take luck but do not rely on it. They import and self-generate two kinds of vitalizing information. One is best management practices. The second is improved technologies and new products emergent through application of superior management concepts.

We are saying, then, that good management is the differentiator. Even economists, who are given to explaining all economic twists and turns in terms of fiscal and monetary policies, have been forced to recognize that management can make a difference. Notably, what catches economists' eyes is, of late, the unusual behavior of inventories, along with a possible dampening of the business cycle. The conventional wisdom is that when the economy booms, inventories grow massively; then, before long, warehouses bulge, so producers retrench and the boom turns into bust—until inventories become

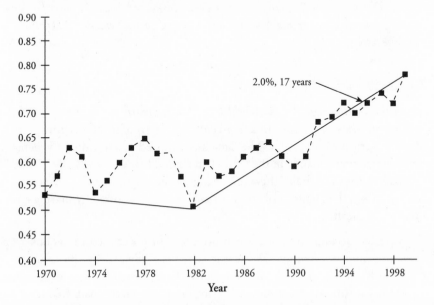

Exhibit 1.2. U.S. Manufacturing Shipments to Inventories, 1970–1999
Source: U.S. Census Bureau, Statistical Abstract of the United States
Shipments and inventories are both measured in dollars.

scarce, which re-ignites the boom. That cycle could be depended upon, until the early 1980s, when manufacturing shipments-to-inventories ratios began to improve. (This is a variant measure of what is known as "inventory turnover.") As shown in Exhibit 1.2, the improvements were stutter-step from 1982 to 1990. Then the ratio rose nearly every year. For the seventeen years between 1982 and 1999, the average annual improvement is 2 percent. (The rate would be higher if it omitted industries, such as extraction, that have no incentives to decrease inventories.) The surprising (to economists) explanation: Industrial companies were making hay with new management techniques that continually drive out wastes and drive down inventories.

INVENTORIES: PROXIES FOR COMPETITIVENESS

For their state-of-the-economy and predictive value, economists keep a close watch on inventories. Investors sizing up a certain company might take a lesson. Of all the pointers of strength or weakness that might be gleaned from a goods-oriented company's financial records, none reveals quite so much as trends in inventory turnover (alternately expressed as days of inventory).[1] Chapter 3 details why that is so. This chapter reviews the inventory patterns themselves.

If you're troubled by the premise that inventory turnover is a worthy proxy for competitiveness, please mark your place here and go read chapter 3. Then come back.

The Good Years

The 1996 Schonberger book, *World Class Manufacturing: The Next Decade,* includes eye-catching results of a half-century analysis of inventory turnovers in manufacturing companies. The database consisted of a few dozen venerable manufacturers, mainly in the United States and France. Nearly all of those companies showed about the same pattern—getting worse on inventory turnover from the 1950s until around 1975 or 1980, followed by sharply rising turns thereafter.

Note: The accountant's measure of inventory turnover is cost of goods sold, found in a company's income statement, divided by the value of on-hand inventory, from the balance sheet. Large amounts of inventory tie up cash and produce low inventory turnover—bad. Reducing inventory and getting lean frees up cash and raises inventory turnover—good. (Exception: If managers simply reduce inventories, without acting to cut wastes and delays, they remain fat—bad!)

Now the companies in the inventory database number more than five hundred and include manufacturers in Canada, Mexico, Japan, the United Kingdom, and several countries on the European continent. The half-century decline-incline pattern holds up well for this much larger sample. Exhibit 1.3 lists some of the companies, the number of years they've been improving, and annual rates of improvement since bottoming out. The increases in inventory turnover generate cash flows at average rates of almost 3 percent per year. (This is as of the end of 2000. A quick re-check as the book went to press shows lower average rates if the most recent "bad-year" annual report numbers are used.) For the typical twenty-plus years of improvement, it is a whopping amount of cash. It is usable for opening new plants or upgrading old ones, funding new product development, raising pay, distributing dividends, or almost any other purpose. Generating cash on one's own—as opposed to borrowing or diluting ownership by issuing new shares of stock—is everybody's favorite way to succeed in business.

Note: The previous exhibit, Exhibit 1.2, tracks *shipments to inventories,* which is okay as a macromeasure of inventory turnover (for instance, for a whole economy or sector). Exhibit 1.3 is for single manufactur-

Inventory Turnovers: A Half-Century Look
Tracking the Decline and Rise of Industry

Examples: 500 manufacturers studied (annual % rise, worst year)

Anheuser Busch (1.6%, 1977)	Lucas Industries, U.K. (3.4%, 1980)
Caterpillar (2.1%, 1971)	Maytag (2.0%, 1971)
Colgate-Palmolive (1.8%, 1974)	Medtronic (2.8%, 1981)
Cooper Industries (2.7%, 1979)	Merck (2.0%, 1977)
Courtaulds, U.K. (2.6%, 1980)	National Semiconductor (3.4%, 1979)
Eli Lilly (2.0%, 1977)	NEC, Japan (2.0%, 1974)
Ford (2.9%, 1974)	Parker Hannifin (1.7%, 1970)
GKN, U.K. (2.8%, 1979)	Philips, Netherlands (3.0%, 1980)
General Motors (2.5%, 1974)	Raven Industries (2.4%, 1978)
Hach (3.3%, 1978)	Renault, France (2.7%, 1980)
Herman Miller (4.4%, 1977)	Smiths, U.K. (2.8%, 1980)
Hon Industries (4.4%, 1977)	Sony, Japan (2.7%, 1979)
Honda, Japan (2.5%, 1975)	Tektronix (3.4%, 1972)
ICI, U.K. (2.4%, 1975)	Tennant (2.7%, 1975)
Ingersoll-Rand (2.9%, 1974)	TRW (3.4%, 1974)
International Rectifier (3.9%, 1982)	Unisys (6.1%, 1970)
Johnson Controls (4.1%, 1978)	Woodward Governor (2.8%, 1982)

Exhibit 1.3. Inventory Turnover Patterns

ers, not sectors. For a single company, the preferred, more precise measure of inventory turnover is *cost of goods sold to inventories.* Cost is
more valid since it removes possible pricing biases present in shipment
numbers.

Chapter 3 will show the actual down-then-up inventory turnover patterns
for a few manufacturers. It will also zero in on the meaning of these common
patterns. We shall see that the period of decline is explained by poor and

Bad News: Many Manufacturers Never Got Off the Mark
(Years of Getting Worse on Inventory Turns)—Examples

Aerospatiale-Matra (France)	General Dynamics	Owens-Corning
Akzo Nobel (Holland)	Genuine Parts	Pentair
Alberto-Culver	Georgia Pacific	Pope & Talbot
Am. Home Products	Gibson Greetings	PPG Industries
Archer-Daniels-Midland	Glaxo-Wellcome (UK)	Quebco (Canada)
Audi (Germany)	Goodrich, B.F.	Ralston-Purina
Bayer (Germany)	Hasbro	Rhone-Poulenc (France)
Brady, W. H.	Hershey	Russell Corp.
Bridgestone (Japan)	Hormel	Sara Lee
Casio Computer (Japan)	International Paper	Scott Paper
Castle, A. M.	Komatsu (Japan)	Sherwin Williams
Conagra	Kyocera (Japan)	Smucker
Crane	Lilly Industries	Standard Parts
Denso (Japan)	Lockheed-Martin	Stone Container
Diebold	Mallenckrodt	Sunbeam
Domtar (Canada)	Mitsubishi Electric (Japan)	Twin Disc
Esselte (Sweden)	Monsanto	Tyson Foods
Fairchild	Nestlé (Switzerland)	Volvo (Sweden)
Fuji Heavy (Japan)	Nissan (Japan)	Wacoal (Japan)
GE	Nokia (Finland)	Whittaker

Exhibit 1.4. Manufacturers Exhibiting Long-Range Pattern of No Improvement or
Worsening Inventory Turnover

Note: The inventory studies reveal three different patterns for this group
of laggard manufacturers: 1) years of improvement followed by, in recent
years, the opposite—signified by the rising, then falling arrow; 2) years of
worsening inventory turns with no discernible change—the continuously downward arrow; 3) no clear pattern, just random rising and
falling in inventory turns—represented by the jagged up-and-down line.

worsening practices in virtually every function of the enterprise; and that the past two decades of renewal are explained by the opposite—a period of industrial renaissance based on an outpouring of new knowledge.

The Flattening

But there is distressing new evidence. First of all, in the midst of a global get-lean movement, about one-third of the world's best-known manufacturers are not. For at least the past ten to fifteen years, those companies either have shown no loss of weighty inventories or have actually fattened up on them. Prominent among the one-third are the sixty listed in Exhibit 1.4. Their names are Audi and Bayer in Germany, Komatsu and Kyocera in Japan, Nokia and Volvo in Scandinavia, Domtar and Quebeco in Canada, and Conagra and Crane in the United States—to name a few.

Second, the other two-thirds—who may have thought themselves among the masters of lean—are having their own problems. This is the group whose annual reports show a long run of inventory reductions. A close look at their recent records, however, shows that nearly 40 percent have ceased to improve. Their inventory turnovers have either plateaued or worsened. Among this group are perhaps the two most admired of all manufacturers: Toyota and General Electric. They are joined by fifty-eight others on the list in Exhibit 1.5. All sixty in the exhibit had averaged an approximate 3 percent per year improvement in inventory turnover for fifteen years or more. But in about the last five to seven years all have plateaued or declined. Appendix 1 ranks twenty-four industry sectors according to their success in sustaining at least a fifteen-year improvement trend in inventory turnover—without that five-to-seven year lapse. Some companies in Exhibits 1.4 and 1.5 have been acquired or merged. In such cases, the data reflect the inventory turnover pattern up to the year of consolidation.

Adding the one-third of manufacturers that have not improved to the 40 percent that were improving but have lapsed provides a not-so-grand total of close to 75 percent. That is 75 percent that are at risk, as evidence by bloated and bloating inventories.

Of twenty-five automotive parts manufacturers in the survey group, guess which one has the worst several-decade-to-the-present inventory performance, as judged by the combination of absolute turnover and rate of change? It is Federal-Mogul, which in late 2000 was teetering on the brink of bankruptcy.[2] The company and the press blamed the financial troubles on asbestos suits from former employees of an acquired company.[3] If Mogul had been generating the kind of cash flow

Bad News: Many Declining/Plateauing on Inventory
Turnover after Years of Getting Lean—Examples

Abbott Labs	Federal Signal	Plastic Omnium (France)
Alcan Alum. (Canada)	Fiat (Italy)	Renault (France)
AMP	GE	Rogers Corp.
Avon	GM	Scania (Sweden)
Badger Meter	Goodyear	Schlumberger (France)
Baldor	Harnischfeger	Siemans (Germany)
Baxter International	Harsco	Storage Technology
Briggs & Stratton	Heinz	Tambrands
Brunswick	ITT Technologies	Textron
Campbell Soup	Jostens	Timken
Carpenter Technology	Kellogg	Toyota (Japan)
Caterpillar	Louisiana Pacific	Union Carbide
Clorox	Mascotech	United Technologies
Cooper Tire	Mitel Corp. (Canada)	Valeo (France)
Corning	Motorola	Valspar
Cummins	Nalco Chemical	Varian
Deere	Pechiney (France)	Volkswagen (Germany)
Dover	Pepsico	Volvo (Sweden)
Dresser	Philip Morris	Warner Lambert
Esterline	Pitne Bowes	Whirlpool

Exhibit 1.5. Manufacturers Exhibiting Recent Pattern of Leveling Off
or Declining on Inventory Turnover

Caveat: Some of the listed companies may have special justifications for their poor inventory turnover pattern of late. Dover Corporation, for example, may cite a recent accelerated acquisition effort: buying manufacturers long on inventory, thus lowering Dover's overall turns, with the intention of helping the new acquisitions to "get lean." Motorola may claim that inroads into China and India, with lengthening inventory pipelines, have temporarily dragged down its overall turnover numbers. Most of the companies, however, should look into the mirror and see the flat or downward trend for what it probably is: poor performance.

that comes from getting lean, however, it might easily have been able to weather the asbestos storm.

These points about decline could be solidified if the disturbing data from Exhibits 1.4 and 1.5 could be backed up by alternate measures, especially

Caution: Inventory is necessary in the absence of process management.
(Other cautionary statements similar to this are placed in later pages of the book. Their purpose is to dispel any misinterpretations of the data on inventories.)

quality. The huge advances industry has made in quality over the past two decades seem unarguable. But has quality suffered in most recent years, along with inventory? There are no handy records to study to find out; annual reports are clear on inventory but say nothing about quality. Anecdotal evidence of quality problems is available, however. There is, for example, this striking news headline: FORD SAYS LAST YEAR'S [2000's] QUALITY SNAFUS TOOK BIG TOLL—OVER $1 BILLION IN PROFIT."[4] Ford Motor Co. is a latter-day quality pioneer, having mounted a company-wide quality program in the early 1980s. It was founded on the works of Deming, Juran, and Crosby, who were hired to spark the effort. Ford is the company that had enough success with quality to dare to make its main advertising slogan "Quality Is Job One."

Ford may not be alone. Jeffrey Garten, dean of the Yale School of Management, says this: "Among the forty top business leaders I interviewed for an upcoming book, the word *quality* wasn't mentioned once as a major strategic challenge."[5]

THE PROBLEM

Each company, of course, has its own story. We can speculate in general, though, on reasons for the tapering off of the encompassing inventory indicator; quality, too. Complacency, already mentioned, is one. Six other causal factors join complacency on the list in Exhibit 1.6 (repeated from the preface). These are briefly discussed below and elaborated on in later chapters.

---

1. Complacency—a societal, industrial, and national tendency.

2. Stock-hyping deals that divert attention from "the basics" of world-class excellence.

3. New managers, no trial-by-fire experience.

4. Retention of old, nonprofitable customers and SKUs.

5. Retention of command and control.

6. Legacies of bad equipment, systems, job designs.

7. Disjointed and narrowly focused world-class implementations.

Exhibit 1.6. Why Manufacturers Lose Their Competitive Way

Tendency to Regress

There is a body of academic research that bears on how industry leaders tend to lose their top rank. It goes by various names, including industrial dethronement and market-share erosion. Studies in 1983 and 1986, for example, found that the majority of market leaders lose their top rank within a couple of decades.[6] Using broad economic data, those studies bear out what this book's inventory research shows for specific manufacturing companies. The issue, though, is not how companies lose. It is how to renew and recover from regression, erosion, and complacency. That is the main theme of the book, taken up in most chapters.

Stock-Hyping Deals

What manager could think about staying the course with stars in his or her eyes? In the late 1990s e-business, silicon-tech, and biotech firms repeatedly sprang up, had their initial public offerings, and made large numbers of youthful people quickly rich in stock options—on paper, if not in the bank. In big industry, one megamerger after another (the majority ill considered) sent stock option prices soaring for layers of executives and managers. The aforementioned Jeffrey Garten, dean of the Yale School of Management, agrees. On what gets in the way of quality, he says, "[Top business leaders] are obsessed with boosting short-term share prices, reaching new markets at warp speed, and ramping up scale through mergers or alliances."[7] In comparison, the rank of continuous process improvement falls low on the priority scale.

There is some method to the madness. Demolition of the Iron Curtain along with momentous trade, political, and single-currency pacts—all in the midst of decades of world peace (blemished, to be sure, by a pack of small wars)—created a wide-open global marketplace of 6 billion people. The clear imperative: Get one's foot in the door.

It is a giant door. The foot needs to be encased in a combat boot—in the form of company-wide, customer-focused excellence. In other words, companies that let their world-class journey slide while rushing to acquire, merge, or partner to build power and a global presence may be the worse for the effort.

New Managers

At the core of the world-class journey are the just-in-time (JIT) and total quality (TQ) methodologies, which migrated to the West in about 1980. Their message was revolutionary. Early practitioners treated them as crusades.

Leading companies—IBM, Motorola, Milliken, and the like—sent scores of high-level executives and managers to Philip Crosby's Quality College. W. Edwards Deming's four-day seminar played to full houses for fifteen years. Joseph Juran's quality-management message had similar prominence. And consultant William Wheeler liked to talk about "born-again JIT'ers" popping up across the industrial landscape.

One reason these complementary approaches—JIT and TQ—had such grand impacts is that they were the only games in town. Not anymore. Reengineering, teaming, agility, mass customization, constraints management, 5S, six sigma, supply-chain management, e-commerce, and so on blur the senses. The crusaders have retired or are small in numbers alongside the legions of new, young, job-hopping managers who populate the hierarchies. The new cadre is quick to develop an initiative but doesn't stick around long enough to see it through. (The ardor for job-hopping may have cooled some in the aftermath of the stock market plunge in 2000–2001.[8]) Moreover, it lacks the fervency of forerunners who had experienced mind-set transformations: for the crusaders, the reigning system of inspector-based quality and big-batch, big-system complexity had to go. In its stead is everyone-a-process-manager, along with quick-change, small-lot, visually managed operations. Even where a group of today's new managers has the process-management zeal of the crusaders, they may not be able to act out their preferences, because they typically work in downsized companies and have overly full plates.

Retention of Old, Nonprofitable Customers and SKUs

Plates are heaped partly because of the way companies continually add new customers and stockkeeping units. Trouble is, as the new arrive, the old do not depart. Chapter 12 expands on this failing and how to deal with it. But new managers with full plates usually must contend with another holdover situation: Their company probably still operates in the command-and-control mode, which gets in the way of best intentions.

Retention of Command and Control

Command starts with commanders—those high up. Control employs a network of specialist-agents who count everything and make reports for the commanders.

Command and control is at odds with employee-driven process management. By one set of standards, it is also out of whack with continuous process improvement, total quality, and flexibility/agility, along with statistical process control, just-in-time, total preventive maintenance, and 5S. These initiatives can be advanced under command-control—but by a small group of specialists and managers, leaving out the bulk of the workforce.

Further limiting workforce involvement is heavy use of external consultants to guide new program installation. Consultants find it easier to deal with like-minded managers and staff experts than with folks in the ranks. Moreover, there is always pressure on the consultants to get quick results, but turning on a whole workforce is anything but quick. Training and prodding managers and experts is much faster.

And it works. The professional staff, with consultants standing by, maps the processes and designs the work cells. Together they install sophisticated work-tracking systems and advanced statistical analysis methods to zoom in on causes of defects and down machines; these are systems and methods beyond the ken or the sight lines of the general workforce. They put improvement charts on walls throughout the plant. And never mind that the charts track remote management concerns, not the things that aggravate or stimulate the troops. It works—at least long enough to make a few competitive inroads and maybe even drive up the stock price. But it doesn't last. Before long, the advantage goes permanently to a superior competitor who takes the time to get all the minds and bodies of the company involved, instead of just a minority of professionals.

Legacy of Bad Equipment, Systems, Job Designs

Years of command-control often leave in their wake misfitting equipment, information systems, and job designs.

As for equipment, there is little point in rehashing the by now well-known arguments in favor of smaller-scale machines and production lines. The outsize, high-volume monuments to the economy-of-scale concept are out of step. Making in small or one-piece lots in synch with customer usage works best with smaller-scale, high-flex equipment. Many manufacturers, however, have large sums tied up in still capable supermachines bought years ago. Continued use of such equipment holds the manufacturer hostage to the batch-and-queue system. Sometimes there are no affordable alternatives. Quite often there are, but executives lack the will or the wits to switch.

Criticizing systems—manufacturing information technology (IT) systems, that is—hits at the giant, well-endowed software industry. IT applications have their place in industry. But the legacy systems that schedule, dispatch, release, track, count, and cost everything that moves are, by today's standards, largely non-value-adding wastes; their use sacrifices hands-on visibility. Best practice calls for a host of visual-management devices—kanban flow management, 5S discipline, process data in the workplace, and so on.

As to job design, Frederick Taylor had it partly right. For any set of conditions there is one best way. Though it can never be found, it must be continually sought, documented, timed, taught, and practiced. In the Toyota system, the result is called "standard work." Employees improvising—doing the work their own ways—causes variation, which, as Dr. Deming beat into our heads, is the root of any number of ills. Since things change, standard work must, too. The workplace should be, to use Robert Hall's language, an improvement laboratory[9] hosting a never-ending sequence of work studies. The main research tool in the lab is 1900-vintage Taylor-Gilbreth process flowcharting.

However, Taylor and the whole reductionist/command-control school has it wrong about who designs the work and what the best way should look like. Job design and job improvement is not, properly, a staff function. As already stated, it must be largely in the hands of those who do the work. Too often, companies give their workforces training in process analysis and problem solving but then retain the system of professional staff and consultants actually to do most of the analyses.

Here the term *reductionist* refers to the common bent of job designers, which includes industrial engineers, human resources staffers, or bosses. They tend to apply the division-of-labor concept down to minute levels of detail. Jobs may end up so squeezed down that any newly hired warm body can be up to speed on them the first day—at minimum wage. This holds down the payroll. It also ensures high turnover, dissatisfaction, and an untrained, nonthinking workforce.

Erratic Application of World-Class Concepts

These days, many companies do spend a lot on training. It's a good thing. The reservoir of best-practice knowledge that exists today, there for the learning, is massive, as compared with the meager, poorly respected offerings of twenty-five and thirty years ago. Companies keep sending their professionals to seminars, launch in-house workshops, and even establish their own versions of Motorola University. Moreover, growing numbers of manufacturers have gravitated toward forty hours per year as a minimum amount of training. It's for all employees, not just professionals.[10]

For all that, our own benchmarking research shows that even best manufacturers have serious blind spots when it comes to application. In the next chapter, that research, called "World Class *by* Principles" (WCP), is summarized briefly. Most of the remaining chapters blend in specific results of the research.

2

Renewal

The first published listing of world-class manufacturing principles appeared in a 1986 book, *World Class Manufacturing: The Lessons of Simplicity Applied*, by Richard Schonberger. It was a seventeen-point list labeled an "action agenda for manufacturing excellence."[1]

Agendas are nice. But, as they say, you get what you measure, and agendas lack that important ingredient, measurement criteria. Therefore, in 1994, the seventeen-point agenda evolved into a sixteen-principle matrix, with measurement criteria and five lowest-to-highest levels of world-class achievement. A benchmarking project followed. Manufacturers self-score their business unit or company on the sixteen principles and forward their scores for entry into the benchmarking database. Each manufacturer then receives a customized report (see box) comparing its scores against those of peer organizations and the whole.

**Contents of World Class by Principles
International Benchmarking Report**

Section 1 (ten or more pages), containing

- Three introductory pages

- Two pages of scoring details organized by type of manufacturer

- One page of results, for selected industries, for each of the sixteen customer-focused, employee-driven, data-based principles

- A one-page bar chart of average scores on each principle for all participating organizations

- Two or more pages of principle-by-principle bar-chart comparisons, customized for your organization (your scores compared with those of peer organizations)

Section 2 (usually two to five pages). Selected competitiveness/leanness data in the form of graphical trends from a half-century analysis of inventory turnovers—for over five hundred manufacturers in sixteen countries—including yours, if available

---

> Section 3 (six compact pages). A listing of all WCP benchmarking participants (about 485 at this writing) from eighteen countries—not including their scores, which are confidential
>
> Section 4. An executive summary (about twenty pages), containing
>
> ■ Rationale for the WCP self-assessment and benchmarking
>
> ■ Analysis by industrial sector and by highest and lowest scorers, plus special findings and anomalous/surprising results
>
> ■ Global and industrial-sector analysis of the spread of "lean" management, as indicated by inventory trends
>
> ■ Three-page set of the WCP self-scoring matrix

WCP BENCHMARKING, PHASES 1 AND 2

The first 130 manufacturers participating in the WCP Benchmarking are listed in the 1996 book *World Class Manufacturing: The Next Decade.*[2] The book presents each of the sixteen principles, the five-step scoring matrix, and summarized results for the 130 manufacturers.

The project continues, now with research partners in fourteen countries administering the scoring for companies in their regions. Around 485 manufacturers are in the database and have received benchmarking reports. Their names—but not their scores, which are held in confidence—are listed in appendix 2. The research population is deliberately biased in favor of companies with a track record of world-class achievements. A significant number were sought out as having received prestigious awards, including the Baldrige national quality award in the United States, the Shingo Prize for North American companies, *Industry Week* magazine's best-plant winners, state quality awards, and counterpart recognition in Europe, the Far East, Australia, Africa, and South America.

The scoring criteria in the WCP matrix are very tough. The idea is that even the best companies should maintain a strong sense of vulnerability, given the wide-open global marketplace, with competitive standards rising ever higher.

And how do companies actually score on the sixteen principles? The top forty in the WCP database—including several best-plant designees and Baldrige winners—average less than three points per principle on the five-point scale. We've observed that some of these companies' management teams react with momentary concern but do nothing. Their companies are making money in a booming economy, and the company hallway is filled with award plaques, so everything must be okay. Other companies are in better hands: their officers see that everything is not okay and get busy, especially on the blind spots—principles on which they've scored only one or two points.

PRINCIPLE 2: COMMON BLIND SPOT

One common blind spot—among the lowest scoring of the sixteen principles— is Principle 2. Its condensed description is "Capture/Use Customer, Competitive, and Best-Practice Information." Exhibit 2.1 shows the principle and scoring criteria, plus a few "fine points" on how to interpret the criteria. Each principle follows the same format. The criteria get progressively more demanding for each step up the ladder, and each step is worth a maximum of one point.

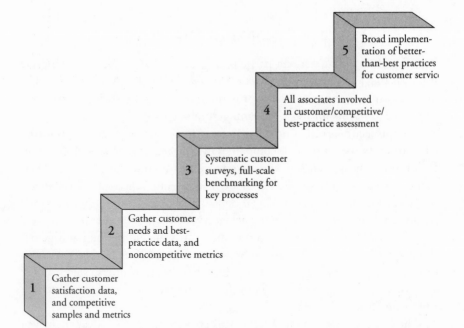

Exhibit 2.1. Principle 2: Capture/Use Customer, Competitive, and Best-Practice Information

FINE POINTS

■ This principle taps outside information/knowledge; it's your main antenna.

■ Information/knowledge (especially external) is the spark of innovation.

■ Aim: Drive your improvement efforts with external data—from customers (customer satisfaction/needs surveys), competitive products (competitive analysis), and noncompetitive best practices (benchmarking studies).

■ Though customer surveys and competitive analysis are old techniques, few companies have done them well or systematically; it's been haphazard.

■ Benchmarking is a newer approach, developed by Xerox, that seeks out best-in-the-world practices (best at supplier sourcing, paying invoices, and so on).

■ Lowest point level (step 1) is getting data from customers and competitive analysis; higher points require benchmarking as well—each done systematically; at the third step, "noncompetitive metrics" refers to data on best practices, most of which will not be found in one's own industry; highest points require all-employee involvement and superior uses of the data.

For the sake of illustration, let us consider two manufacturers that participated in the benchmarking in 1997. Each scored in the top 20 of some 485 participants, and the lowest score for each—2 to 2.5 points—was on Principle 2. They represent the following industrial sectors: machinery and large appliances, electrical, metalworking/machining, sheet metal, and electronics. (In the WCP, each manufacturer is categorized in up to three sectors.) Their total scores are 52 and 57.5, an average of 3.25 and 3.6 points per principle. Here is a closer look at the "blind spot" effects of lower scores on Principle 2 at each of the two manufacturers:

Manufacturer A, maker of building control products:

■ Gave itself a full point on Principle 2, step 1, "Gather customer satisfaction data, plus competitive samples and metrics." A point here just means that now and then they gather feedback from customers; bring in competitors' products for reverse engineering; and know something about competitors' lead times, on-time performance, and so on.

■ Gave itself one-half point on step 2, "Gather customer needs and best-practice data, plus noncompetitive metrics." A half point means, "We do it somewhat. That is, we delve a bit into customer

needs (which goes beyond customer satisfaction). And we've been
known to look beyond our competitors (who may not be best at
anything) at best practices and metrics of noncompetitors."

■ Gave itself one-half point on step 3, "Systematic customer surveys
and full-scale benchmarking for key processes." The word *systematic*
distinguishes the third step on this principle (the same is the case at
the third step for several other principles as well). Systematic means
"We don't just take a look once in a while; we have a system for doing it (for instance, customer surveys) on a regular basis. It's built in,
like the payroll."

A half point at steps 2 and 3 suggests this for Company A: Being only
marginally aware of its customers' wants, competitors' capabilities, and out-
siders' best practices may set off an erosion of its strengths on other principles
(scores of 2.5 to 4.5, plus two 5s). Quality, for example, is the main focus of
Principles 10 and 11. But Company A is probably viewing quality through its
own eyes. It is not quality in the eyes of customers, or in the gun sights of
competitors, or based on superior best-quality practices of noncompetitors,
none of which Company A systematically assesses.

Manufacturer B, maker of medical instruments:

At fifty-seven total points, this manufacturer is one of the highest scorers
in the WCP benchmarking database. Its scores on the other fifteen principles
are all in the 3-to-4.5-point range, which makes the two points on the second
principle stand out. Possible explanation: Like many companies, Manufacturer B probably has a history of being inwardly focused. That won't do for a
company so bent on excellence by highest global standards.

A saving grace: This company has received a number of public honors.
That brings its managers into contact with other award-winning companies
at honors conferences. Those contacts may help the company develop better
awareness of best practices outside its industry. They also provide contacts for
benchmarking visits to other highly regarded firms.

In summary, Principle 2 is a weakness for both Manufacturers A and B. A
key benefit of participating in any kind of benchmarking is finding one's
blind spots—before getting blindsided by a more aware competitor. Blind-
spot elimination is an effective pathway to betterment.

We have looked closely at only one of the principles in the WCP. All sixteen
are included in appendix 3. (Manufacturers wanting to formally participate

in the WCP International Benchmarking receive the set of principles and self-scoring criteria, along with other explanatory "invitation to participate" materials.) The principles are intended to cover most of what a manufacturer does—from design and development, to purchasing, to human resource management, to presentation, promotion, and marketing. To justify the label *world class,* all the principles and five-step scoring criteria have the same overarching three-part theme: they are customer-focused, employee-driven, and data (fact)-based. The intent is that they define competitiveness not by today's standards, but by the much elevated standards sure to arise in the future under unfettered world commerce. We look at competitiveness more closely, and through other lenses, in chapter 3. But first, in finishing this chapter, we reflect on the sources of the lore of renewal.

KNOWLEDGE-BASED INDUSTRIAL RENAISSANCE: ITS SOURCES AND FUTURE

The rest of the world owes Japan a debt of gratitude—actually, not Japan, but a modest number of elite manufacturers in that country. Led by Toyota, the giant automotive and textile machinery company, their contribution, besides fine products, was management innovations. Their products invaded the West. Ten or twenty years later, their management innovations made the voyage.

Japan Decade and Western Decade

The names of those innovations from Japan are mostly well known. The eleven under "Japan Decade" in Exhibit 2.2 are standouts. In the far right column are seven equally notable innovations, these from the West. Each lines up with a key business process. It is no surprise that Japan's contributions were mainly in operations and engineering, the West's favoring the managerial side: strategic/competitive and collaborative.

Innovations in human resource management arose in both decades. The three from Japan serve to breach barriers that squelch ideas of the general workforce. The two in the right column respond to the question "What's in it for me?" Front-line employees in Japan may not ask the question, but independent-minded operatives in the United States, Canada, and Western Europe will.

One of the items on the right side of Exhibit 2.2 deserves special mention. Design for manufacture and assembly (DFMA) is surely the most signifi-

	JAPAN DECADE: 1960–1970	WESTERN/U.S.DECADE: 1985–1994
Operations:	Total quality Just-in-time/kanban	
Engineering:	Cellular layout Joint product/process design Target costing Total preventive maintenance	Design for manufacture and assembly
Financial:		Activity-based costing
Strategic/ competitive:	Quality function deployment	Benchmarking Business process reengineering
Collaborative:	Supplier partnering	Quick response/Supplier- managed inventory Continuous replen- ishment
Human resources:	Employee involvement Cross-careering Visual management	Employee ownership/ gainsharing Broad-band pay systems

Exhibit 2.2 Two Decades of Management Innovation

cant of the West's innovations—at least equal to any innovation from Japan. Developed in the early 1980s by University of Rhode Island professors Boothroyd and Dewhurst, DFMA quickly became a hit among Western electronics and automotive manufacturers.[3] Rivals in Japan have been the laggards. Still today, fifteen years after Ford and Chrysler embraced DFMA, Toyota seems bent on taking a less promising road. (Though an early champion of DFMA, Chrysler became distracted by its own success. As one news story put it, "Instead of taking advantage of economies of scale by using the same parts in different cars, [powerful platform teams] bought their own components."[4]) Toyota's benchmarking studies show that it generally pays more than other automakers for purchased parts, but its reaction, according to one report: "[Toyota] spurned the growing industry practice of installing standardized parts in a range of car models: No sharing of door locks in Camrys and Corollas, if you please." (Note: Better that the writer had said "wellestablished" instead of "growing.") Instead the company is "figuring out the lowest prices paid by carmakers for 173 commodity-type components, from rearview mirrors to the bearings inside shock absorbers." Then, Toyota holds the pricing data over the heads of its suppliers. "For example, Toyota wants to cut the number of bearings it buys to as little as ½₀ of current levels by asking suppliers to design simpler parts."[5] Using cost clout to drive out waste is contrary to the Toyota system itself, which is famed for direct attacks on root causes. The DFMA guidelines give engineers the tools directly to attack root causes of design excesses; no need for cost analysts to tell the engineers what to do, if you please.

Regarding the dates in Exhibit 2.2, let's backtrack. Some of the early work—on just-in-time, supplier partnering, and so on—began in the 1950s. The developments had taken root, largely in the Toyota group, by 1970. Other Japanese automakers and suppliers would learn their lessons later, and other industries still later. The manufacturers that learned best became an export juggernaut, attacking the giant United States market first, then Britain, then the European continent and beyond. Survivors of the onslaught went though a mind-opening experience. Status quos blown, they, along with various consultants, began to innovate themselves. Best emergent ideas make up the eight items in column three in Exhibit 2.2.

While it took a couple of decades for Toyota's innovations to find homes on another continent, the lag time is much less today. See the box on page 22 for a reason why.

Knowledge Base for This Book

The potent base of knowledge generated in the Japan and Western/U.S. decades is elemental in this book. In addition, the book draws upon three streams of new research:

1. The continuing World Class *by* Principles (WCP) Benchmarking—self-assessment data from, so far, some 485 participating manufacturers.

2. A related survey of best-practice applications that lead to good scores on the WCP: how manufacturing companies are doing in applying those practices. The survey includes 105 questions and was administered during seminars from 1997 through 2000. Par-

Free Trade—Ideas Follow Products

Economists love free trade: it yields plentiful goods of wider variety at lower prices for consumers. The public is not so sure. Not with all the fuss about the errors and excesses of the International Monetary Fund (IMF), World Trade Organization (WTO), and World Bank.

Lost in the debates is this: Wherever products move, competitive alarm bells ring and roust laggards from their naps. The main beneficiary of U.S. openness to Japanese cars and cameras, machine tools and copiers, ceramics and memory chips, was not the consuming public, nor even the Japanese producers. It was Western manufacturers that were forced to react or give up. They reacted by learning the customer-focused competitiveness formula themselves and applying it. Wide-open trade policies are what transformed U.S. industry from critically sick in 1980 to global powerhouse fifteen years later. Next, the same thing happened in the United Kingdom: trade barriers down, products in, competitiveness up, new management innovations implemented, industries revitalized. And so on in each country that lowered its barriers— so far including about two-thirds of the world in terms of population (about 4 billion of the globe's 6 billion people are now in free-enterprise economies, compared with around 700 million before the fall of communism[6]).

Conclusion: The main benefit in each import country is not affordable, high-quality goods coming in. It is knowledge-based resurrection of their own industries, which then produce their own affordable, quality goods. High competition fosters industrial renewal.

By all means, let's fix the IMF, WTO, and World Bank. And ensure that free trade builds, not trashes, countries, their consumers, their workforces, and their environments. Bringing out the best is the essence of world class.

tial survey results are threaded among the sixteen principles in appendix 3.

3. The inventory turnover research—data from over five hundred manufacturers covering their performance in the last half of the twentieth century.

There was no attempt to include the same manufacturers in the three research projects. However, a preference for larger, prestigious companies—the better to represent top-notch performance—ensures that many of the same ones do appear in all three research databases.

Exhibit 2.3 provides a few pertinent characteristics of the two main databases: the WCP and the inventory study. The charts show U.S. manufacturers making up around three-quarters of the manufacturers in both databases. Remaining participants in the WCP come from, in descending order, the Americas other than the United States, Europe including the British Isles, South Africa, and Asia and Australia. As the WCP project continues, the aim is for the research partners in various countries to build the non-U.S. component of the database.

The inventory database includes, besides the 407 U.S.-based manufacturers, 38 from European countries (other than the British Isles), 31 from Japan, 23 from the United Kingdom, and 19 from Canada and other countries

Percentage Participation in WCP Benchmarking, by Region

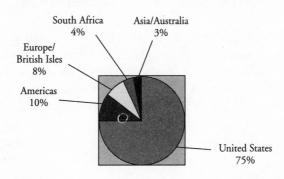

Numbers of Manufacturers in Inventory Database, by Region

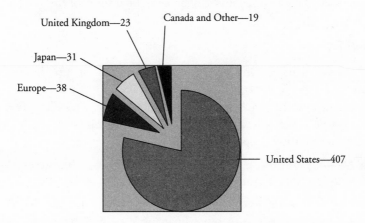

Exhibit 2.3. Characteristics of Research Populations

(such as Israel, Mexico, Korea). The inventory turnover data are from published financial records, mainly annual reports. Records are complete for some of the five-hundred-plus companies: those that have been in existence as publicly held entities for the entire study period, 1950 through 2000. More commonly, the records are less complete: some in the database, especially in electronics, were established as businesses more recently. Others have been public for part of their history and taken private (no public inventory records available) for other years. Another portion have been acquired or merged in recent years, thus curtailing their publicly available inventory data. And in earlier years some companies' books included a "costs and expenses" category, then later split the category into "cost of sales" (or "cost of goods sold") and other expenses. Since cost of sales divided by value of inventory is the formula for inventory turnover, the "costs and expenses" years of data were not usable.

Inventory records are more readily available, and for more years, for U.S. and Canadian companies than in other countries. The *Mergent* (formerly *Moody's*) *Industrial Manuals,* a primary source, include other countries but for a limited number of years. Computer databases, also used, were generally more limited than the manuals. Thus, most of the data from other than the United States and Canada cover less than the full half century. Despite the uneven coverage of the fifty-year target study period, the sheer numbers of companies in the database provide clear indications of the competitive trends featured in this book.

Both the WCP and the inventory trend databases will continue to grow. The research will continue beyond the publication of this book. And what of the knowledge renaissance itself? That is the final topic of this chapter.

Global Era

The sixteen elements and assessment criteria making up the WCP give prominence to the contributions of the Japan and Western/U.S. decades. But, as they say, excellence is a journey. There are many festering problems in industry still to be resolved for which the WCP principles, current version, do not provide solutions. Here is a sampling:

- *Demand forecasting.* There is no "world class" breakthrough here; item forecasting remains a vexing problem.

- *Performance appraisal.* No one is satisfied with how it's done, whether strictly boss-to-subordinate or 360-degree appraisal.

- *Motivation and leadership.* As much may have been spent researching these issues as on finding a cure for cancer—and more progress may have been made on the latter than the former (leaders come in fifty-seven varieties).

- *Management of innovation and invention.* We are no more enlightened here than on performance appraisal and motivation and leadership.

The above are how-to-manage issues. Add to those such broader socio-economic problems as the following:

- Alarming executive-to-working stiff pay differences, especially in the United States.
- Continued stock market distractions.
- Buying and selling of companies beyond all reason.
- Reduced loyalty—can't be a good thing.

These are only a few large issues. Many smaller ones, some old, some blowing in on the Internet, beg for help. Novel solutions are sure to arise, and from any region. The developed economies no longer have a knowledge advantage: we are in a global era of continuing management innovations.

That makes a difference. It used to be that a manufacturer with mediocre management but a decent product line could carry on for generations. Consultant Tom Archer offers three reasons: 1) Company owners accept wide variations in profitability. The best thrive and bank their gains; others keep making and selling widgets year upon year, though their after-tax profits on sales or book value are often less than U.S. Treasury bond yields. 2) When manufacturing costs rise to prevailing selling prices, companies have plenty of other costs to slash: sales expenses, product engineering, R&D, administration, and so on. So companies chop away at those costs and manage to stay afloat. 3) Inefficient manufacturers can often just pass on their high costs to their customers and get away with it. That is "thanks to the fact that a surprising number of [their customers] are reluctant to switch to, or even investigate, new vendors."[7]

Not any more. An obvious reason is the Internet, which provides ease of investigating new suppliers—and may freeze out high-cost ones that don't have compensating advantages. A more bedrock reason is that the air is filled with today's and tomorrow's potent, quick-to-migrate new concepts on how to compete. The typical average manufacturer will be at risk, playing catch-up. These might include, for example, an electronics company just discovering lean concepts twenty years after Hewlett-Packard did; or a polymers manufacturer that plunges into six sigma, having missed out on statistics-based quality in the 1980s. Those are the average companies. The below average won't have a chance.

What about manufacturers admired as much for their management as their products—GE, Motorola, and the like? We return to this chapter's opening point. Companies on top tend toward complacency. Their best protection is doing, at an accelerated pace, what they've been best at: learning, learning, learning.

3

Competitiveness

Is industrial competitiveness a moot issue? In an information economy it may seem so. Industrial companies, these days, have all the glamour of sand. Come to think of it, however, sand is derivative of silicon, and silicon morphs into processor and memory chips, which underpin the information economy.

The services-replacing-manufacturing viewpoint bears further scrutiny and is the first chapter topic. We continue with research findings central to this book's mixed (good-bad) message: that best manufacturers, having found the keys to competitiveness, have tended of late to lose track of them. What companies must do to regain, or gain in the first place, a competitive edge is the closing message of the chapter.

THE TILT TO SERVICES: NOT FOR EVERYBODY

Even as services employ greater percentages of the working populace, sober realists remind us of what we all do with our paychecks and capital gains. We buy and use goods: durables, including big-ticket houses and cars; semi-durables, such as CDs, books, and mobile phones; and consumables. When we go to a movie, we pay not only for the intangible audiovisual experience. The price also includes costs of the theater's bricks, mortar, and furnishings, along with semidurables such as the film itself, and consumable candies and popcorn.

Eamonn Fingleton makes these kinds of points in his book, *In Praise of Hard Industries*.[1] Fingleton asserts further that manufacturing is where wealth is created. Services, he says, create lots of lowball jobs, but only small numbers that pay well and require high intelligence and talent. When Western manufacturers outsource production to low-wage countries, he continues, they give away the source of wealth. What is left are services, which, he says, do not export well.

Too much, I think, is made of these goods-versus-services distinctions. Good management is much the same in either: take care of the customer by keeping in touch and taking out wastes, delays, and rework. Companies that follow this formula can compete anywhere, and the best may move quickly to establish a multinational presence. Some do so by setting up operations in other countries, others by exporting from a home base of production. Either generates wealth for the host company.

As to Fingleton's point that services are not exportable, the competitiveness formula certainly is, and it works for services as well as goods. For example, some of the world's most competitive service companies—expanding globally as quickly as trade agreements allow—are North American airlines, banks, insurance companies, fast-food restaurants, overnight mail services, and chain retailers. Service multinationals, from U.S.-based Starbucks to Canada's Laidlaw, repatriate profits and grow wealth just as surely as goods multinationals such as Coca-Cola and Honda.

Manufacturing Red Ink

A provocative newer viewpoint has it that manufacturers don't make money anymore. This is said to be the case for Coca-Cola and Honda, as well as component makers down through the supply chains. Global competition has pinched and squeezed to the point where little is left but physical assets and brand names.

What to do? The title of a *Harvard Business Review* article provides an answer: "Go Downstream: The New Profit Imperative in Manufacturing."[2] To make money, the authors advise, it is necessary to forward integrate into higher value-adding services, à la GE Capital. That business unit provides financing to General Electric's customers and has cash-cow equipment leasing operations all over the world; only some of the leased equipment is GE-made.

Plenty of other manufacturers are taking steps in the same general direction and making money at it. IBM's resurgence is owed largely to its transformation into an information services powerhouse. They'll design and run big systems for the customer, using IBM and non-IBM equipment. Boeing, Airbus, and other plane makers may make little or nothing selling aircraft but clean up on major repairs and retrofits. They make even more on sale of parts over the long lives of the planes.

Component makers are forward integrating as well. Consider electronic manufacturing services (EMSs), lately among the fastest growing and most profitable of industrial sectors. EMS companies such as Jabil Circuits, Flextronics, and Solectron all started out assembling printed circuit boards for major electronics companies. They've grown by acquiring plants, equipment, and workforces from Hewlett-Packard, NEC, Nortel, and other big customers. Along the way, the EMSs have moved up the food chain, to assembly of whole PCs, routers, and printers, and up some more into design of components and repair of end products.

Overcapacity and Undermanagement

In other manufacturing sectors, if there's no money to be made anymore, the main reason is global overcapacity: too many carmakers, paper mills, foundries, and textile/apparel companies. That goes for services, too. There is excess capacity in banking, insurance, leasing, health care, airlines, movie theaters, and government agencies.

The difference is this: Most services are at an earlier stage of management development than manufacturing. The services sector has not generated its own equivalent—in impact—to manufacturing's driving force, the Toyota system. Lean, uniformly high-quality services, therefore, are still relatively rare. That state of affairs won't last. Wal-Mart's entrée into Germany in 1997 has been having effects similar to Toyota's and Mazda's plant openings in the United States in the early 1980s and the United Kingdom a few years later: as local laws allow, supply systems, labor practices, quality management—most of what companies do—get transformed. As of this writing, Wal-Mart had not even ventured into France; yet Carrefour, the giant French department store chain (number two retailer in the world, after Wal-Mart), was already reengineering itself in preparation.

For a manufacturer, a balanced, forward-integration strategy often means contracting out at the other end. Motorola could shed some of its production or design in order to make way for hawking its six sigma expertise; Xerox could do the same with benchmarking. Toyota could farm out some production in order to spend effort marketing its famous core competency, the Toyota system itself. These are examples of forward integrating into services. Trouble is, competitors can materialize much more quickly and surely in services than in manufacturing. Every major management consultancy the world over already offers expertise in six sigma, benchmarking, and the Toyota system; they were able to develop and market these kinds of expertise virtually overnight. (An International Society of Six Sigma Professionals exists, with its own newsletter and Web page, www.issp.org.)

Anyway, all services are derivative. Many of the dot.coms actually sell food, shelter, and clothing.

Conclusion: There is no safety in a manufacturing strategy of going downstream to tap higher value-adding services. The few manufacturers that are first to do so may make hay, but it won't last. Where profits are, tough competitors enter, especially in services.

Besides, in services it is hard even to measure competitiveness. Manufacturers, complex as they are, have a convenient, omnibus metric, considered next.

INVENTORY REDUCTION: SURROGATE FOR COMPETITIVENESS

Chapter 1 presented industry's typical down-up inventory turnover pattern over the last half of the prior century. But so what? Inventory is just an intermediate performance indicator, isn't it? The real world revolves around earnings, return on equity, and share prices, not operating metrics.

For purposes of running the business, those real-world, high-impact indicators all have weaknesses. It's the old saw about steering the ship by watching its wake—or, more realistically, steering the ship by the wake it left two years ago. That is, today's earnings generally have more to do with beginnings two years ago than any recent management moves. Chapter 6, "Performance Management," gives full treatment to the subject. That chapter makes the point that the lean/quick-response/high-quality/high-flex way of managing requires a new set of performance measures. Our narrower discussion here—of inventory turnover as a good, universal indicator—dovetails with that chapter 6 discussion.

Decline

Inventory turnover is a performance collection point for much of what an inventory-intensive business does. Exhibit 3.1 lists the many manufacturing management elements that impact inventory performance, in this case negatively. In the exhibit, a downward stairs and arrow depicts industry's widespread 1950–1975 pattern of decline. By about 1980, the Western business press had already about given up on the manufacturing sector. It was on a sharp down-slope in the direction of Japan and developing Asian "Tigers."

The causes were many. We may tick off the contributors to decline one by one, starting at the top left point on the stairway. In each case, worsening performance shows up as wasteful, non-value-adding inventory.

■ *Quality.* What may be the most widely quoted reference on quality in the last two decades is not a journal article or book. It is a 1980 documentary on U.S. television: NBC's two-hour prime-time *News White Paper: "If Japan Can, Why Can't We?"* Manufacturing's dirty little secret, its sad state of quality, was out in the open. The top items in Exhibit 3.1 reflect those quality woes and their inventory effects:

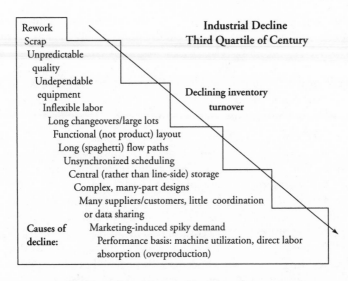

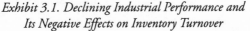

Rework
Scrap
Unpredictable
quality
Undependable
equipment
Inflexible labor
Long changeovers/large lots
Functional (not product) layout
Long (spaghetti) flow paths
Unsynchronized scheduling
Central (rather than line-side) storage
Complex, many-part designs
Many suppliers/customers, little coordination
or data sharing

Industrial Decline
Third Quartile of Century

Declining inventory
turnover

Causes of
decline:
Marketing-induced spiky demand
Performance basis: machine utilization, direct labor
absorption (overproduction)

Exhibit 3.1. Declining Industrial Performance and
Its Negative Effects on Inventory Turnover

▶ *Rework and Scrap.* Every unit of bad product, to be reworked or scrapped, ties up that much inventory.

▶ *Unpredictable quality.* More inventory must be on hand just in case the next lot is bad—the unpredictability factor.

■ *Unpredictable equipment.* By the 1970s engineers often were no longer running manufacturing companies. An era of mergers and acquisitions had put financial people in charge. Armed with sharp pencils, they sought costs to cut, and maintenance was an easy target. With poor maintenance, machines won't make good parts, adding more inventory in a state of rework and scrap. And still more just in case the equipment totally breaks down—the unpredictability factor again.

■ *Inflexible labor.* Training costs were another easy target. Without sufficient training, the workforce has less flexibility to move to where the work is. So manufacturers kept people busy in place, making more and more parts for orders pushed ever further into the unpredictable future.

■ *Long changeovers/large lots.* Changing over a production line or setting equipment for the next job requires extra skills. With plant maintenance and training budgets cut to the bone, the skills were in short supply. Manufacturing's response: Reduce the frequency of changeovers and setups via longer production runs of each job, driving inventories still higher. Overhead-absorption cost accounting—all about labor costs, not inventory wastes—favors the practice. So lot sizes kept getting larger—until the West had its first Toyota system lessons on the methods and merits of quick setup/changeover and small-lot, quick-response manufacturing.

■ *Functional (not product) layouts and long (spaghetti) flow paths.* Narrowly trained employees cannot operate multiple kinds of equipment. So manufacturers laid out their plants in "critical mass" clusters of common skills, equipment, tools, and functions. A consequence: To get any job done meant long moves from one cluster to the next; transport lots and total inventory in transit and in intermediate stockrooms grew accordingly. This, too, was standard practice before the West heard about Toyota's better idea: the work cell. By co-locating a flow path's resources, the cell makes a complete item with scarcely any inventory in transit, in intermediate stockrooms, or in queue.

■ *Unsynchronized scheduling.* The functional layout clusters, called shops in the plant and departments in the office, act as fiefdoms. Each is separately scheduled to maximize its own performance: sub-assembly shop C is starved of a critical part; oblivious to that, its supplier, fabrication shop B in the next building, has scheduled itself for a long production run of a different part. Inventories swell. A computer routine called "material requirements planning" (MRP), perfected in the 1970s, helps get feeder and user shops better synchronized, but only a little. Western manufacturers would learn later about the very tight synchronization that comes with the kanban system—still another Toyota innovation.

■ *Central (rather than line-side) storage.* In the 1970s, to qualify as a "class A" MRP user, a plant had to have locked stockrooms between the separately scheduled fiefdoms. Multistep paperwork to receive, put away, log, count, value, pick, load, and release added to the time outsize inventories would spend in their lockups. Storing small quantities line-side, with no trips in and out of stockrooms and no transactions, would come later as part of the Toyota system.

■ *Complex, many-part designs.* If left to their own devices in developing a new product, engineers will feel it's their job to redesign every part. After all, shouldn't a good engineer be able to think of some way to make a design better? Each new part, of course, must be stocked— more inventory. Moreover, marketers, if left to their own devices, keep adding features, sizes, and colors, and each must be stocked— still more inventory. The antidote for design excesses, called "design for manufacture and assembly," arose from the work of Boothroyd and Dewhurst,[3] but not until the 1980s. Proliferation from the marketing side is a more complex issue—one being partially resolved by value-driven megaretailers (such as Office Depot, Wal-Mart, and Costco) who refuse to stock every brand and model.

- *Many suppliers/customers, little coordination or data sharing.* With uncertain quality from suppliers, companies protected themselves by lining up multiple sources. For cost, quality, and delivery reasons, companies would play one supplier off against the others. The upshot: Each supplier had to hold high inventories in case they should be favored with the next big order; suppliers' inventories grew under this industry-wide way of doing things. Moreover, customers could not develop trust in such large numbers of suppliers. Absent trust, customer companies upped their own protective stocks of purchased materials.

- *Marketing-induced spiky demand.* Promotion is one of the "four Ps of marketing," long a bedrock topic in Marketing 101 classes. *To promote,* the verb form, is good business. To promote and to advertise serve to inform the customer. *Promotion,* the noun, however, raises demand artificially: cut the price and get people to buy more than they need. Then, however, customers will not want to buy again for some time. A cycle of up-and-down demand spikes is the result. Some retailers and wholesalers do not know any other way to do business. Manufacturers should know better but are easily caught up in the promotion game. It's the easy way to "make the numbers" when end-of-the-period panic sets in. Manufacturing and the supply chains respond by adding capacity, and inventory, to meet the upspikes; then, during downspikes they have to keep producing—and adding inventory—just to keep the costly extra capacity busy.

- *Performance basis: machine utilization, overhead absorption (overproduction).* Faulty performance management is our final contributor to the twentieth century's third-quartile industrial decline. Companies turned a blind eye to the wastes of making too much of the wrong things; measuring performance was reducible mainly to keeping equipment and people busy. A business magazine reports on how devastating these practices have been to major Korean manufacturers. The story attributes the Korean economy's ills in the 1990s to the dominant strategy of the *chaebols* (megacompanies). Their way was to go for production volume while paying little heed to such matters as inventory and waste. Before its renewal, under frugal-minded new president Yun Jong Yong, Samsung was typical:

> In TVs, the company was carrying up to three months of excess inventory by 1997. [And, under fierce global competition, Sam-

sung's prices for electronics products] were often 30% lower by the time they were sold. "In the past," explains supply-chain management director Park [Sung Chil], "we were evaluated by unit manufacturing cost alone, . . . so we produced and produced, not caring whether or not it was sold."

Samsung's embrace of more of a just-in-time production approach has enabled the company to cut its inventory and accounts receivable costs by $3 billion, according to Park.[4]

Plenty of manufacturers in other countries have followed the Korean practice of putting production volume ahead of all else. Nissan's disastrous decade of the nineties comes to mind. Jed Connelly, Nissan North America's top executive, offers his insight: While Nissan dealers were offering rebates and cutting prices to move excess cars from bloated lots, the Nissan plant in Smyrna, Tennessee, was running full blast and being praised for productivity.[5]

Ascendancy

To sum up the above points, the growing ills of industry were mirrored by bloated inventories. Happily, old, wrongheaded concepts were replaced by new knowledge, and the downslide turned into a roaring era of industry rejuvenation. Exhibit 3.2 with stair steps going up instead of down, shows the reversal: All the causes of decline were flip-flopped, becoming driving forces

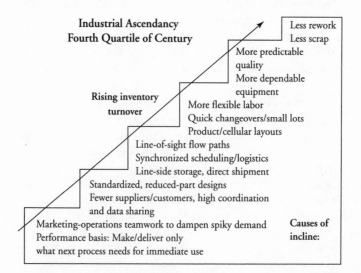

Exhibit 3.2. Rising Industrial Performance and Its Positive Effects on Inventory Turnover

of improvement. The words in Exhibit 3.2 are nearly opposite to those of 3.1 and may be quickly summarized:

- *Less rework and scrap.* Less tied up as non-value-adding inventory.

- *More predictable quality and equipment.* Less inventory just in case the quality is bad or equipment down.

- *Flexible labor.* Multi-skilled employees move to where the work is rather than staying in place building currently unneeded inventories.

- *Quick changeover/small lots.* Less lot-size inventory.

- *Product/cellular layouts with line-of-sight flow paths.* One of today's tools of improvement is the "spaghetti chart," which traces convoluted, crisscrossing flow paths laden with inventory in transit. Spaghetti-chart analysis leads to formation of multiple, self-contained, product-focused productive units with short flows and little in-transit stock.

- *Synchronized scheduling/logistics.* Visual kanban tightly links feeder and user work centers. It does the same with external suppliers and customers. Inventories plunge.

- *Line-side storage, direct shipment.* Here, three more factors drive inventories downward: 1) On-site feeder work centers and off-site suppliers deliver right to production lines. No need for inventories to spend time in an in-process or receiving stockroom. 2) Some purchased materials ship direct from the supplier to the user company. This eliminates need for inventory to route through distribution warehouses. 3) Other materials go to a distribution warehouse but employ "cross-docking": they are not stored; rather, an inbound truckload of one item unloads, and those items move immediately to multiple outbound trucks for delivery in small quantities to multiple customer sites.

- *Standardized, reduced-part designs.* The work of the aforementioned Boothroyd and Dewhurst teaches product developers to use standardized parts, unless there are good reasons not to. Modular, mix-and-match designs hold down part counts further and still provide the wide-variety options that sales needs to attract more kinds of customers. Fewer parts to manage means less overall inventory.

- *Fewer suppliers/customers, high coordination and data sharing.* These days, reducing suppliers to "a few good ones" is normal, and cutting the customer list is gaining adherents. The same item stored in fewer supplier and customer locations means less inventory. In addition, fewer suppliers give trust and data sharing a better chance. By using the same demand data, suppliers and customers can avoid making excess inventories of wrong items based on guesswork.

- *Marketing-operations teamwork to dampen spiky demand.* This is a work in progress. When marketing and operations are on the same page, inventories shrink.
- *Performance basis: Make/deliver only what next process needs for immediate use.* "Only . . . for immediate needs" is intended to mean in the right quantity, quality, and time—for the customer. No more inward focus on keeping busy growing inventories of uncertain demand.

MRP and IT

Notably missing from Exhibits 3.1 and 3.2 are information technology and inventory management itself. The latter is absent for this reason: Inventory managers do not manage inventory. Their role is to keep watch on it (record it, count it, reconcile it, and so on). It is not the inventory manager's job independently to lower/raise buffer, lot-size, or in-transit stocks. Such actions make sense only following resolution of process issues: quality, upkeep, layout, cross-training, and so on. So good inventory management is not the reason for the industrial ascendancy. Nor may poor inventory management be blamed for the earlier industrial decline; it was complacency-based deterioration in everything else.

Phil Duncan, assistant general manager of manufacturing at Toyota's powertrain plant in West Virginia, would agree, commenting thus on the way too many companies strive for just-in-time: "The first thing they do is drop their inventory and they crash and burn, they can't make production, and they're running out of parts and lines are shutting down, and they think, this stuff doesn't work. Well just-in-time is a result of doing all other things well—preventive maintenance, logistics, quality approach, safety—all those things done well end up allowing you to run with low inventory."[6]

IT, on the other hand, has had and is having its impact on inventories. First effects were in the 1970s when material requirements planning took off. A research paper dated 1980 reports the results of a study of over one thousand MRP-using manufacturers. Typical gains in inventory turnover were 20 to 35 percent.[7] Those gains, however, are a onetime shot. Moreover, some of MRP's main features (work orders, purchase orders, shop-floor control, stockrooms) became obstacles in the way of just-in-time (visual orders, visual flow management, no stockrooms). JIT's gains often include inventory reductions of 80 percent, gains on top of those that came from MRP.

In these regards, it is instructive to look at the inventory performance of three companies that enjoyed fame as pioneers of MRP and were among the first to achieve "class A" MRP status: Tennant Company, Tektronix, and Twin Disc (the "three Ts"). Exhibit 3.3 shows the inventory turnover patterns for each.

We see that in the 1960s all three were doing as most others did: loading up on inventory as a cover for mounting ills. Then, aided by MRP, all improved in the 1970s and into the 1980s. Finally, all three more or less ceased to improve in the 1980s and 1990s. Of the three manufacturers, Twin Disc was the first to lose its way, suffering declining inventory turnover since 1982. In contrast, Tektronix and Tennant actually accelerated their improvement rates through most of the 1980s. Having had close contacts with the two companies during that time (as invited presenter), I may know why: Both were early, active advocates of JIT/TQ/"world class." The minimal rate of incline at Tek and Tennant since 1988–89 suggests each has, generally, lost its way. As noted in chapter 1, other high-performing manufacturers became complacent, too, but not until around 1995.

Finding the Way

Now let's consider a manufacturer that *found* its way. Typically in industry, materials account for 30 to 60 percent of costs. The leanest of the lean push that much higher. (Lean is not the absence of inventory; it is the absence of high expenses related mostly to slow, wasteful movements of inventory through the company pipelines.) Foxboro Company's Intelligent Automation Systems plant, Foxboro, Massachusetts, cut overhead from 27 percent in 1992 to just 16 percent in 1999. At the same time it raised the inventory

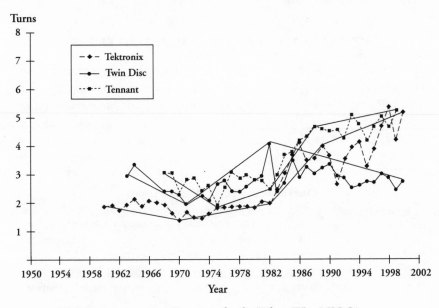

Exhibit 3.3. Inventory Turnovers for the "Three Ts"—MRP Pioneers

component of cost from 70 to 82 percent. (The unreachable ideal is inventory as 100 percent of cost: bring it in and move it out with no delays, overhead, or conversion costs.) This plant is paperless and, via very nearly zero changeover time on surface-mount circuit card lines, produces one-piece lots to order. It is the first two-time designee, in 1993 and 1999, as an *Industry Week* "best plant."

> *Caution: Inventory and related overhead expenses are necessary where processes are inflexible—and vice versa.*

Another company, Hewlett-Packard (H-P), was among the West's first manufacturers to find its way. An academic journal article reports on the importance of inventory in H-P's overall financial results. The researchers scoped a number of major H-P projects and conclude:

> *For many of these projects, the inventory cost category outweighed all others in terms of impact on the decision. At most HP businesses, inventory-driven costs (which include devaluation, obsolescence, price protection and financing) are now the biggest control lever that the manufacturing organization has on its business performance, measured in terms of ROA (return on assets) or EVA (economic value added). In the highly competitive electronics and computer industry, where product life cycles are short and commodity prices erode quickly, inventory is a tremendous cost driver and the most variable element on the balance sheet.*[8]

HOW ELSE TO MEASURE COMPETITIVENESS?

Control lever and cost driver, yes. But the reader will be uncomfortable with the idea that measuring inventory measures competitiveness. I am, too. If we place first emphasis on inventory turns, companies will game the system to make turns look good. The accompanying box offers one example; chapters 6 and 7 elaborate on tendencies to flim-flam the numbers.

Outsourcing Your Way to Lean

Getting lean is easy: just turn over your production to a contract manufacturer. This can elevate the materials component of total cost from the usual—less than 50 percent—to 80 percent, or even 95 percent. Hank Zoeller explains why: "Accounting. When product was made almost entirely in house, the material, labor, and overhead were tracked separately, resulting in a lower percentage of material content.

> [Under outsourcing, accounting] includes those products and assemblies as material only."[9]
>
> The high inventory turns that come from doing this can translate into a perception, in the stock market, of "world-class . . . inventory management and a higher PE ratio on your firm's stock price."[10] What goes up, though, comes down—at least if what made it go up was phony. If the outsourcing does not make for quicker, more flexible response to customers, the higher price-earnings ratio is gained on false pretenses. Reversal will not take long.

The real nubs of competitiveness lie in customer-sensitive factors, especially, quality, speedy response, flexibility, and value (QSFV). And what about customer retention? New products generated?

Customer Retention and New Products

Customer retention is a strong measure, and three manufacturers I admire excel in it:

■ Varian Vacuum Products, Lexington, Mass.—Recipient of Massachusetts Quality Award; named *Industry Week* "best plant" partly for its 95 percent customer retention over a five-year period; and a participant in the World Class *by* Principles International Benchmarking.

■ Senco Products, Cincinnati, Ohio—Named an *Industry Week* "best plant" partly for its 99.6 percent customer retention over a four-year period; and a participant in the WCP Benchmarking.

■ Cooper Automotive-Wagner Lighting—Named an *Industry Week* "best plant" partly for its 100 percent customer retention over a five-year period; and a participant in the WCP Benchmarking.

If present customers stick with you, you must be doing things right. But wait a minute. In this global economy, markets and channels for many products are expanding rapidly. Whole new markets—for example, India with its nearly 1 billion people—have opened up for products or brand names not seen there before. In some cases retention may be less vital than new customer attraction.

What about ability to turn out new products? Some business sectors live and die by this attribute (mobile phones and women's clothing, for example). On the other hand, new products are not at all the keys to competitiveness for Senco Products, which produces nails and nail guns, staples and staplers. Wagner Lighting, making lights for automotive interiors, needs to generate new products at about the same rate as the auto companies turn out new car models—but no faster. For thousands of manufacturers, design stability—with intensive process improvement—is more of a key to competitiveness than new product generation.

Quality, Speedy Response, Flexibility, and Value

QSFV defines competitiveness in the eyes of the customer. (QSFV, in five upward steps, make up Principle 3, which is the "attainment principle." The five-step self-assessment criteria for this principle are included in appendix 3.) They are what the world-class renaissance is, mostly, about. All are measurable, too—in thirty or forty or fifty or more ways. Speed, for example, includes time to market, cash to cash, setup time, order-fulfillment time, supplier lead time, and more.

It is good for manufacturers to employ several such measures. Your industry trade group may provide benchmarks to compare with your own company's numbers. Alternatively, your company may have membership in the International Benchmarking Clearinghouse, apqc.org; The Benchmarking Exchange, benchmarking.org; the ASTD (American Society for Training and Development) Benchmarking Forum, astd.org; the National Association of Manufacturers (United States) and its benchmarking services; or others.

Benchmarking, however, comes in different forms. Two broad categories are fact-finding and prescriptive. Fact-finding, by a trade association or benchmarking service, is the most common type. For example, your trade association's benchmark for scrap and rework may be 1.1 percent, whereas the figure for your company is 3 percent—a lot higher. Such factual comparison is useful. It may trigger a call to action and roughly suggest direction—for example, do something to improve the process.

Benchmark numbers (facts) have their place. Prescriptive benchmarking is different.

PRESCRIPTIVE BENCHMARKING

The alternate benchmarking method prescribes high standards in the form of written criteria. Your company is assessed against those criteria. The Baldrige, Shingo Prize, and European Quality Model award are of this type. So are the criteria for the World Class *by* Principles (WCP) Benchmarking. The ISO 9000 series has always been prescriptive as well. Earlier versions, however, did not have much to do with process improvement or competitiveness. The drastically revised set of standards known as ISO 9000:2000 changes that.

In this kind of benchmarking, scrap and rework would not be a subject.

Rather, a prescriptive track for workforce training might take care of the issue: train the workforce in how to reduce scrap and rework. A quality track and an equipment maintenance track likewise should lead to less scrap and rework. In other words, prescriptive benchmarking is mainly about *means* of becoming competitive. By demonstrating a certain level (means) of competence on a given track, a company receives points. In the Baldrige, the European Quality Model, and the Shingo Prize, maximum points possible are one thousand; maximum for the WCP are eighty (five points per principle, or track; sixteen principles).

It is probably unwise for a company to settle on any one kind of benchmarking, since each yields its own special benefits. That point should be kept in mind in the following comparative discussion.

WCP Benchmarking

In general, the World Class *by* Principles (WCP) system of assessment and improvement advocates "proven," time-tested, widely accepted best management practices. It allows points only for following *those* practices, not a different set. The practices are stair-stepped upward, easiest-cheapest to hardest-costliest. (Appendix 3 presents each principle and the stair-stepped self-assessment criteria.)

The layman might expect rather wide differences of opinion about what constitutes best practices—or whether there even can be a standard set of them. However, these days most of the esteemed business and manufacturing books, articles, and consultancies echo each other rather than argue over what good management is. (Who would argue against continuous process improvement; high levels of employee involvement; quick, flexible response; or getting lean?) Several hundred companies, most of them with strong "excellence" credentials, have studied and/or used the WCP criteria. In a few cases, their suggestions have led to small wording changes in the scoring criteria. Otherwise, the principles and criteria remain stable but are basic enough as to embrace best ideas from new management initiatives.

The WCP has several unique features, as follows:

- *"Pure play" process management.* The WCP criteria track *how to do it*— in specific terms; no intermixing of the how with ultimate financial success; the pure-play approach embodied in the WCP follows the premise that if you do the right things, and stay with them, the bottom line will take care of itself.

- *Quiet benchmarking:* The WCP is "quiet"—no public exposure (company scores are kept confidential), therefore no need (or cost) for external auditors and their fees. (In its first four years, the WCP service was entirely free to participants; today, a small fee is often charged by WCP International Benchmarking partners—to help defray the costs of bulky mailing, database administration, and production of customized benchmarking reports.) A business unit's purpose, in participating, is to develop and sustain world-class rates of improvement, not to win an award.

- *High validity.* Managers doing the self-scoring have no incentive to inflate scores—since there is no public award, recognition, or release of scores, except in the aggregate (or by special permission).

- *Quick.* A small cross-functional team of managers often can complete its self-scoring on the sixteen principles in about forty-five minutes; the give-and-take (arguing) over the scores is itself valuable.

- *Tough.* The WCP criteria are extremely tough; even the top-scoring companies are giving themselves twos and threes (out of a possible five points) on a few of the sixteen principles—which reveal their blind spots.

- *International.* While most benchmarking services are national, regional, state, or industry-specific, the WCP is international, with research partners headquartered in fourteen countries.

- *Elite sample.* The manufacturers submitting scores to the WCP database are an elite group; many have received recognition such as a Baldrige or other national or state quality prize. Though any company may join the benchmarking, the research partners seek out the best, so that composite benchmarking scores reflect best practices of companies with forward vision. Of this sought-out elite group, nearly 50 percent have accepted our invitation to participate in the WCP (this compares with about 10 or 15 percent acceptances for the typical survey sponsored by a prestigious university, consulting company, or professional society).

- *Award enabler.* The breadth and depth of the WCP criteria define pathways to excellence that can help a business unit win a prestigious public award—valued for promotional purposes and for the assessments that lead to the award.

- *Total business benchmarking.* The sixteen principles in the WCP stretch from stem to stern, including most of what manufacturers do (from focused organization to continuous process improvement to promoting and marketing every improvement).

- *Total workforce.* The WCP criteria are crafted to give high emphasis to contributions of every employee; the idea is to avoid heavy reliance on leaders—to build in some immunity to the risk of gains lost if key leaders depart for greener pastures.

The theme of the previous chapter is that after success, companies fall into the complacency rut. This tendency applies as well to companies that receive awards. Informal research on this point suggests that the year of receiving the award is often the company's best year (to some extent, the award may contribute to the letdown). An intent of the WCP is to humble even the best. Its top score—five points—defines not what the best are achieving today. Rather, it is projective. Highest-point criteria define what companies must achieve to survive and thrive under global hypercompetition in the twenty-first century's upcoming decades.

The Shingo Prize, administered by Utah State University (shingoprize.org), has much in common with the WCP. It should. Shigeo Shingo, after whom the prize is named, was a mastermind of the Toyota system and the industry's leading expert on quick setup. In addition, Shingo, who died in 1990, was the world's leading advocate of two powerful quality techniques: fail-safing (*pokayoke*) and source inspection. Of the 1,000 possible points in the Shingo criteria, about 750 are in the realm of "pure play" process improvement, which, as noted earlier, is a feature of WCP self-assessment. We often advise the higher-scoring WCP companies to apply for a Shingo Prize. The purpose is to gain public recognition of their strengths. For manufacturers that already have received a Shingo, participating in the WCP can help avoid the after-prize complacency effect. The challenge of going for the next point on some of the sixteen principles prods continuity.

The Baldrige and the European Quality Model, considered next, are like the WCP and Shingo Prize in some important ways, considerably different in others. ISO 9000:2000 is now worth mentioning in the same breath.

The Baldrige, European Quality Model—and ISO 9000

About half of the one thousand possible points in the Baldrige award are consistent with concepts underpinning the WCP, but the other half are not. Briefly, the WCP's focus is on respected, highly specific "basics" of customer-centered process management. The Baldrige and the European award started out in that direction, but their criteria have been modified over the years. A *Quality Progress* article notes, for example, that in the new, revised European Quality Model, the word *quality* does not appear in either the areas to address or the subcriteria.[11]

Ironically, while the Baldrige and European awards have moved away from process improvement, ISO 9000 has moved sharply toward it. ISO 9001:2000 is based on eight principles. Notable among them are customer focus, involvement of people, process approach, factual approach to decision making, and mutually beneficial supplier relationships.[12,13] By their sound, these principles could have come right out of the W. Edwards Deming playbook.

Getting back to the Baldrige, in its year 2000 revision, about 50 percent of points are on what to do (manage the processes). Most remaining points are for outcomes of what to do—that is, see if managing the processes actually produces important results, including financial success. In effect, each Baldrige company serves as another testing ground to prove/disprove the viability of managing the processes. This redundancy in the Baldrige—necessary for political and other reasons—does not discredit the award, though it does inject an element of means/ends confusion. These comments apply as well to the European Quality Model. (Among other quality awards, Australia's had stood out for its high emphasis on bedrock customer-focused process improvement. The award's revision in 1999, however, shifted emphasis to conform to the U.S. and European models.[14])

There are good explanations for the means-ends redundancy in the Baldrige and the European Quality Model. Being prestigious national and continental awards, they must admit a certain amount of compromise. They are obliged to offer something to each major supportive constituency—four in particular.

1. *The quality community.* This is the original constituency, still supplying most of the awards' support, examiners, lore, and impetus for use. (The American Society for Quality, asq.org, administers the Baldrige, with oversight and partial funding supplied by the National Institute of Standards and Technology, U.S. Department of Commerce.) This constituency's mind-set is that continually improving processes in the eyes of customers is the key to every genuine, long-lasting measure of success.

2. *Executives.* The Baldrige and European awards must court the favor of executives, inasmuch as they have veto power over the awards' application in their companies. Thus, it is tactical to include as award criteria various characteristics of the executive art, some being controversial. For example, executives may be bent on maximizing shareholder value and, as shareholders, their own compensation—in partial conflict with overall stakeholder interests. The high influence of executives is reflected by the ease with which newly favored executive-level programs find their way into the criteria before they have stood the test of time. Examples: stretch targets, economic value, and notions about leadership.

3. *The investment community.* The majority of investors may care deeply about building real value. The "owners of the moment" segment, however, holds sway, and its interest is in short-term fi-

nancial success, which conflicts with the build-the-infrastructure affinity of the quality community. In the Baldrige, assigning a large percentage of points to business results tends to guarantee good business results for winners; see the accompanying box.

"Baldrige Stock Index Once Again Outperforms S&P 500"

The above is a news item headline in the April 2000 issue of Quality Progress. The note explains that in 1995 the U.S. National Institute of Standards and Technology set up a hypothetical stock market fund made up of Baldrige award recipients. Each year $1,000 is "invested." In 1999 the Baldrige fund outperformed the Standard & Poor's 500 by 4.8 to 1.

And why not? Of the 1,000 maximum Baldrige assessment points, 450 are for business results. (Five other categories get a maximum of 85 points each: customer and market focus, human resource management focus, information and analysis, and process management; leadership gets 125 points.)

It's like assessing the sports excellence of, say, teams of the National Basketball Association based half on "how" factors and the other half on outcome numbers. The hows would include player selection, conditioning, drill and practice, competitive analysis, and so on. Main outcomes numbers would be won-lost records, number of times winning their division, and number of times winning the championship. The Chicago Bulls, 1990s version, would score very high on this assessment. As my eleven-year-old nephew might say, "Duh!"

These points are made with some reluctance. Baldrige winners are highly deserving of their recognition: they are examined exhaustively. Existence of highly visible national and international awards also serves a valuable public purpose: it proclaims that this company is great to do business with. Having a prestigious, independent body tell us this is far better than trial and error (that is, buy from or sell to a company and get burned). We think more companies ought to apply for the Baldrige—and the Shingo, the European Quality Model, your state or province award, and your country's magazine-sponsored best plant award.[15]

---

4. *The news media, general public, and political community.* The general public, and by extension the political establishment, reacts to anything, however sensational or unfair, that is expounded in the news media. The Baldrige and European criteria contain a rather complex mix of measures. Then, when (not if) any one of them receives bad press—such as someone claiming process management doesn't lead to success—other positive criteria are there to deflect the criticism.

To sum up these points, the Baldrige and European criteria, and the Shingo and WCP Benchmarking, are around 50 percent similar in content but are distinctly different in many ways. For their public value and rallying-point impact, the Baldrige and European awards are peerless; so is the Shingo Prize. On the other hand, the WCP offers practical courses of action for building a competitive engine to thrive in this century.

SUMMARY

For any given manufacturer, gaining a solid edge is a rocky road. Surest, though imperfect, pathways follow the kinds of excellence models that have been discussed. Other formulas, such as moving "up" to services, are riskier.

One advantage of sticking with manufacturing is that it offers a single, telling measure—inventory turnover—of multiple kinds of performance. When tracked as a multiyear trend, the measure tells a lot about a manufacturer. To those who still have their doubts, please (as they say) *do the math.* Here the math is simple: Just add the number of causes of the industrial decline and rise in Exhibits 3.1 and 3.2. They total fourteen—fourteen critical activities of a manufacturer that if done poorly make the inventory metric poor, and vice versa. Outside of manufacturing and other inventory-intensive sectors (wholesaling/distribution and retailing), reliable indicators of competitiveness trends are harder to pin down.

Caution: Inventory is necessary where processes are subject to high variation.

Chapters 4 and 5 carry this discussion of competitiveness forward. The management program "disease" gets our attention in chapter 4, faulty success formulas in chapter 5.

4

Programs and Their Half-lives

New management programs are like new product models: everyone wants one; then before long, almost nobody does. Not only that, but the time between everyone and almost no one is ever shortening. This is not to ridicule the phenomenon. Rather, the purpose of this chapter is to find what is solid in each fading initiative and ensure that it is preserved.

The oldest notable management program is scientific management, now over one hundred years old. A comparable old product is the Honeywell round thermostat. Each enjoyed almost total market dominance, in home markets, for decades.

Now consider a modern pair: In management, business process reengineering is a good example, as is the notebook computer on the product side. Within a couple of years of reengineering's genesis in 1990, every management consulting firm worldwide was professing expertise in it, but by 1996 it was collecting figurative dust in PowerPoint archive files. As to notebook PCs, they are like women's skirts, obsoleting themselves with each new advance in technology or fashion.

This does not mean that reengineering is an obsolete idea or that clunky, three-year-old notebooks are museum pieces. There is still value in each, but the opinion makers have gone on to other things.

What comes to mind is the half-life principle in nuclear physics. It refers to the time required for half the atoms in a piece of radioactive material to disintegrate; half its power is gone. In business, half-life works, too. It is the time it takes for a management program to lose half its potency or cachet.

This chapter, after reviewing program half-lives, poses ways of dealing with related excess demands on management. Among these are folding core concepts and enduring techniques into a master program, anchoring to an honors/awards regimen, and building a critical company history.

LOFTY-NAMED PROGRAMS AND THEIR EVER-SHORTENING HALF-LIVES[1]

Let us consider some of the last century's best-known management initiatives and track the compression of their half-lives. The ones selected have enjoyed prominence in manufacturing companies. In the process, we'll keep tabs on the worthy concepts that emerge and endure from each. The remainder of the chapter will propose a cure for a rampant, modern disease, *programitis:* the practice of flitting from one short-half-life program to another, generating confusion, leaving important work undone, and sapping energy along the way. Scientific management serves as a starting point for this half-life analysis.

A Sixty-Year Half-life

Management was scarcely recognized as a profession or field of study until scientific management emerged, in the late 1800s, from the works of Frederick W. Taylor, Frank and Lillian Gilbreth, Henry Gantt, and others. (We are not counting impressive planning and control practices for building Egypt's Pyramids or producing sailing ships at the Arsenal of Venice; they were historical blips, not management movements.) Briefly, scientific management means work study. One tool is time study. Another is methods or motion study, which employs process flowcharting. Some economic historians have offered scientific management as a prime reason why the United States became industrially supreme. It originated in the United States in an age when ideas took decades to migrate across seas.

Interest in time study and methods study peaked during World War II, when the industrial world had a single-minded objective: more. To squeeze out more, industrial engineers in many factories were using motion-picture technology. They filmed jobs being performed; then, in the plants' film laboratories, isolated non-value-adding wastes. After the war, the film labs quickly disappeared, along with the dominance of "more." In fact, by the early 1950s in the United States (though certainly not in bombed-out Europe and Asia), excess capacity was emerging as a problem. That ushered in marketing as a new business function: find ways to sell the excesses.

These days, scientific management is called Taylorism. In testament to the notion that its half-life has passed, Taylor himself has become a pariah, a favorite whipping boy among promoters of any brand of enlightened management. Taylor may lie uneasy in the grave, but time standards and methods studies are bedrock tools of industry:

- *Standard times.* In a just-in-time environment, precise timing is all the more important. Moreover, good time standards are a necessary input to a newer technology—computer simulation of factory operations. At Monarch Marking Systems, Miamisburg, Ohio, operator teams do their own time studies.[2] Monarch is recipient of a National Association of Manufacturers 1999 award for workforce excellence and an *Industry Week* "best-plant" award in 2000.

- *Standard methods.* Elemental in the Toyota system and *kaizen* events, both enjoying resurgent popularity, is "standard work"—same as standard methods.

- *Process flowcharting.* Non-value-added analysis (popular enough today to be shortened to its initials, NVA) has process flowcharting as its main fact-finding tool. Process flowcharting has three lives. The first was as originated about one hundred years ago. Its second life began some thirty years ago in Japan, when Kaoru Ishikawa named process flowcharting as first of the seven basic tools. (Ishikawa is also originator of the fishbone chart and the quality circle concept). Its third life began around fifteen years ago when it was renamed "process mapping," then slightly renamed again as "value-chain mapping" or "value-stream mapping."[3] Whatever the name, it is a top-notch tool for exposing non-value-adding elements in the process.

Other aspects of Taylorism are at odds with good business practices as we know them today. For example, Taylorism tends to focus on more output, whereas just-in-time aims for just enough output—no more—to meet customer demand. In addition, Taylor would have the production function split into thinkers, who do the analysis and set the standards, and doers, who just do. Today we reserve our admiration for companies that empower the direct labor force to think for itself.

In summary on scientific management, we may conclude that it held sway for about sixty years (say, 1890 to 1950), then quickly lost about half its steam. In other words, its half-life was sixty years. Exhibit 4.1 leads off with scientific management and follows with programs having progressively shorter half-lives. Discussion of those programs continues.

Thirty- to Ten-Year Half-lives

The next major management program, operations research (OR), arose during World War II. OR's main tools are mathematical models such as linear programming and queuing, along with Monte Carlo simulation. Early applications included finding optimal sites for radar installations on the British Isles and safe-from-U-boat configurations of ship convoys crossing the Atlantic. After the war, OR migrated out of the defense agencies. It found new homes in think tanks such as the Rand Corporation and university depart-

60 Years:	Scientific management
30 Years:	Operations research
20 Years:	Just in time
15 Years:	Total quality management
10 Years:	Benchmarking
Toward <5 Years:	Business process reengineering, demand-flow technology, theory of constraints, *kaizen,* activity-based management, agility/mass customization, self-directed work teams, balanced scorecard, open-book management, supply-chain management, six sigma, lean manufacturing, any initiative called "breakthrough"

Exhibit 4.1. Program Half-lives, Ever Shortening

ments of industrial engineering. Soon, schools of business added OR to their quantitative course offerings, usually calling it management science (not to be confused with scientific management). Graduates set up OR or management science offices in big industry and government agencies. Their charge was to apply OR modeling in studies of problems in complex organizations. By about 1970, the budget cutters were taking hard looks at those high-salaried offices that manipulated hard-to-understand math models; as a result, most of the special studies offices were downsized or eliminated.

Academic departments still turn out math-model-literate graduates, and the models continue to find uses in industry. But OR and management science enjoy nowhere near the esteem they did in their glory years between 1940 and 1970. The half-life of OR: about thirty years.

Now we close in on the present. What is the half-life of just-in-time? JIT made it out of Japan in about 1980. Though still alive, another program employing most or all of JIT's features has taken over—namely, *lean.* JIT's half-life: twenty years. (It takes only an offhand remark in one prominent source to accelerate the predictable sinking of a popular program. See the box for one such remark in a business magazine, concerning JIT's deflation.)

JIT R.I.P?

Fortune magazine relates how Japanese manufacturers are selling their plants or turning over production to electronic manufacturing service (EMS) providers, most being

U.S. based. According to the piece, an approach called "demand-flow technology" (DFT) has been instrumental in the success of some of the EMSs. (DFT is a term coined by the John Constanza Institute of Technology.) Demand flow, states the article's author, "does away with that mainstay of Japanese manufacturing, the just-in-time (JIT) delivery of components . . . ," and so, the article continues, perhaps "it's time for just-in-time to rest in peace."[4]

Notwithstanding the fine work of the Costanza Institute, most insiders know that demand flow is firmly rooted in JIT. While having its own special wrinkles and effective training regimens, demand flow contains virtually all of JIT's elements, notably cellular organization of plants with kanban methods of restricting work-in-process inventories; one-piece, mixed-model production; and quick changeover and other methods of gaining flexibility.

The half-lives of total quality management (TQM) and benchmarking look to be about fifteen years and ten years, respectively. Judging by the many times that someone has, in print, dismissed TQM as a "failure," some might say that its *whole* life was fifteen years. ("What's as dead as a pet rock? Little surprise here: It's total quality management": *Business Week,* June 1997.)[5] That view will not stand up, however, unless we are ready to invalidate TQM's main features: take care of the customer, continually improve quality, use statistics-based process analysis, and work together in multiskilled teams.

Benchmarking's launching pad was Robert Camp's 1990 book on Xerox's origination of the practice.[6] Attempts to dislodge benchmarking from our favor revolve around this argument: Aiming for a best-practice benchmark gets you only parity, not competitive advantage. By 2000, that idea had made the rounds of professional conferences sufficiently that benchmarking, as a program, had reached its ten-year half-life.

The substance of benchmarking, searching for best ideas beyond one's own little world, cannot be cast off. Failure to stay abreast invites complacency and also duplication of effort. Consider, for example, a manufacturer seeking best ways of handling employee performance appraisal. It arranges a benchmarking visit to a hotel chain that masterfully employs 360-degree performance appraisal. The benchmarking team returns fully informed about the hotel's trial-and-error period. So armed, the manufacturer avoids going through the same wheel-spinning sequence.

Benchmarking offers another benefit: New innovations are generally more likely when you have thorough knowledge of best old ones. Existing knowledge, especially from external sources, is often the spark of innovation.

Note: It is unreliable to do an Internet search of published articles to judge when a program has reached its half-life. Articles continue to pour forth for years after a program has gone over the hill. Benchmarking, for example, has an academic journal devoted to the subject: *Benchmarking: An International Journal,* published quarterly, first issue in 1994. Such journals do not die easily.

Toward Five-Year (or Less) Half-lives

The following is a partial list of management initiatives approaching half-lives of five years or less: business process reengineering, demand-flow technology, theory of constraints, *kaizen,* activity-based management, agility/mass customization, self-directed work teams, balanced scorecard, open-book management, supply-chain management, six sigma, and lean manufacturing.

Regarding lean, Jeff Sabatini, writer for an automotive industry magazine, offers testament to its shortening half-life. He had attended a large industry conclave featuring the president of Toyota–North America as keynote speaker. After the president's talk, on the Toyota/lean system, Sabatini overheard two listeners say, "He didn't say anything," and, "The Toyota Production System is old news." Sabatini counters that "the lessons . . . of TPS/lean will never be 'old news.'"[7] Right. Still, its half-life may have been reached. The same may be said of six sigma, which was called into doubt by the *Fortune* piece directed to investors, "Why You Can Ignore Six Sigma."[8]

Add to the five-year list any program touted as "breakthrough." This is not to demean the programs carrying the label. Sort through the hyperbole, and there often is plenty of good content. With so many programs being launched, sometimes the only way to muster up attention is to attach a tag such as breakthrough, which, the purveyors hope, will be seen as something grander than continuous improvement/*kaizen.*

> *An academic study of sixteen management programs since 1950 partly substantiates the decreasing half-life notion. It found that the average time span between inception and peak for a program was 14.8 years from 1950 through 1970. It fell to 7.5 years in the 1980s, then to 2.6 years in the 1990s. That study included only four of the manufacturing-oriented programs cited in this chapter. The rest were general management programs such as quality of work life and core competencies.*[9]

What's Next?

More programs, yet to be heard from, are on the drawing boards. Still others have budded out, and whether they blossom is still uncertain. One of the latter is called "strategic quality management" (SQM). R. J. Ricardo proposed it—as a step up from total quality management, in his 1994 article, "Strategic Quality Management: Turning the Spotlight on Strategic as well as Tactical Issues."[10] Other references on SQM can be found. Still, in terms of applications, the clock has not yet started on SQM's half-life. Will the clock start? The defender of TQM might claim that SQM is just a way to take quality away from the *total* workforce. The advocate of empowerment might suggest that propping up the tottering command-and-control system is SQM's hidden agenda. Both might argue that TQM is already strategic and that the proper executive role in it is to provide visible support and funding. These points of view may or may not be influential in determining the fate of SQM. They point, however, to the tougher kinds of tests likely to be applied to each new initiative that begs our attention.

Not included in this half-life discourse are software programs, such as the critical path method, material requirements planning, enterprise requirements planning, and many others, including those on drawing boards and in the bud stage. They get into the computer system, and you can't get them out. (The previously cited academic study includes PERT, which originated in the 1950s. The study noted that, unlike the other fifteen programs, PERT never has run out of gas.[11] [PERT stands for "program evaluation and review technique," which is about the same thing as the critical path method.])

Inasmuch as a small industry of educators and consultants attends each of the programs named in this section, the list may be seen as offensive. It should not be. Half-life is not death. Rather, it means that while the pot may not be boiling anymore, it still simmers.

STABILITY

Bubbling forth from all those simmering, by-no-means-dead programs are enduring features that build the body of world-class knowledge. The features are of two types, core concepts and techniques:

Core. The enduring core concepts are customer focus, a turned-on workforce, management by fact, and continuous improvement. All of the sixteen principles making up WCP have features that incorporate these four core concepts. (See appendix 3 for descriptions of each principle and assessment criteria.)

Techniques. The enduring techniques are work cells, kanban, small-lot production and transit, quick setup/changeover, the seven basic tools, design for manufacture and assembly, basket of values, target costing, value engineering, *takt* times, process capability index, quality function deployment, cross-careering, and many more. Each of these techniques finds a home in one or two of the sixteen principles.

The core concepts appear to be unimpeachable. It is hard to imagine that they could be superseded or revoked. A program at its half-life is out of the limelight, not out of favor; favorable support for the core concepts hangs tough.

Nor is it easy to see how any of the techniques should become obsolete. If that should occur, the wording of the scoring criteria for one of the principles may have to change. The criteria are as highly specific as the present state of understanding of "best practices" allows. That is why the principles advocate, and press manufacturers to adopt, all of the enduring techniques. To make the list and find their way into the criteria, the techniques must have been time-tested in many industries and companies. As such, the enduring techniques should be thought of as, simply, good management.

Some companies, typically the stronger ones, have not been program chasers. They stay aware, and they extract and incorporate best ideas. Toyota's system carries on, and was never supplanted by, say, total quality. Yet Toyota folded out its own company-wide quality effort and was able to win Japan's Deming Prize for quality in 1965.[12] Similarly, important Western innovations such as design for manufacture and assembly, benchmarking, and activity-based cost audits fit easily into the Toyota system (though Toyota was a bit slow to recognize each of these, probably because of their non-Japanese origins).

An enduring and stable system builds on a special kind of framework: one focused on universal customer wants. As noted in chapter 3, those wants are ever better quality, speedier response, greater flexibility, and higher value (QSFV). By universal, we mean that all customers, internal (next process) and external (outside user), value them.

Some have raised questions about the internal customer concept. Ackoff, for example, distinguishes between internal consumers and customers,[13] meaning those using the final product or service. The latter are the real objects of a business. But how can an employee or supplier who never sees a final user relate to that user? The elegant answer is to improve that employee's own contribution to what the final user is sure to want—ever better quality, quicker response, greater flexibility, and higher value.

What about *cost* and *service* as universals? The accompanying box explains.

Universal Customer Wants/Needs

Pick up any number of business textbooks. Look for competitive priorities. You are likely to see the following: quality, cost, service, and—a newer addition—flexibility. No big argument here, only small ones.

- The current industrial renaissance appears to be as much about quick response (S, for speed, in QSFV) as the classic competitive priorities.

- Service is a lot of things, but it breaks down fairly well into quality (quality of service), speedy response (quickness of service), and flexibility (service agility). So there is no pressing need to list service as a separate universal.

- As originally posed (mid-1980s), the World Class by Principles agenda listed low *cost* as one of the four "golden goals" desired by all customers. Later, *value* replaced cost. Reasons include the following:

  ▶ Customers talk about value all the time; so do retailers, who are closest to customers.

  ▶ Value includes cost.

  ▶ Eliminating non-*value*-adding wastes and delays is a basic of lean/world-class management; so is value analysis/value engineering. These techniques provide ways of improving and managing for value.

  ▶ Too many sins have been committed in the name of cost reduction: blanket layoffs, budget cutting through the fat and into bone, and failure to pursue worthy avenues that might cost money. Moreover, cost is an internal measure, unlike quality, speedy response, flexibility, and value, which are outward, customer/competitive concerns.

PRESCRIPTIONS: MASTER PROGRAMS, AWARDS, AND HISTORIES

Commonly, what deflates a thriving program, shortening its half-life, is someone with an alternate agenda. Often enough, that someone does so by authoring an article entitled, "Beyond TQM," "Beyond Reengineering," or "Beyond" any other popular program. It takes only one. That one article, regardless of credibility of the source, gets quoted and requoted, and TQM or reengineering is a has-been. Then, the herd stampedes toward the new, improved model (or an old one rebranded).

The chorus "We Are Like Sheep" in Handel's *Messiah* comes to mind. Businesses, in defiance of supposed high rationality, are quick to follow, like sheep, each casting off the old for a frenzied embrace of the new.

How can a company protect itself from that energy-sapping practice of leaping from initiative to management initiative? Best answer is adoption of a stable *master program* and sticking with it. Pursuit of any of the prestigious prizes and awards can offer further protection. It helps, as well, to maintain a company history so that initiatives have the benefit of memory of what has already transpired and to what effect. The chapter winds up with further remarks on these three stabilizing approaches.

What's in a Name?

Emerson Electric's master program, dating back to the early 1980s, is called "Best Cost Producer." It is a commitment to quality, customer satisfaction, competitive knowledge, focused manufacturing, and so on—not at all just cost reduction.[14] As would be expected the typical automaker's superprogram is named (fill in the blank—Ford, Kawasaki, Toyota . . .) "——— Production System." Or, other than in the auto industry, there is the Aeroquip Production System, and others.

Other stable-named management systems center on the word *quality*, such as Baxter International's long-standing Quality Leadership Process (QLP). Baxter launched QLP in 1985 and rolled it out company-wide in 1988–89. QLP is robust enough to absorb new initiatives, six sigma being Baxter's latest.

Sealed Air Corporation's choice, stable for over ten years, is tried-and-true World Class Manufacturing. (Except that it makes the term a bit cumbersome, the word *Company* might be added—the WCM *Company*—so as to emphasize the whole enterprise as the unit of improvement.) Any generic term that easily admits each new, worthy innovation will do. How about Customer Focus, Continuous Improvement, or Global Competitiveness as the title of your company's management supersystem—for the duration?

Two fine new books provide another pair of possibilities. One is Johnson and Bröms, *Profit Beyond Measure*,[15] which hammers away at the idea of "management by means." Chapter 7 of this book is devoted to the same notion: that management by results is unworkable, because good results follow only from having the means. So your master program might be called Management by Means. The other book is Ruffa and Perozziello, *Breaking the Cost Barrier*.[16] In this book on lean in the aircraft industry, the dominant theme—and another good super-program name—is "deviation management." The authors' point, backed up with research, is that there is too much talk about averages and too little about deviation—in time, quality, output, or any aspect of managing the means of production and service. (Dr. Deming, were he still alive, surely would enthusiastically agree.) That same idea was front and center in my own 1986 book, an excerpt from which is included in the accompanying box. Standard and Davis echo this viewpoint in their 1999 book; they provide examples in most chapters of why variability is the enemy.[17]

Variability Reduction[18]

If a ticket taker can sell a ticket in "exactly" thirty seconds nine out of ten times, but then the machine jams and it takes three hundred seconds to sell the ticket to the tenth customer, consider the effects. Not only has the tenth customer been poorly served, but at an average rate of one customer arrival every thirty seconds, ten new customers will have appeared, only to get in line and wait while the jammed machine gets fixed.

Varying only once in a while from the thirty-second standard requires wasteful solutions: extra space for customers to line up; staff to manage the queue and soothe the customer; and perhaps an extra, mostly redundant ticket seller to keep the line from getting too long.

Costly solutions of that sort are called for in response to variability regardless of the setting. The cutting tool that must be searched for sometimes, the assembler who does the task the wrong way sometimes, the part that arrives late sometimes, the blueprint that is wrong sometimes—all of these and many more require costly sets of "solutions." They are not true solutions, because they provide for living, poorly, with the problems.

Manufacturers that have been flitting from program to program don't need to be told that the practice is irrational. They do need to do something about it—to make a start toward stability. Honeywell's merger with Allied Signal in 2000 presented an opportunity, because the two companies' dominant programs went in different directions. Allied, under Laurence Bossidy, a GE alumnus, had committed itself to the GE total immersion version of six sigma. Honeywell liked that but knew better than to abandon its own years of commitment to alternative initiatives. What evolved is a program called "Six Sigma Plus." It neatly absorbs Honeywell's three thriving initiatives, lean, ABM (activity-based management), and total preventive maintenance (TPM). As in GE, the program requires employees to be trained and involved. In the new Honeywell wrinkle, they can earn certifications in several "core areas": six sigma green, black, and master black belts; lean expert and lean master; ABM expert and ABM master; and TPM expert and TPM master.[19] The program's name, Six Sigma Plus, may not stand the test of time very well, but the name is less important than giving strong backing to the enduring basics: the quality sciences (in six sigma), eliminating wastes and delays (lean), keeping facilities in tiptop shape (TPM), and keeping everyone involved (as the program has been set up). (Here, ABM appears to be a bit of a misfit, since it overlays the other program elements with cost data and analysis. Cost analysis has value in some improvement projects but in most is redundant—non-value-adding waste.)

The Steadying Influence of Honors Programs

There is further merit in rallying around the concepts underpinning notable honors programs, such as the Baldrige award, European Quality Model award, International Asia Pacific Quality award, Shingo Prize, "best plant" recognition (such as that from *Industry Week* magazine in North America or *Management Today* in the United Kingdom), and World Class *by* Principles. Though each of these has its own features, and the criteria for each get updated, they all put the customer on a pedestal.

States and provinces in many countries operate their own Baldrige-like awards.[20] In addition, a number of larger manufacturers devise their own. One that closely parallels the WCP is Allied-Signal's Total Quality Maturity Path. Business units score themselves in six areas on a scale of one point (lowest) to four points (world class). The six areas address several of the sixteen principles. A more complete summary of the Allied-Signal model can be found in an earlier Schonberger book.[21]

These kinds of honors and awards are more than just programs. They have legs in that they generally commit award recipients to various follow-through activities. Winners may be obliged to send presentation teams and speakers to conferences, serve on boards that oversee the awards, host benchmarking teams from other companies, and submit updated performance results. This can go on for years, which helps the company toe a consistent path. (The awards maintain high levels of interest. NIST sent out 112,000 copies of the Baldrige Criteria for Performance Excellence in 1999. In 2000, the number was about 80,000-plus; NIST doesn't know how many more were downloaded from its Web site.)[22]

A more apparent benefit of awards is that they help impel a company toward excellence in the first place. One more benefit, this one not so obvious, is that better information breeds stronger partnerships. That is, information about an award winner and the nature of its excellence saves time for others who must size up the company as a potential ally. It fosters or improves the bond with potential and existing customers, suppliers, employees, regulators, and other stakeholders.

For these reasons, receiving recognition and awards earns points in WCP Benchmarking. The points are included in steps 3 and 4 of Principle 16:

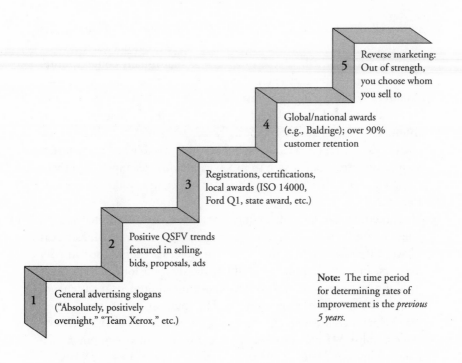

5 — Reverse marketing: Out of strength, you choose whom you sell to

4 — Global/national awards (e.g., Baldrige); over 90% customer retention

3 — Registrations, certifications, local awards (ISO 14000, Ford Q1, state award, etc.)

2 — Positive QSFV trends featured in selling, bids, proposals, ads

1 — General advertising slogans ("Absolutely, positively overnight," "Team Xerox," etc.)

Note: The time period for determining rates of improvement is the *previous 5 years.*

Exhibit 4.2. Principle 16: Promote, Market, and Sell Every Improvement

"Promote, Market, and Sell Every Improvement." That principle, in the stair-step format, is included in Exhibit 4.2. Registrations, certifications, and local, state, and other awards qualify for one point at step 3; and global/national awards (along with over 90 percent customer retention) qualify for a point at step 4.

Note, also, that step 3 of Principle 16 specifically names ISO 14000, the Organization for International Standards' series on management for the environment. The ISO 14000 series sets forth criteria for becoming registered as conforming to the standard. ISO 9000, the standard for quality, does not qualify for credit at step 3 of the principle. That may seem odd, since quality is one of the golden goals of customer service (quality, speedy response, flexibility, value). The differences are these:

ISO 9000. The ISO 9000 series can stimulate a company to improve quality. But it is a weak way as compared with approaches that employ total quality, the quality sciences, and initiatives such as six sigma.

ISO 14000. There are all too few ways to get companies to pay heed to the environment. But the WCP is intended to project competitiveness well out into the future. ISO 14000 fits the bill. Before ISO's drafting of the 14000 series standards in 1992, manufacturers generally failed to see the here-and-now savings that usually come from reduced use of water and energy and increased reuse and recycling of resources. Those savings generate value, the fourth golden goal. Companies also tended to overlook future liabilities for damage to the environment. Those liabilities, especially in companies that heavily use chemicals, can render a company's otherwise valuable real estate unsalable. Worse, they can absorb so much capital for cleanups as to drive a company out of business—the ultimate in negative value for the customer.

Sometimes the tangible savings come from an unexpected source. The chemical division of Canon Virginia, Inc. (CVI), of Newport News, Virginia, makes components for toner cartridges used in laser printers. In its pursuit of ISO 14001, the division found that a great deal of manufacturing waste occurred during equipment maintenance to correct a manufacturing problem. The solution was to increase preventive maintenance and cut reactive maintenance in half. CVI reports these results: Maintenance work orders to fix failed equipment fell from 85 percent in June 1998 to 28 percent later in the year. Work orders for process improvements increased from 4 percent to 35 percent. Defects dropped by more than 70 percent. Substantial cost savings resulted from increased yields. And, of course, CVI saw considerable improvements in environmental impact.[23]

ISO 14000 is not comprehensive, like the European Quality Model award and the Shingo Prize. But it is both an honors program and good business.

Histories

Another prescription for combating programitis is building a history book. We are not talking about the kind of cream-skimming business histories that revolve around the company's officers, demographics, and financial results. Rather, a good history is filled with details on analyses done, decisions made, and postmortems completed. It is not for public consumption but is for improving future decisions in light of past mistakes. Strategic matters should make up part of the history, operational matters another part.

On the strategy side, a company in the snack food business provides a good example. The company had been expanding and opening new plants for years—thirteen of them. Too many, however, turned out later to be poorly located. Why? Company management decided on a formal plan of action to find out. A small group of senior people was charged with doing a deep search. They pored over company records and interviewed everyone available who had been involved in the original siting decisions. The result of the study was a highly revealing history. Some of the insights and conclusions drawn were

"We picked the wrong products for sites [X, Y, and Z]."

"We built plants too early."

"Our accounting methods overly influence [our choices]."

"We should build each factory grounded in a profitable product."

"We equalize all the businesses we add to the company culture rather than keeping them competitive with their local competitors or job market."

"We allow our investments in new business to be affected or driven by our core business; we should do it the other way around."

If this history just ends up on a shelf, it is a waste of time. What needs to be done with a good history is to build its lessons into a new, systematic procedure. Each new factory planning initiative, then, must follow the procedure.

The operative word is "systematic." Given the high turnover of both managers and programs in many companies, good management practices need to be made systematic instead of catch-as-catch-can. Elevating a principle to systematic status was illustrated in chapter 2, using the second principle as an example. Companies with systematic procedures—if well aimed at competitive/customer issues—will have an edge over the typical seat-of-the-pants managed company.

Operational activities also deserve to be documented for posterity. My initial exposure to this was on my first trip to Japan in the early 1980s. I returned with an impressive remnant of the trip. It is a book of an entire year's worth of studies done by quality control circle teams at Japan Radiator Company (Nihon Chukoko). Study reports in the book include before and after process data and drawings, often cartoon-like; schematics; improvement graphs; and team photos. Previous years' books populate the company's bookshelves. Before going very far, a team working on, say, a quality issue on a punch press will check all the previous books to see what studies have already been done on that issue. Lacking such histories—as is the case with even most top-ranked manufacturers—and systems of using them makes for a lot of wheel spinning. Process improvement, when it has already been done before, is non-value-adding waste.

SUMMARY

This chapter has viewed competitiveness programs through a wide-angle lens. It has been about tendencies of the whole business sector. Companies do the right thing: searching, searching for new ways to gain an edge. But they do so jerkily and without memory and records, the keys to thorough learning. A few broad-brush prescriptions have been presented: How to extract the enduring from the fleeting. How bootstrapping to honors programs can tone down the instability. And the need for keeping and using decision histories.

Next chapter's lens narrows. Main subjects are prominent manufacturers and what they need to do to solidify their strengths and attend to their shortcomings.

5

Success

Twenty-five years ago my wife and I accepted one of those free-vacation offers. You go to a resort area, agree to sit through a real estate sales pitch, and
get three free nights in one of the units, plus other amenities. The salesperson
had us one-on-two in a drive through the development. He started out in a
pleasant soft-sell mode, learning in the process that we were educators. But in
response to our repeated "No thanks; we aren't interested in buying," he got
increasingly aggressive. Finally, when it was clear that all was lost and time
was up, he hurled an outright insult: "You know what they say: 'Those who
can't do, teach.'" My fast retort, of course, had to be, "Yes, and those who
can't teach, sell!"

Actually, I didn't say it—not being that quick-witted. But the story is relevant here. It pertains to what does and does not drive business success.

Yes, good selling drives success. But selling is a secondary mover—though
of a higher order than financial wheeling-dealing and legal maneuvers. The
primary drivers of genuine success—sustained competitive advantage—are
on the customer side of the ledger. This means a product line that has high
value in the eyes of the customer, made and delivered when, where, and how
the customer likes it best.

A theme of this and other prominent writings on excellence is that "the
basics" offer the surest path to success. That was not the case in the past era of
retarded, nonglobal competition. Companies could high-pressure customers
into buying what they really did not value. They could keep doing it year
upon year. They could be chronically late and slow in deliveries, consistently
ship quantities different from that ordered, offer an unchanging take-it-or-
leave-it product line, and ship lots high in defects.

This chapter brings success up-to-date. It contrasts conventional and contemporary success formulas, with prominent manufacturers as examples. Included is an example of how small-pocket actions can trigger small but
meaningful chain reactions. Last, the chapter rank-orders, by average scores,
the industry sectors that have participated in the World Class *by* Principles
International Benchmarking.

CONFOUNDED SUCCESSES

In an earlier era, companies with limited capabilities could get by. The 1990 Schonberger book, *Building a Chain of Customers,* identified three common types of companies and why they were just getting by—or flying high: cowboy companies, Keystone Kops companies, and blue-suit companies. We'll revisit these three types. For the cowboy and Keystone Kops categories, discussion is more extensive than for blue-suit companies. We begin with the cowboys. Included is a look at a few admired manufacturers and their soft spots as well as strengths.

Cowboys

Let's scrutinize five companies that were or are remarkably successful. Three of them, Boeing, Nucor Steel, and Lincoln Electric, are classic cowboy—but have lost their competitive dominance. The other two, Nypro and Wainwright Industries, are cowboy-with-a-difference. First rank in their industries, both supplement their can-do cowboy personas with superior dedication to the customer—but not just any customer.

BOEING, PRE-1990.

Today's Boeing is working hard on the world-class basics. After a couple of its worst years in decades, Boeing emerged in 2000 as one of the stock market's bright spots. Instead of just selling airplanes, says Seddick Belyamani, head of sales and marketing, "We're running it as a business." A *Fortune* special report states that every Thursday Belyamani and other managers meet with Commercial Airplane Group president Alan Mulally. Together they "pore over a color-coded spreadsheet of the commercial business's vital signs: material costs, inventory turns, overtime, defects, and so forth."[1]

It took most of the decade for the company to develop a management system containing a diverse set of good business basics. In comparison, pre-1990s Boeing was one-dimensional. It was admired for its can-do cowboy character but was seriously plagued by a complacency complex.

A brief digression. Friends in the United Kingdom say that the term *cowboy company* elicited confused reactions. Isn't the cowboy the Old West's buffoon? No, no, I say. We Americans much admire our cowboys. A range boss, hired to drive an unruly 2,500-head herd hundreds of miles across the Llano Estacado, would make the rounds of dusty West Texas towns, collecting about eight to ten cowboys. Most had never met or worked together before. Yet they could successfully guide the herd past hostile tribes of Comanche and Pawnee through largely waterless, treeless expanses all the way to the Kansas City train terminus. No management system. The cowboys just knew what to do and did it.

Plenty of manufacturers have had success the same way. At Boeing proficient engineers were the cowboys. We all had confidence in the planes they designed and built, and had high admiration for the Boeing Company.

Today the world is too complicated for the cowboy formula. Boeing was successful with it because of light competition.

NUCOR STEEL.

Throughout the 1980s and into the 1990s, Nucor Steel progressively invaded the integrated steel companies' markets with innovative technology for processing scrap iron. Nucor became the United States's second-largest steelmaker. The company's nonunion, cowboy workforce, motivated by huge productivity bonuses, made Nucor hum. With global steelmakers finally getting lean in the 1990s, Nucor's simple formula was no longer sufficient. In the industry it has lost its standing as "most admired."

As to Nucor's cowboy roots, we may consider a *Business Week* story: in June 1999, Nucor's CEO, John D. Correnti, was replaced. The magazine quotes Correnti as saying later that he feared the new CEO's plans for a strategic planning staff would stifle the company's spirit. Correnti's worry was over loss of a can-do, localized way of operating. The Nucor way was one in which plants handled "everything from sales to purchasing and are often the fount of Nucor's best ideas."[2] Doing it locally plant by plant is the cowboy way, whereas a strategic planning staff has the look of a blue-suit company.

LINCOLN ELECTRIC CO.

Best precedent for Nucor's "spirit" surely is Lincoln Electric of Cleveland. In many years, Lincoln's proficient, cross-trained, cowboy-like front-line workforce received productivity bonuses near to 100 percent of regular wages. That bonus system dates back to 1934. Lincoln was also one of the world's first companies to offer employee training, health benefits, a pension plan, and a suggestion program. Its management innovations covered enough ground that business college students could encounter a Lincoln Electric case study in several different courses. The TQ/JIT era, however, passed Lincoln Electric by, as it rested on its laurels.[3] Meanwhile, competing welding equipment manufacturers reorganized into cells, slashed setup times, and populated the work centers with process control charts. In the late 1980s and into the 1990s, Lincoln began to lose market share, especially to JIT-savvy

Miller Electric. Stories in the business press about Lincoln's growing competitiveness problems[4] replaced stories about high pay and innovative management.

NYPRO.

Nypro Inc. is the world's largest plastic injection molder, with plants in about a dozen states and ten countries. Esteem for closely held Nypro today is like that of Boeing, Nucor, and Lincoln Electric fifteen years ago. Like them, in some respects, Nypro is a cowboy company: its technical people know what to do and go out and do it, in each new plant. Nypro adds plants much as Intel does with its "copy exactly" formula: replicate good practices over and over again. In other respects Nypro is unlike Boeing, Nucor, and Lincoln. Its excellence is owed, in large part, to its early dedication to statistical process control of quality and customer/product-focused factories and plants-in-a-plant.

Being customer- and product-focused does not mean letting the total population of potential customers out there dictate terms. Rather, it is the opposite. Focus on a few good products for a few good customers, then intensively serve and deliver. That describes Nypro to a T. In the late 1980s Nypro was floundering a bit. The senior staff pondered the problem and concluded that the company was cutting too wide a swath. This led to a bold act: Nypro reduced its customer list from six hundred large and small customers to thirty-one large ones. Its new, focused policy was to accept a new customer only if there was the likelihood of $1 million in sales within two years. If so, Nypro would often build a plant right next to that customer's facility. Ever since, Nypro has been a growth engine—in both size and reputation.[5]

> In the WCP, a focus on customer or product families is the first and most important of the sixteen principles. (See appendix 3 for a full description of Principle 1, along with the other fifteen principles.) One criterion for scoring on this principle relates to the Nypro strategy of slimming the customer base to a number that can be treated with dedication.

Impressively, Nypro has pursued these key aspects of global competitiveness in an industry low on competitive pressure to excel. There are no other injection molders that come close to Nypro in size or commitment to training and customer-focused quality. But can it last? Nypro's success formula is just "basics," which are well known. Predictably, therefore, tough competition will emerge, and soon. In light of that, it is urgent for Nypro to press forward with the full world-class agenda. Like nearly all best-in-class manufacturers, Nypro has its weaknesses and blind spots. Its management teams know them inasmuch as most of Nypro's plants have self-scored on the sixteen elements in the World Class *by* Principles International Benchmarking. The scores point to step-by-step pathways for closing gaps. Competitors are likely to be shooting at a moving target.

WAINWRIGHT INDUSTRIES.

Wainwright, a smaller St. Louis–area manufacturer, received a Baldrige national quality award in 1994. Wainwright has no obvious technical edge. Its conventional presses stamp automotive and aerospace parts out of metal, like a few hundred other stamping shops. They are the best of the lot simply because, cowboy-like, they do it better.

As we would expect of a Baldrige winner, Wainwright has a multifaceted customer-focused improvement system—though with a few gaps that need filling (as with Nypro, Wainwright has self-scored on the WCP Benchmarking). The way it runs its low-tech business bears some similarity to a cattle drive. Instead of each drover keeping watch over his or her own space alongside the herd, each Wainwright machine operator keeps watch individually over a stamping press. Consultant Michael Simms, formerly a Wainwright officer, says that 50 percent of Wainwright's success comes from having every employee owning his or her twenty-five-square-foot area of influence. The company backs this up with plenty of training, support, and recognition for results.[6]

COWBOY COMPANIES IN PERSPECTIVE.

Yes, we cherish our cowboys. We've always admired their counterparts in industry as well—whether a giant company like Boeing or a wizard of an auto mechanic who can fix anything on any car. These days, though, it is not enough just to be highly proficient at making something or providing a service, a superlative one-trick pony. Each of the five companies just discussed has several tricks in its saddlebags. All five need still more. To gain and keep a competitive edge, companies need forty, fifty, or sixty tricks. Or, to be more specific, mastery of a full set of the tools of continuous, customer-focused, employee-driven, data-based improvement. Nypro and Wainwright are on the right track, combining their cowboy competencies with many of the tools. Boeing got a late start but is working on it. Nucor Steel and Lincoln Electric need to make up lost ground fast.

All five of these companies have exceptional attributes yet must be challenged to change and improve. Nonexceptional manufacturers—cowboy or otherwise—are far more severely at risk.

Keystone Kops Companies

Opposite from the can-do stability of cowboy companies is the helter-skelter Keystone Kops category. Cowboyers promote from within; Keystoners don't keep their people—not even their company name and marque—long enough for that.

We run into companies like this often. They've been repeatedly destabilized: bought and sold, privatized and made public, relocated, fattened up and downsized, and churned in their professional ranks. ALARIS Medical is a recent example, though not even close to a worst case. ALARIS's family tree sprouts quite a few branches. Without showing the linkages, here are some of the names and dates of the players: IVAC (public) 1968, IMED (private) 1974, Eli Lilly (public) 1977, Warner-Lambert (public) 1980, Fisher Scientific (public) 1987, Henley Group (public) 1990, River/DLJ (private) 1995, Advanced Medical (public) 1996, ALARIS (current parent, public) 1997, Instromedix (acquisition, public) 1998.

In such companies, we may ask some of the current incumbents how long they've been there and hear four years, two years, eighteen months, and just hired. Their new people carry with them a diversity of valuable experience and know-how. On that score, they have an advantage over cowboy companies, which sometimes suffer from inbreeding and lack of exposure to the wave of ideas emergent from the knowledge renaissance. The trouble is, the ideas are too numerous and their lives too short to take hold. The professionals in these businesses are like the Keystone Kops of silent film days, who—to quote my encyclopedia—"dash off to the chase in jerky, speed-up tempo, collide with one another around corners, and become entangled [in whatnot], their facial expressions of dour dignity never changing."[7]

IMPORTING THE RIGHT EXECUTIVE.

It may not be possible for a manufacturer embroiled in such disorder to become, say, a Shingo Prize winner. They may, however, be able to tone down the turbulence enough to beat the blue-suit competitor. A strong, experienced guiding hand at the top for a while or a few like-minded, seasoned professionals might show the way. In ALARIS's case, the appointment of Dave Schlotterbeck as CEO of the multimerged business has the look of the right kind of guiding hand. Schlotterbeck was on the management team at Cal-Comp in the mid-1980s when that business unit, then of Lockheed Corp., was receiving awards and publicity for its JIT/TQ way of running a business.

Schlotterbeck went on to turn around a couple of other manufacturers by overseeing implementations of the same best-practice basics. One of them, Pacific Scientific, parent of thirteen operating companies, was in financial turmoil when Schlotterbeck hired on as president. He handed out a dozen different books to a management team and asked them to pick one. They did, and it became the subject of monthly progressive reviews and study groups. The studies led to rapid improvements, including, within four months, a 20 percent reduction in wasteful inventories and a 50 percent rise in the value of the company. That piqued the interest of a competitor, who launched a hostile takeover bid. Seven months after Schlotterbeck's arrival, Pacific's share price had tripled in an auction that generated $350 million in shareholder value.

By now, there must be a few hundred people with, more or less, Schlotterbeck's sure-handed ability to make a difference. Some are top-executive level, others somewhere down the ranks. Keystone Kops companies need to find and hire a few. Maybe the same goes for blue-suit companies, soon to be discussed, although their problems are different.

POCKETS OF "WORLD CLASS."

Without a Schlotterbeck-like executive, a Keystone Kops manufacturer will have a tougher time. A saving grace is that world class is large doses of good sense and small doses of money. Therefore it can develop in pockets, without funding and without strong top-down leadership. For example, a single turned-on machinist might plunge into machine setup-time reduction. Or a supervisor might cross-train all her subordinates. Either action is a start (and not likely to get the person fired).

Exhibit 5.1 is a flow diagram that shows a large number of possible pockets. It also shows how a small-pocket action (any box) can trigger little chain reactions. The cause-effect arrows flow from any action to the final objective, the box on the far right. While every box needs effective implementation to reach "sustained competitive advantage," each activated box is a small start, worth doing.

There are many pathways flowing left to right in Exhibit 5.1. A winning pocket initiative may start with any box. It does not seem to matter which; in our experience, every company seems to begin where it will and take its own path. (In contrast, management consultants tend to want clients to follow a certain pat sequence.) Examples follow:

Manufacturer A.

The sheet-metal shop starts with setup-time reduction, followed right away by lot-size reduction, which improves flexibility. (The three affected boxes are near the bottom-center of the exhibit.)

In the assembly shop, on the other hand, first step is to slash assembly lot sizes, thus improving flexible response. That action increases frequency of assembly-line changeovers. The costs of more changeovers are unacceptable, which presses the shop, before long, to cut setup/changeover times (the arrow between setup time and lot size goes both ways).

Manufacturer B.

The first pocket initiative is in accounting. A cost accountant launches an attack on inaccurate costs (second box from the left, top row). The method is activity-based costing audits of key product models. The results flow into sales and marketing, which sharpen the company's product-line decisions and pricing and enhance product-line expertise. Sharper pricing also cuts the non-value-adding wastes of bidding on—worse, booking—jobs that cannot pay their way. Elimination of the wastes lowers average unit costs.

None of the pocket initiatives is risky, and the only one in Exhibit 5.1 that costs real money is better equipment selection.

Though any of the boxes is a worthy starting point, there are two that vastly outshine the rest in total impact: the two at the extreme left. When a manufacturer takes early steps to form product-focused value chains (e.g., plants-in-a-plant and work cells), everything else falls into place naturally. Products are what customers buy. A rather self-contained work unit geared to

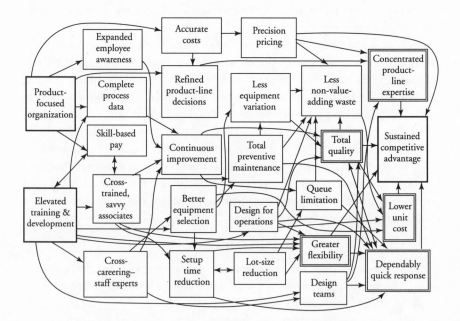

Exhibit 5.1. Interlinked Manufacturing Agenda

making just one product family elevates customer visibility. People in the unit can see the customer effects of cross-training, queue limitation, total preventive maintenance, and so on. There is no such visibility in the conventional organization, which is cut up into shops and "silos," each with its own narrow function.

The other left-most box is training and development. Without large amounts of it, people do not even know about quick setup, process data collection, and design teams.

Another point about the pockets approach: Executives and consultants like to precede any project with an analysis of its cost or profit or revenue impact. That's okay. But often it makes just as good sense to go with paths of least resistance. For example, the biggest bang for the buck, pound, or franc often is in design for operations (generic equivalent of design for manufacture and assembly). Say that in your company a cost/earnings analysis indicates just that. But the design engineers are not ready for DFMA, not up to speed on it. What should be done, force it down their throats? Or fire and replace an engineer or two? Maybe first projects should shift to total preventive maintenance, or queue limitation (kanban), where key people already have some awareness and readiness.

A final note about Exhibit 5.1: Five double-bordered enabler boxes immediately precede the ultimate box, sustained competitive advantage. Three of the five correspond to "golden goals" of customer focus: quality, speedy response, and flexibility (QSF). The fourth and fifth bring on value (V) in the eyes of the customer: lower unit cost (just below "sustained competitive advantage" in the exhibit) accounts for a key element in the value equation. Concentrated product-line expertise (upper right corner of the exhibit) represents the business link to the customer.

Say that your company has superior product-line expertise. Sales and marketing persistently and effectively convey that expertise. Dependable delivery of QSFV—in a state of continuous improvement—backs up what sales and marketing convey. That adds up to sustained competitive advantage.

The pockets in Exhibit 5.1 are all elements in the world-class journey. The trouble is, manufacturers are too easily distracted from staying with that journey. That is particularly the case for the blue-suiters, which tend to adopt every distracting program that comes along.

Blue-Suit Companies

Most large, old-line manufacturers are, or were, blue-suit companies: their professional ranks overflowed with suited-up program managers, department heads, accountants, and staff analysts. Their names were Kodak, General Motors, AT&T, Campbell Soup, Texaco, British Steel, Philips, and Olivetti. For another perspective on blue-suit versus cowboy, see the accompanying box.

Some of these and similar manufacturers have gone dress casual (out with the suits) and downsized. Regardless of uniform, their tendency to plan things to death persists. The suits keep abreast of what's new in management—to a fault. A "modernization" program spends enormous sums on inflexible factory automation, while a flexibility/agility thrust is in the opposite direction. A program to train the entire workforce on lean/JIT, with *elimination* of shop-floor transactions, collides mightily with an enterprise requirements planning implementation *requiring* shop-floor transactions.

The siren song of size—growth by merger and acquisition—worsens these problems. It becomes blue-suit company A's conflicting programs clashing doubly with those of acquired companies B, C, D. . . .

More than anything else, the suiters need to go on a diet of no new programs. Or, more accurately, bring best ideas from emerging programs prudently into the fold. As noted in the previous chapter, the "fold" is a tailored superprogram with a stable name and a full array of core concepts and enduring techniques. Manufacturers seriously lacking in even one of the concepts can lose ground quickly. A few examples follow.

MANUFACTURING FAILURES

"You can be sure if it's Westinghouse" was a mid-twentieth-century slogan known to every American. It lasted far longer than, say, "Things go better with Coke." Today, you can be sure Westinghouse no longer makes anything. We will consider its demise, as one of the world's premier manufacturers,

---

Blue-Suit (Low-Context) and Cowboy (High-Context)

Robert Hall presents "the eighth waste": the waste of excess information. His discussion of it offers insights that bear on the blue-suit and cowboy distinction.

The cowboy company fits with what Hall labels "high-context." This is where there is "well-developed visibility" and "an integrated view of space." Large amounts of information are wasteful and unnecessary because "if a person . . . already knows what to do, all that must be conveyed is job priority, a simple action message."

Low-context—the blue-suit organization—is opposite. "People are less aware of their environment, so action messages are more detailed and explicit," requiring "many communications intermediaries."[8]

along with that of International Harvester. We will also look at some other famous manufacturers that fell off a cliff but arose and are healing; and at still others that are weakened with recoveries delayed.

The Fallen

Why did Westinghouse drop out as a manufacturer and megacompany? A brief history: In the early 1980s, the Westinghouse Productivity and Quality Center turned its sights generally away from high-cost factory automation. Its officers had become converts to JIT and total quality. Westinghouse factories were the beneficiaries. Four of them made the "honor roll" in Schonberger's 1986 book. To qualify, a manufacturer had to have reduced its throughput time at least 80 percent (eighty-four manufacturers made the list).[9] While the manufacturing side of the company had its head on straight, senior management had stars in its eyes. After a few years of buying TV and movie studios, Westinghouse's fortunes began to sink. Plunging deeply into red ink in the 1990s, the company lost little time in selling off all its manufacturing businesses. The Productivity and Quality Center's fine efforts were for naught. The Westinghouse debacle is owed to the head's loss of interest in manufacturing, while the body tried futilely to keep it going.

International Harvester (IH) fought labor "forever," while its main competitor, Deere and Company, for the most part kept the peace.[10] Caterpillar, another similar business, fought labor, too, and took a 17½-month strike in the mid-1980s. IH, though, had a more severe failing: Its factories stayed stuck in the batch-and-queue mode with unfocused plants. After mostly red ink in the 1980s, IH's assets were sold off and the famous brand was dead. Meanwhile, Caterpillar's fortunes soared under its "Plant with a Future" strategy. Main features included total reengineering to form focused factories and work cells, with emphasis on cell-size rather than monument-size equipment.

The Recovering

While Westinghouse and IH were dying, three much larger manufacturers, IBM, General Motors, and U.S. Steel, were ailing. U.S. Steel was the first of the three to show its ailments; General Motors was next. IBM was actually the first to sicken but the last to show it.

IBM.

Our inventory research tells the IBM story: In 1961 IBM was turning its inventory a phenomenal 24.8 times per year. That means on average its stocks—raw materials, work in process, and finished goods—spent less than two weeks inside the company. Is there another sizable firm in the world that had a number that good? We don't know of any.

Exhibit 5.2 highlights IBM's inventory turnover since 1961—a sharply downward, and finally upward pattern. From the trend line, we can see this: The handwriting was on the wall. By 1985 inventory turns had sunk all the way down to two, which means stocks were spending six months, not two weeks, inside the company. That plunge says that IBM had rapidly lost its ability to manage itself.

Through much of this period, however, sales skyrocketed. Between 1956 and 1985, sales were doubling every four years. Share price, too. The popular phrase "If only I had bought . . ." was probably applied to IBM more than any other stock. Then sales growth slowed sharply—to doubling every six years, then seven, then eight or nine years. IBM's common stock price peaked in 1983, earnings per share in 1987. The company hit bottom in 1991, 1992, and 1993, suffering $16 billion in losses in those years. In the early part of the period since 1961, when inventory turnover peaked, financial results looked fantastic. Underlying performance, though, was crashing. But nobody knew.

In leanness, IBM's peak performance year was 1961. Another milestone occurred the same year: the company launched what may be the most successful product of all time, the IBM 360 series of mainframe computer. That success, ironically, contributed to IBM's undoing. Big business everywhere wanted a 360 model. IBM had to ramp up faster than any company's ability

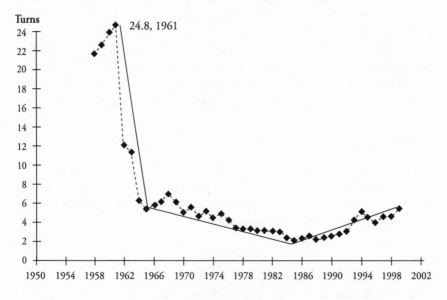

Exhibit 5.2. Inventory Turnover at IBM

to do it well. IBM and supplier plants sprouted and grew fast around the globe. Each new order meant more inventory in transit and in queue. IBM, the information company, could not manage the information necessary to coordinate the massive complexity.

This is not for lack of trying. IBM was among the earliest Western advocates of the JIT/TQ/lean agenda. The Schonberger seminars and workshops played at IBM sites in several European countries, as well as, repeatedly, at IBM's White Plains, N.Y., training center and its leading-edge business unit in Raleigh, N.C. One IBM plant manager's reaction: "The first thing we have to do is get rid of COPICS."

There hangs another dragging anchor: IBM's own manufacturing system software, one called COPICS, the other MAPICS. Both are large, complex material requirements planning packages. In those years MRP's heavy requirements for scheduling and work-flow transactions and reports weighed against the simplicity of kanban and rate-based scheduling. Later MRP versions (from IBM as well as other software companies), though still tending toward excess transactions, became friendlier to JIT/lean management. (Earliest attempts to use kanban at Toyota also were foiled by requirements for work-flow transactions. In that case it was the Japanese tax office levying the requirement "on the grounds that the system did not document accurate accounting records for each transaction.")[11]

GENERAL MOTORS.

The story at GM is quite different from that of IBM. GM's difficulties may be owed in large part to its 1980s' leapfrog-the-Japanese strategy. GM would automate its production, thus slashing payrolls (beat Japan on cost) and tightly controlling processes (equal Japan on quality). Its $50 billion–plus investment fell far short; the GM frog couldn't leap. Worse, GM lost years of time. While it plunged into robotics and automation, Ford and Chrysler worked on total quality, supplier partnerships with kanban deliveries, and removal of non-value-adding wastes.

U.S. STEEL.

Big Steel, it was called. Nobody had to ask the company name. Today, U.S. Steel, owned by holding company USX, is one of the crowd. Like other steelmakers in the United States in the 1960s and 1970s, U.S. Steel did the opposite of modernizing and upgrading its workforce. Its technology became outdated, its factories run-down, its labor-management relations miserable. The company had been doubling sales every seven or eight years. That came to a halt in the late 1970s. With modern mills and technologies, first Japanese and then Korean steelmakers became the new global champs. In the

1990s, U.S. Steel, along with others in the industry throughout the world, modernized and became more or less competitive equals. The whole industry, however, has been a laggard in adopting a customer-focused competitiveness model. More will be said of this in the last chapter topic.

From these examples of recovering manufacturers, we go to some that, of late, have faltered.

The Weakened

It is ironic: the Japanese auto industry, birthplace of the ongoing manufacturing renaissance, has not kept pace. Nor has Japan's electronics industry, whose early excellence also caused global competitive havoc. The giant performance gap with the rest of the world has been for the most part closed. The two industries in Japan are still strong. In relative terms, though, they are weakened. Some of the failings noted below are current, others projective.

- *Product design.* The most critical failing is in product design and development. Both industries in Japan were late in discovering the power of design for manufacture and assembly. Having been "invented" in the United States in the early 1980s, DFMA lore found homes in U.S. companies first. Briefly, DFMA simplifies product designs. It calls for fewer parts, less variety of parts, multiuse parts, more standardization, more modularity, elimination of fasteners, unidirectional assembly, and so forth. In the auto industry, U.S. producers gained roughly a ten-year DFMA head start over their Japanese competitors. The American electronics industry's time advantage was only a bit less.

- *Restructuring.* In the face of global overcapacity, industries everywhere have been forced to downsize. Big industry in the United States, in league with the investment community, seemed almost to relish shuttering factories and laying people off, in many cases ten thousand people at a time. This began in the late 1980s and continues today, though at a slower pace. The United Kingdom quickly followed with its own redundancy actions. Continental European industry, too, has chopped plants and bodies, despite more restrictive labor laws. Finally, Japanese manufacturers had to restructure— a bitter pill in view of Japan's cherished lifetime employment policies. Companies like Nissan, which lost money in almost every year of the 1990s, had to close plants just to survive.

    In electronics, Hitachi, NEC, Panasonic, and others had their own reality checks. They've been downsizing five thousand and ten thousand employees at a time, plus farming out component production to Solectron, Celestica, and other contract manufacturers—but years after Hewlett-Packard, IBM, Compaq, and other Western manufacturers did so. (The "farming out" in many cases is selling out. That is, Cisco, Sony, and the other majors are selling whole plants to the electronic manufacturing service companies. This trend, handing over plants to the EMS specialists, finally has taken root even within Japan. There the rub was that manufacturing was long thought of as a core competency. Moreover, there were concerns as to whether Western owners would be able to develop an "understanding of Japanese employees," as a news story put it.)[12]

■ *Modular plants.* In industries assembling complex products, the chronic weakness is too many parts. The solution is a vast reshuffling from assemblers that have far too many parts to suppliers that have too few. (Chapter 12 elaborates on this movement.) Any single plant that has to juggle thousands of parts is a plant rife with wastes, and auto assembly plants have long been among the worst cases. With so many components, they bear multiple burdens. They include too much complexity, too much non-value-adding investment in storage and handling apparatus, too many people whose jobs are just to manage all those items, and too much risk of a single wayward part or lot causing havoc. In the modular system, suppliers of preassembled modules grow their part counts but within reason, while final assemblers shrink theirs.

Finally, the auto industry is taking action. But the leaders are not Toyota, Honda, and Nissan. In the vanguard are Ford, Volkswagen, General Motors, and DaimlerChrysler. These Western automakers have all opened modular assembly plants, at first mostly in Brazil. Lessons learned from those plants may revolutionize the industry. The birthplace of lean manufacturing concepts is the automotive industry, but it can never approach real leanness until that revolution takes place. That said, the modular shift does carry with it some degree of risk, as noted in the box on the next page.

The intent here is not to pick on Japanese industry, but rather to show how easily tables can be turned in a world alive with management innovations. (And though Western industry has a bit of a head start with modular systems, automakers in Japan and Korea won't be far behind; a 1999 report indicates that Honda fully intends to adopt modular assembly.)[13] No company's past history of success will stand the tests and challenges of today and tomorrow. To disagree with one of the best-selling business books of the 1990s, no company is built to last. The point bears further discussion.

Design of Modules, Design of Systems

The auto industry wants to be like Mike. Michael Dell, that is. Different modules of Dell's computers plug-and-play just fine. Each module can be rather independently optimized, and still the modules come together as a system. And it works—discounting the occasional "fatal exception error" message.

Carmakers want the same thing. There is a problem, though. A fatal exception error, if the modules don't mesh right, may end as a highway fatality.

As first-tier suppliers take on responsibilities for module design and manufacture, what must be done to ward off fatal exceptions? Brett Smith, senior staff member at the Center for Automotive Research, has an answer: Automakers must maintain a strong grip on design of the system as a whole. This is not just to optimize fit and finish. It is to minimize the chance of modules that do not perform as they should when functioning as a hurtling two-or-more-ton vehicle. As an example, Smith cites the finger-pointing that occurred regarding deaths due to tire tread separation of Firestone radials on Ford Explorers.[14]

NOT BUILT TO LAST[15]

Consider the following companies. What is special about them?

CBS

Digital Equipment Corp.

Dow Jones

Du Pont

General Motors

Hallmark

Hilton

J. C. Penney

Kodak

McDonald's

Pan Am

RCA

Reader's Digest

Sears, Roebuck

U.S. Steel

Westinghouse

Yesterday, Today, and Tomorrow

Answer: They are among yesteryear's most admired corporations. Why? What are the genes that make for especially long life among corporations? Say that in the 1960s or 1970s a professor of business decided to undertake research to find out. Of the large population of companies to examine for such genes, the above sixteen might have emerged.

CBS, the Tiffany network, made TV what it is. Dow Jones was in the catbird seat as a repository of investor news. DEC was the highest flyer of high tech. Du Pont was "better living through chemistry." General Motors invented, and was past master of, the business world's most influential form of decentralized line-staff organization. Hallmark was nirvana for commercial artists and where you went for a card when you "care enough to send the very best." Hilton was to hotels as Callas was to coloratura arias. Penney, perhaps the first company to call its people "associates" (dating back to 1902),[16] was where retail folks wanted to work. Kodak prints were what you grabbed first if your house was on fire. Generations of families were raised on McDonald's dependable fare. Pan Am was to air travel as Hilton was to hotels. RCA, an electronic technology Vesuvius, was dominant in home radios and TVs. *Reader's Digest* had coffee table prominence. Sears, Roebuck had pioneered a form of empowerment via a very flat, broad-span-of-control organization structure—and, according to rural mythology, its catalogs were staples in America's outhouses. We've already commented on U.S. Steel, the elephant in the industrial menagerie, and on the Westinghouse "You can be sure [of]."

Fast-forward to 1994. That is the year that Stanford professors James Collins and Jerry Porras revealed a different set of "visionary companies," which, by their research, were *Built to Last*. American Express, Boeing, Citicorp, Ford, General Electric, Hewlett-Packard, IBM, Johnson & Johnson, Marriott, Merck, Motorola, Nordstrom, Philip Morris, Procter & Gamble, Sony, 3M, Wal-Mart, and Walt Disney.

Fast-forward again to, say, 2020. At least two of these sixteen will have shot themselves in both feet, à la Westinghouse or, worse, Pan Am. One or more will have been saved by being acquired (DEC'ed?). If another research team engages in another research project to get to the bottom of business longevity, their sixteen-odd companies will scarcely resemble those of Collins and Porras.

The point is, the Collins-Porras companies are not built to last. They are all excellent companies. But none has what it takes to survive, say, a CEO like Roger Smith, whose belief in leapfrogging through automation and high technology shrank GM's domestic market share from nearly half to a precarious 28 percent.

The criticism notwithstanding, *Built to Last* deserves respect. Its research basis is more extensive than that of nearly any of the other top-selling trade books of the past two decades. What the authors tell us about the diverse strengths of each of the sixteen companies makes for high-interest business-book reading. It is too bad the conclusions do not begin to live up to the title.

Flaw

Why not? A fatal flaw is the book's lack of consideration of the current and ongoing business renaissance. To reiterate, headliners of the emergent knowledge are just-in-time and total quality. Closely related are time-based competition, focused factory, plant-in-a-plant, empowered work-cell teams, quick-change flexibility, total preventive maintenance, design for operations, continuous replenishment, and supplier partnership. This collection of drive-out-the-waste concepts and techniques has become essential for survival in many industries. Why did *Built to Last* exalt Ford while listing GM as its hapless foil? The book doesn't mention it, but, as we've already noted, Ford got started on the lean agenda early while GM dithered. And by the way, is any manufacturer better built to last than Toyota (which is absent from the Collins-Porras list)?

Lean management cannot be assumed to be that which will separate the enduring from the receding. But it has become a key requisite, rating consideration equal to the mores, cultures, and habits cited as vital in *Built to Last*. There is much more to the longevity equation, much of it awaiting more rounds of innovation, learning, and implementation. Some industries have been up to the challenge, while others lag badly. The final chapter topic provides a current ranking.

INDUSTRIAL RANKING

The main message of this chapter is that success goes to those that learn. The World Class *by* Principles Benchmarking offers its own support for that message. We've grouped the 480-odd manufacturing units participating into twenty-six sectors and averaged the scores in each. Participants were asked to place themselves in up to three different sectors. Thus, an auto parts maker might be in the vehicular components, metalworking/machining, and electronics sectors. Out of the 80 points maximum (sixteen principles, up to five points each), the grand average score is just 33.1 points. That average is

MANUFACTURING SECTOR	AVERAGE SCORE	NUMBER OF MANUFACTURERS
Aerospace/defense	39.9	20
Vehicular components	37.8	48
Electronics	36.8	130
Electrical	35.8	36
Textiles	35.8	8
Telecommunications	35.6	22
Medical devices/ pharmaceuticals	34.7	75
Semiconductors	34.6	11
Sheet metal	34.3	65
Metalworking/machining	34.1	154
Liquids, gases, grains, powders	33.1	33
Grand Average	**33.1**	**480+**
Vehicles	33.0	11
Motors & engines	32.8	12
Pump, hydraulic, pressure	32.7	29
Sheet stock, including textiles	32.4	23
Wire & cable	32.4	14
Printing	31.7	14
Plastics, rubber, glass	30.7	67
Machinery, large appliances	30.5	30
Furniture, wood products	28.0	14
Distribution	27.7	6
Basic metal processing	27.6	7
Basic wood & paper products	27.3	5
Remanufacturing/reconditioning	26.4	6
Apparel, sewn products	25.6	8
Food & beverage	23.6	14

Exhibit 5.3. WCP Benchmarking Results

shown in Exhibit 5.3, nested between eleven sectors with higher mean scores
and fifteen with lower scores.

High-Scoring Sectors

Sample sizes for about half of the twenty-six sectors included in the exhibit
are not yet large enough for high validity. Top-ranked aerospace/defense
(AD), averaging 39.9 points, is, with twenty participating manufacturers,
nearly large enough. That sector, though, may be upwardly biased in that it
includes three or four especially outstanding companies. The AD sector has
its hands tied somewhat by the restrictions of government contracts. For that
reason we should not expect its scores to be among the highest. On the other
hand, AD is characterized by ultrahigh tolerances needed for space rockets
that won't blow up, aircraft that will fly, and weapons that hit targets precisely.
Those attributes bless AD with highly capable equipment and commitments
to well-trained workforces. Excellent equipment and workforces push scores
up on several of the sixteen world-class principles.

Rounding out the top five manufacturing sectors (not counting sectors of
fewer than ten participants) in the WCP—averaging thirty-five or more
points out of eighty—are vehicular components, electronics, electrical, and
telecommunications. No surprises here:

- *Telecommunications.* Like aerospace/defense, telecom has a natural,
  well-developed commitment to precision, quality, and training—
  raising scores on several of the sixteen principles.

- *The others.* Vehicular components, electronics, and electrical were
  the first Western industries that had to face up to the Japanese export
  juggernaut. Those industries began developing their world-class responses twenty years ago.

Low-Scoring Sectors

Lowest sectors, averaging thirty or fewer points include: plastics, rubber, and
glass; machinery and large appliances; furniture, windows, doors, wood flooring, other wood products; and food/beverage. Among the first three of these
bottom-most sectors are a few exceptional manufacturers. They are well-
known companies (anonymous, since their scores are held in confidence) that
were early birds in their industries. Prominent examples include a few plastic
molding, "white goods," medical device, and office furniture producers.
Manufacturers in those industries have had their stories—of JIT, TQ, employee empowerment, and supplier partnership—told in such sources as

Quality Progress and *Target* (the journals of the American Society for Quality and Association for Manufacturing Excellence, respectively).

In the plastic/rubber/glass sector, these reasons for the low average score suggest themselves:

- *Plastics.* As noted earlier, except for Nypro the plastics sector is made up of thousands of small molders. They mostly compete locally and succeed or fail more with machine tools than with management tools.

- *Rubber.* Tire producers, one part of the rubber products sector, most assuredly have not been protected from global competition. Historic bad blood between labor and management in that old-line industry, however, may have been holding down the rubber goods sector.

- *Glass.* Not being readily shippable across oceans, glass as an industry has not had to face the kind of global competition that elevates performance.

As with plastics and glass, low scores for wood products and food/beverage may be explained mostly by localism. These sectors saw only modest international competition prior to the current era of regional trade pacts and multinational mergers.

To sum up, the low-scoring sectors, including those with fewer than ten participants, were "late to the party." Take basic metal processing: In that sector, only seven business units have signed on to the WCP Benchmarking thus far. No surprise. We've seen scarcely any mention of this industry in published articles on applications of world class/lean/total quality. Moreover, until the late 1990s this industry was—in my recollection—completely devoid of companies receiving national awards, attending seminars, and receiving training and advisory services in "world class" management applications. The common mind-set had it that success revolves around melting and refining technologies, not management concepts.

The first five chapters have squeezed and massaged obstacles and pathways to industrial competitiveness. The remaining eight get at the details, first—in the next chapter—at the most critical resource: people.

6

Performance Management: The Human Side

I'm sad. I was invited to make a one-day presentation for managers of Sealed Air Corp., a Fortune 500 company. A dozen years earlier the chief executive officer had had me do the same thing. My charge this time was to help rejuvenate the company's world-class manufacturing effort, especially for all its new people and new acquisitions. The now-retired CEO, call him Mr. Smith, signaled his strong support for the message in several ways, even staying through the whole presentation. So why the sadness? Two times, Mr. Smith got up and interposed himself at the mike to articulate polite but firm disagreement. Once the topic was employee suggestions, and the second time it was productivity charts. The two are related.

CYCLE OF IMPROVEMENT

Smith had led Sealed Air through a long period of sustained growth in sales and profitability. The company enjoys a whopping market share and an international presence. Smith was a strong, pragmatic executive who was admired also for his humanity. Thus, his expressed skepticism about the role of employee suggestions surprised me. He wasn't disapproving of suggestions. He just stated his view that the professional and technical staff would always be the dominant drivers of improvement and that suggestion systems were low on his company's long must-do list.

Building an All-Company Human Improvement Engine

Yes, we all know that most suggestion programs are duds. But I thought I had spun a convincing web of rationale for, if you will, total continuous improvement. Suggestions would not be the centerpiece but just one of several critical elements. Summarized in brief in Exhibit 6.1, it goes like this:

1. All front-line employees receive application-linked training in process improvement and "sense of the customer" view of competitiveness.

2. All employees gather process data.

3. Via data collection, employees become process managers.

4. Formatted data point to root causes.

5. Solutions become suggestions, often implemented by suggestors.

6. Trend charts in the workplace track direct-effect results.

7. Recognition closes the loop.

8. Derivative intrinsic rewards equal monetary awards in motivational impact.

Exhibit 6.1. Total Continuous Improvement

1. *Training.* The workforce receives many hours of training. Task and cross-task training is part of it. But emphasis here is on training in 1) the problem-solving process itself; and 2) the customer-focused keys to competitiveness: quick response, elimination of non-value-adding activities, nearly perfect quality, cellular layout, cross-trained teams, and so on. Without the training, forget about getting good suggestions.

2. *Application.* Each training session on problem solving interweaves with application. (This is the so-called just-in-time training approach.) Application starts with all employees becoming data collectors. They record, on check sheets and chalkboards, as they occur, every glitch and hiccup in their processes. Rely only on the technical staff (quality engineers, production controllers, maintenance technicians, and so on) for this role, and large amounts of problem data never see the light of day.

3. *Process ownership.* For the employees, the mere act of recording problems gives a sense of taking control, of becoming a part of management. (Operators use cutting tools; managers use recording tools.) Charles Handy refers to the reverse of empowerment: employees *taking* control instead of having it bestowed upon them.[1] Recording problems starts this reversal; more steps, below, plant that reversal more deeply.

4. *Data to information.* The collected data readily rearrange into Pareto charts. Along with other tools of process analysis, the Paretos point to root causes and suggest solutions. The professional

staff can do this analysis (to the extent that they have the time). But if the front-line associates are left out, the following steps are left out, too.

5. *Suggestions and their implementation.* In analyzing the data, the work teams generate suggestions, which they formally record and, in many cases, implement themselves. At companies that achieve high suggestion rates (for example, Baldrige award winners Milliken and Co. and Wainwright Industries, and Shingo Prize winner Exxon Chemical-Baytown), implementation is often just documenting the new method and training one's teammates in it. Or it may be buying a needed work tool out of the team's monthly cash stipend.

6. *High-visibility trend charts.* Operators plot the direct-effect impacts of each improvement—shortened flow time, distance, or setup time; reduced scrap, rework, or downtime—on large trend charts within the work center. The charts visibly mete out praise when the trend is in the right direction, and they scold any long absence from another trend-extending improvement.

7. *Recognition and celebration.* Various informal and formal kinds of recognition follow. They may include logoed T-shirts, pizza, restaurant dinner for two, or chances to win in a lottery with odds favoring those who submit the most suggestions. Exceptional improvements get special notice. That may include the team making presentations to senior executives at award ceremonies and a photo on the company's "wall of fame."

8. *Intrinsic value.* The employee's heightened intrinsic feelings of self-worth may count more—as motivators and factors that bind the employee to the place of employment—than the external recognition. Moreover, intrinsics are much cheaper than pay raises, bonuses, and other monetary rewards.

Mr. Smith heard me walk through this whole interwoven set but still saw fit to express his reservations about suggestions, fifth item on the list. I was at least hopeful that he bought the rest of the set—though leaving out any elements degrades the result. (Jeffrey Pfeffer, offering his own eight-point set of improvement factors, says, "Firms often attempt piecemeal innovations." He sees most firms, therefore, as having only a one in eight chance for success.)[2] Later in the program when the performance measurement topic, item six on the list, came up, I had another chance to gauge Smith's level of buy-in.

Measurement and Motivation

Few companies, it seems, have performance measurement right. To the extent that they clue in the workforce at all about the state of the business, it is with the wrong performance measures. They bombard the employees with measures of labor productivity, unit costs, and machine utilization, which the customer cares nothing about. Moreover, each of those metrics is distant, the aggregate of multiple factors—including some beyond the sight lines of any one group—and easily manipulated. It is okay for management to track these measures as a rough signal of trouble if, over several months, they trend the wrong way. But their long-standing, wide use as tools of control and management of operations has been an utter failure. The accompanying box speaks to the negative reactions of the workforce to one of them, labor productivity. Continuing discussion suggests that prominent display of measures such as productivity and utilization can adversely affect costs—and worsen customer service.

Labor Productivity

The workforce wants feedback. Wants to know how it is doing. Sometimes management gets the message. They decide regularly to post key performance metrics on the wall. First one that comes to the mind of management is productivity. One measure of it is simply units produced in the period of measure. Others are units against plan, units per person, units per direct-labor hour, and actual hours versus standard hours.

Posting these measures, however, has no valid purpose. The workforce is of two minds about it: One says it's great to be productive, and maybe that will improve job security and even lead to higher compensation. The other says more productivity just means they are working us harder. The latter view dominates whenever there is bad blood between those who manage and those who do. Ironically, the posting of productivity numbers can, itself, contribute to trickles of bad blood.

Why? For one thing, it has a manipulative aura, especially when great numbers trigger ice cream for all. Even school kids know manipulation when they see it. More important, productivity looks like someone else's goal, not ours. And when the productivity number turns out to be substandard, just the posting of it turns on the resentment reflex—because "it's not our fault!" Low productivity has no end of causes (late parts, down equipment, wrong prints, and so on), and poor effort ranks low among them.

You get what you measure, yes—if you can de-elevate that which is measured. Bring it down to the level of people and processes and what actually allows/does not allow them to be productive.

Confused Connections

Illustration: Senior management tells me, the supervisor, that unit costs must fall by 5 percent. No problem. I just put off training, maintenance, and operator involvement in problem solving and prohibit use of overtime until the cost drops by 5 percent. No overtime means some customers will not get their goods on time, and my other actions will, before long, recoil in the form of growing incidence of quality, machine, and operator error problems. But I will have made my numbers.

> *When the performance of the parts of a system, considered separately, are improved, the performance of the whole may not be (and usually is not) improved.*[3]

Financial feedback has the same weaknesses, only worse. Financial results are even more remote, aggregated, and manipulable. A financially literate workforce is an asset, but feeding the workforce a regular diet of financials—revenue, earnings, return on investment, common stock price—opens the door to cause-effect confusion: "We thought last month was our best month since I've been here," says a middle manager or team leader, "yet now we hear that we lost market share and were in the red. What gives?"

Cause-effect is not a problem for a very small company. Some years ago my son worked at a family-owned, mostly take-out, pizza restaurant. Every day the owners told employees what the prior day's total take was. The owners sought to build esprit de corps and group pride for contributing to high-revenue days. Employees in any business know that continuing need for their services depends partly on sufficient sales revenue. In that sense, the owners had their staff's attention. What's more, being in so small a business, the pizza shop employees had nearly total visibility. They could see every customer, hear every ring of the cash register, and note every burned pizza or wrong order. And they could discern cyclic customer arrival patterns that cause revenue peaks and valleys. The daily take was easily related to what was visibly happening.

But this is the exception. Put, say, fifty or more people into a business, throw in multiple shifts, staff departments, and a diverse product line, and clouds of confusion roll in. No more clarity of cause and effect.

SPHERE OF INFLUENCE

So, what can be done in the latter situation—the normally complex manufacturer? Best answer is to build performance measurement around what is within the sphere of influence, or zone of attention, of each employee. Still, no measurement system is worth much unless it ties closely to overall business success. Thus, the trick is to seed low-level spheres of influence with business-success factors; then, measure successes within the low-level spheres and follow with recognition and reward.

These days, we know how to do the seeding. Root-cause management, continuous process improvement, *kaizen* events, and total quality are proven ways for the workforce to drive, at the same time, low-level and business-level successes. Cross-training and cells as businesses-within-the-business raise the effectiveness of those tools.

The follow-through—measuring and recognizing the right things—is the hard part (or the easy part consistently done wrong). Companies measure the jet stream instead of how well the hatches are being battened down here on Earth.

Let's return to Sealed Air Corp. and presume it has done all the right things to enable the workforce to continually attack and fix root causes. Let us say, as well, that CEO Smith accepted the view that the old measures—cost variance, unit cost, labor productivity, and the like—are ineffective, even detrimental. But he wouldn't toss those conventional measures until presented with better ones.

Loading Dock

Here is a case from one of his own plants, a strictly make-to-order facility in Hodgkins, Illinois. Reggie's job at Hodgkins is to load trailers lined up at the plant's outbound truck docks. He works from pick lists, one truck at a time. If the item is on the pick list, it has been produced and is in the open storage area in the vicinity of production lines and loading docks. The problem was that, fairly often, Reggie could not find one or more items on the list. The driver is getting testy, but Reggie may not release the truck until every item on the pick list is in the trailer. Here is what Reggie sometimes did when his frustration level rose high enough: He would take the problem to one of the production lines and cry for help. And they did, interrupting the job in progress so as to run off enough of the missing item to complete the loading and get the truck on its way!

I heard this from Reggie (not his real name) while on a plant visit in preparation for Sealed Air's management meeting. The plant's manager said I was free to talk to any employee. He was proud that this plant was among Sealed Air's most advanced in implementing a "world class" agenda. Reggie, it turned out, was a prime beneficiary of that implementation. Reggie said that, for years, the job was wearing him down because of the chronic missing-item problem. Nor did he feel right about pleading with operators to interrupt jobs in progress. But now the job was great.

The solution, he said, was that all items for a given truck now go directly from production lines to a marked-off floor location. It is a large kanban square roughly in the footprint of the trailer right in front of the dock. This eliminated the two non-value-adding steps: pick lists and intermediate storage. The problem of "lost" pick-list items and interruptions of production lines was history, as was Reggie's angst.

Relevant Measures and Root Causes

Reggie was not the one who came up with the kanban-square idea. But he might have been the innovator under a modified system of performance measures. In the loading bays at the Hodgkins plant a standard productivity measure might have been items picked or loaded per hour. If a chart tracking one of these measures were tacked up on a wall in the picker-loader area, what would be the reaction? Would it inspire Reggie to innovate? Work harder? Be happier? Encourage him to stay at Sealed Air instead of defecting for higher wages down the road? Hardly. Higher productivity is not what sticks in Reggie's craw. The aggravations of the job are.

To zero in on those aggravations, a better wall chart would track missing items or trucks delayed per day. Frequency of interrupting a production line is another possibility, if it occurs often enough to track. Alongside charts plotting one or more of those measures goes a white board or flip chart. Then, whenever an item is missing or a truck leaves late, Reggie has a medium for tallying reasons why: Can't find pick-list item, pick list incorrect, found item but insufficient quantity, found item but damaged, and so forth. (Such a tally chart is called a "check sheet," one of the "seven basic tools" of process improvement.) In his small zone of influence, Reggie had high visibility of reasons for the delays, and being able to tally the root causes on check sheets is, first of all, frustration relief. Recording the reasons, in turn, provides grist for problem solving. Fixing the problem is intrinsically satisfying and motivating and grounds for recognition by teammates, senior managers, and perhaps customers. This example takes in most of the eight items called "total continuous improvement" in Exhibit 6.1.

Competency Development: For the Professional and Technical Staff

The example of Reggie, the stock picker/loader, has its limitations. The zone of concern for most front-line staff is restricted. Because of that, developing natural, limited, relevant performance measures for front-line people is doable. For the knowledge-oriented employee, however, influence zones generally are broad. Therefore, designing relevant performance measures for accountants, engineers, technicians, and the like is much tougher. If machines are breaking down, should the maintenance technician be accountable? Should manufacturing engineering? Should finance, which puts up hurdle rates that block acquisition of better equipment? Maintenance technicians perform maintenance, but many others bear responsibilities for the most critical, related measures of performance.

The quest for zone-of-influence measures must extend to the knowledge employee. But since that quest is made difficult by the wide-zone factor, performance measures cannot be relied upon heavily for improving those employees' effectiveness.

For an alternate approach, let us look to training and development, which is the first step of the eight-step improvement sequence of Exhibit 6.1. Consider, however, its application to the knowledge employee. That first step, as modified, will read: "All professional and technical staff receive appropriate training to develop their competencies and a 'sense of the customer' view of competitiveness." Customer-sensitive competitiveness is the dominant theme of this book. Developing competencies is what Johnson and Bröms have termed "management by means."[4]

Abbott Diagnostics, a Dallas-based division of Abbott Laboratories, has the right idea. In about 1993 the division began its "competency-based development initiative." Thirteen job families for salaried people from engineering to quality are included. The object is to try to define competencies the employees will need five years out. Competency definitions have been published as grids with technical, human, and strategic categories, and the division's internal database makes the grids available to employees. According to Steve Broermann, manager of employee development, competency-based employee development "alters the emphasis from results (only) to how . . . and what competencies. . . ."[5]

Even though intellectual jobs entail broad zones of concern, broad company metrics, such as customer retention and sales revenue, are not fair and effective measures of performance for any group of those jobholders. The competency/management-by-means approach is not only fair, but also effective.

STATE OF THE BUSINESS

Speaking of broad company metrics, let us, at this point, reconsider the mom-and-pop pizza place. Just as Reggie has visibility as to causes, so would the pizza crew, who could see burned pizza, late employee, or slow day of the week as the cause of a low-revenue day. Too bad there was no system in place whereby the employees could keep track of those causes on check sheets. The daily take was measured and reported to the employees, but all eight elements of total continuous improvement, Exhibit 6.1, were missing. This is an example of a high-level performance measure (daily sales) that, while not harmful (small shop, no confusion), is not very beneficial, either. If the employees had been trained to collect data on mishaps and conditions likely to cause sales ups and downs, then the owners' hoped-for effect—a highly motivated, problem-solving staff—would have a good chance.

The pizza store owners were practicing what is being called "open-book management" (OBM). OBM became an *Inc.* magazine crusade beginning in summer 1995.[6] Springfield Remanufacturing Company (SRC) was *Inc.'s* model for OBM. Jack Stack, SRC's chief executive, had been on the book-and-lecture circuit, advocating his company's system of making all employees "financially literate," then giving them daily and weekly financial reports.

Open-book management is a fine idea—if done right. Feeding the workforce a heavy diet of financial results, though, is overkill. Not only does this incur confusion, for reasons already mentioned, but it also diverts people's attention. They tend to put improvement of their processes on the back burner, while trying to make numbers that are well out of their influence zones. Then, too, it tempts "gaming" the numbers.

The right way is to consider open-book management as bipolar. On one pole are the processes and on the other aggregated results:

1. *Process data, process-improvement activities, and direct-effect results.* These are generated and tracked by operating teams and are on display for professional, technical, and sales staff; visiting senior management; and customers. For the operating teams, process-improvement literacy is of first importance; financially literacy is nice, too, but down the priority list.

2. *Aggregated results.* Costs, sales revenue, market share, earnings, and the like are presented to the entire workforce at regular, but not too frequent, intervals.

Frequency of Review

U.S. taxpayers get a state of the union and state of the state address from their top public officials only once a year. In a manufacturing company, which needs to be sensitive to changing product lines, customers, and programs, yearly is probably not often enough. At the other extreme, daily, weekly, or monthly reporting is too often. Costs, profits, market penetration, and other markers of business success are not meaningful in the short run. It takes several quarters reliably to judge the degree of success of a product launch, a new plant or distribution center in China, or implementation of, say, an e-business or supply-chain management system.

For grander strategies, it may take not quarters but a few years to reliably judge success. In the United Kingdom, should successors to the Margaret Thatcher regime in the 1980s get credit for the country's rapid industrial ascendancy in the 1990s? See it instead as the Thatcher administration's open market policies kicking in in the years following her departure. Similarly, perhaps IBM CEO Lou Gerstner (for all his good ideas) has enjoyed the fruits of tough-love actions taken in prior years by his predecessor. Whether in government or business, overall success generally lags major change by years, not quarters or months.

The workforce certainly should be kept abreast of the state of the company. In most businesses, a semiannual report delivered to all employees is probably about right. Senior executives review their favorite measures of value—sales revenue, earnings, return on equity, stock price. Managers of business units, programs, and plants follow on. They review successes and failures of new and old products, us versus the competitors, status of new programs, and so forth. Hewlett-Packard has generally followed this formula for years.

In some companies, the state-of-the-business report is issued quarterly, which in the United States is when, by law, publicly held companies must release financial results. At Raytheon, Tucson, Arizona, an executive spends a full day each quarter delivering a series of reports to all of the plant's seven hundred first-line supervisors and team leaders. In this "flow down" communications process the supervisors and team leaders must relay the information personally to their employees within thirty days.[7]

Far more relevant to most of the firm's people is the ongoing state of the business: What's going on in the process? What are the critical process failures? What is being done about them? How can the processes be improved? And how *are* they being improved? These kinds of questions and their answers are part of the jobs of all employees. Ownership of process knowledge and its upkeep resides, properly, at low levels in the organization. For this aspect of the state of business, the spokespeople are not the senior managers but the process operatives.

Exhibit 6.2 summarizes the above points. The columns are not equal in significance—and do *not* make up a "balanced scorecard" (see the *un*balanced scoreboard discussion in chapter 7). The *processes* column reflects real, manageable actions, whereas the *business units/departments* and *whole company* columns refer to complex aggregations. The *time relevance* row clarifies: The processes cast off immediate, direct-effect information, whereas the business units/departments and whole company offer information of much-delayed relevance.

	PROCESSES	BUSINESS UNITS/ DEPARTMENTS	WHOLE COMPANY
Time Relevance	Immediate Direct effect	Semiannual or annual	Multiyear trends
Typical Measures/ Topics (examples)	Mishaps Scrap and rework Flow time and flow distance	Unit costs Sales per employee Downtime Warranty costs	Company-wide initiatives (how they are faring) Sales revenue Earnings

Exhibit 6.2. State of the Business

Next on the horizontal are typical measures and topics for feedback presentations. For processes, they include check-sheet tallies of mishaps, by type; and trend charts on scrap and rework, flow time and distance. Business unit and departmental results include unit costs, sales per employee, equipment downtime, and product warranty costs, to name but a few. Finally, in Exhibit 6.2, are reviews of the state of the business (whole company). These include how new initiatives and any acquisitions are doing, sales revenue trends, and measures of earnings.

Limited Role of Money

Yes, it is nice for employees to be financially literate—capable of understanding return on sales and cash flow to pay down debt, for example. One kind of monetary number that strikes closer to home is expenses. It is well within the zone of attention of the individual employee. I admire companies that include a budgeting module in their employee training repertoire. Seagate Technologies in Oklahoma City was doing this a dozen years ago (it was Control Data's small disk-drive business at the time), and Miller Brewing Company's Trenton, Ohio, facility includes budgeting as one of the training targets under its "star-point system."[8]

Instead of just supervisory responsibility for the budget, every employee gets into the act. As budget watchers, front-line operatives may, for example, try to avoid wasteful usage of power and water and offer ideas for reuse of scrap. If payroll expenses are over-shooting the budget, the work team may step up the pace in order to avoid costly overtime. At Boeing's Renton, Washington, Door Center, the plastic trays that hold hundreds of small fasteners and other hardware have the per-unit cost marked on every tray. Employees become conscious of the substantial value of a single bolt, which at the hardware store costs 50 cents but might cost $10 in its precision, high-test form for holding an airplane together.

The budget should be everybody's business. At the corporate level, the finance department must manage cash, arranging lines of credit or selling stock when necessary to ensure that bills can be paid and programs launched. Middle managers and supervisors have line-item budgetary responsibilities and must keep tabs on expense buildups as often as weekly. Front-liners are the ground troops, avoiding unnecessary expenses hourly and daily. Beyond cash management and the budget, however, money should not be an object to be managed. Manage the customer-sensitive processes, and monetary results will take care of themselves.

CYCLE OF WOE

This chapter began by spelling out an eight-step cycle of improvement. To end it, let's look at the opposite: a cycle of disillusionment. It is a commonplace in newly industrializing parts of the world. The cycle is triggered by the prospect of sharp cost cutting through very low-wage labor. A multinational opens a plant and applies the division-of-labor concept with a vengeance. An average assembly plant has around one thousand production employees, each with a ten-second task. That unit of work repeats nearly three thousand times per day, day after day, week after week—if the employee can stand it that long. (In a ten-hour day, it works out to more than three thousand repeats; in an eight-hour shift with coffee breaks, it is around twenty-five hundred.)

Exhibit 6.3 shows what usually happens. The double-bordered rectangle on the left represents the mindless, three-thousand-times-a-day job (1). Repetitive-motion problems (2) are certain. The combination of physical and mental trauma drives employee turnover sky-high (3). Ask what the turnover is at a typical maquiladora (plants on the Mexican border with the United States), and the likely answer is somewhere between 6 and 12 percent. Sounds rather high by the standards of industrially developed countries. But wait! The maquiladoras' measure is per month! Thus a 10 percent turnover means the equivalent of the whole workforce replacing itself more than annually. With such high quit rates, employee involvement (4)—contributions to process improvement—is unlikely.

Stuck in a hateful task (1) and lacking such involvement (4) ensures that the employee will derive little, if any, personal fulfillment. In other words, the system provides pay and benefits, but nothing in the way of intrinsic rewards (5). Being self-generating, they exceed the extrinsic kind (such as praise from a boss) in motivational effects. Their lack makes defections still more likely.

All this is bad for business. Hiring and training costs (6) are high. Performance—quality, timeliness, output rate—may be okay, even good. Rates of improvement, however, will be substandard: with no employee involvement, improvement is driven only by the professional staff, who are too few in number to yield more than sluggish progress. High personnel costs and relatively static performance (7) add up to cost and competitiveness weaknesses (8).

The ninth factor in Exhibit 6.3 is friendships. In any culture, on-the-job socialization is important to the average employee. In most Latin American cultures, socialization—in neighborhoods, within families, and at work—is far more important. As multinationals open dozens of plants yearly in Mexico, Central America, the Caribbean, and points south, the dominant work design—mindlessly repetitive jobs—flies in the face of those social needs.

The many factories that spring up each year on the U.S.-Mexico border and, increasingly, inland beckon young people from poor villages throughout rural Mexico. They come, in ones and twos, to the industrial cities, hire on, and begin to make wonderful new friendships; many other young people from similar circumstances provide a rich environment for job-centered socializa-

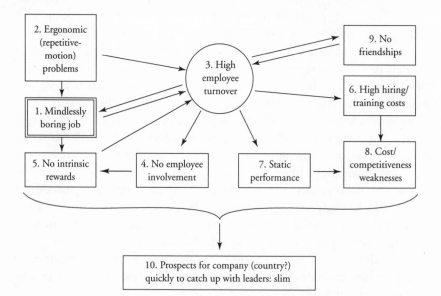

Exhibit 6.3. Unfit Jobs Lead to Marginal Results

tion. With greater than 100 percent employee turnover, however, new friends soon disappear, one after another. No friendships (9) push employee turnover still higher, with even greater adverse effects on the other eight factors.

Finally, prospects for this business unit to catch up and maintain parity with global leaders are slim (10). Prospects for industrial development in the country are negatively affected as well.

Mexico has been mentioned. But nearly half the planet's population faces this bleak scenario. Take China, for example. According to an estimate in *Business Week,* perhaps 100 million peasants are on the move—off their small farms and villages and toward the cities and their new factories.[9] Many of these millions experience the above-described disenchantments of badly designed factory work. There are some signs that they are becoming a tinderbox of growing resentment.

It is not necessary. Manufacturers that are mastering the cycle of improvement—the eight steps in Exhibit 6.1—have no good excuse for implementing it in their mother plants but turning their backs on it in their subsidiaries in Mexico, China, India, Indonesia, the Caribbean, Africa, South America, and elsewhere. This discussion continues in chapter 9 in the context of good plant design. It will be shown that good design of the physical environment can cure many of the work-related miseries that have been ticked off. Emphasis in that chapter is on high-work-content, high-variety, ergonomic jobs; familylike teams; enhanced friendships; continuous process improvement; and stable growth.

Conclusion

The late M. Scott Myers's book, *Every Employee a Manager,* was published in 1981.[10] He was ahead of his time. Today, above-average manufacturers globally are making the effort to empower their employees. Every employee cannot, however, be a manager of the top or bottom line, or the middle lines either. Expecting them to relate to performance as measured by distant, aggregated productivity and unit-cost numbers, and very distant, highly aggregated financial numbers, is futile. Bring your performance management system down-to-earth. And weave it in with the full apparatus of process improvement, including training, data collection and analysis, suggestions and their implementation, charting, and recognition. Include, as well, self-actualization, ergonomics, and building work-related friendships.

Performance management is many things. It is benchmarking. It is harnessing human potential—the topic of this chapter. And it is a whole complex array of measures, in numbers. Chapter 7, next, attempts to make better sense of the complexity.

7

Performance Management: Control Without Controls[1]

Control is a virtue. Lack of it is destructive—among nations, in markets, on the streets, interpersonally, and within the firm. On the other hand, too much control is odious—robs us of individuality and freedom. And it can rob the firm of ideas and motivation, while at the same time costing money. Control's role in performance management, the topic of this chapter—carried over from the last—is also two-sided.

DECLINE OF CONTROL

Until recently, it would have been hard to find authoritative exposition on manufacturing, management, accounting, or quality that did not give emphasis to *control*. Henri Fayol, the original management theorist, said controlling is the fifth of five management functions. His other four are planning, organizing, commanding, and coordinating.[2] Control gets two out of three for Robert Anthony. His widely cited hierarchical framework for running an organization consists of strategic planning, management control, and operational control.[3] Organizations, at least the larger industrial ones, all had their departments of quality control, whose professionals may have been members of the American Society for Quality Control (ASQC) and affiliates in other countries. The American Production and Inventory Control Society (APICS) and affiliates represents still more control specialists.

When, in the 1970s, companies renamed their departments quality assurance instead of quality control, it signaled nothing much. Nor was it momentous in 1992 when APICS adopted a new mission, called "integrated resource management," since the traditional production control and inventory control tracks remain. However, by the time, in 1997, that the ASQC membership had voted to drop the C, making it the American Society for Quality, a few other signs of critical thinking about control per se had surfaced.

Thomas Johnson, in *Relevance Regained*[4]—sequel to global business best-seller *Relevance Lost*[5]—attacked his own field of management accounting: "Control," he said, "is the major theme of what companies practice and universities teach under the name of management accounting. . . . [However], accounting goals should not be used to direct and control workers or managers." Companies that cling to the command-and-control model, he continued, "will not survive in the global economy."[6]

Business managers may have a hard time with the idea that there could be anything wrong with control. For the layman, however, negative images arise easily—from Huxley's thought police in *Brave New World* to Nurse Ratched in *One Flew Over the Cuckoo's Nest* to neighborhood informers in any number of countries in the old Soviet bloc.

If not control, however, what? Or, put differently, how can we have control's virtues (avoiding chaos) without its excesses? We offer four responses:

1. *Self-adjustment.* First is the engineer's concept of control: the self-adjusting system that does without external or secondary assistance. Management devices that are in tune with the self-adjustment idea include kanban, statistical process control, fail-safing, and self-inspection.[7]

2. *Negentropy.* Second, we borrow from general system theory[8] the concept of negative entropy. As noted in chapter 1, negentropy as applied to business is the importing of information for process or system improvement. When this takes place at the level of middle or senior staff, it entails long lag times. At their best, in contrast, information-driven improvements take place at the root, and quickly.

3. *Visual management.* Third, complementing the first two, is interposing visual management, thus nipping the main trappings of control: transactions and reports.

4. *Process management.* Fourth, following from (better yet, leading) the other three, is shrinking the executive oversight/control role. This comes about by shifting the locus of performance management toward front-line, intensive management of processes. Chapter 6 was all about the measurement of that shifting. In the broad sense, process management includes self-adjustment, negentropy at the root, and visual management.

The four points may be summed up as follows: *The best control requires the fewest controls.* This is the economy-of-control concept, which takes lean thinking all the way up the hierarchy.

ECONOMY OF CONTROL

By "controls," we mean the kinds of measures usually embedded in a command-control system: off-line, lagging reactions to events not taken care of at the source. It requires interventions and special investigations by technical and professional people. Administered remote from the action and reliant on indirect, highly aggregated data, this form of control is usually of limited effectiveness. It is also costly. These points about command-and-control are listed in the upper section of Exhibit 7.1, labeled "General Characteristics." In the same section, the exhibit further notes how economy of control differs: It promises quicker and better control, and more of it, via direct action at lowest levels in the organization, near to root causes.

The lower section of Exhibit 7.1 details how the two modes differ with regard to application. Economy of control makes use of self-adjusting devices for well-defined situations, and data-driven continuous improvement where problems are ill defined. The higher-cost, less direct command-control way is to rely on firefighting technicians or on professional experts conducting special studies.

But these differences between top-down command-control and low-level economy of control are old news. The gist of this chapter relates to the last two items in Exhibit 7.1: management oversight fed by information.

Management Oversight: Time-Relevant Metrics

Conventional business oversight is management by remote control. The remotes take the form of periodic performance reports, one type for senior executives and another for middle managers. Exhibit 7.2 lists some of the typical kinds going to each level of management.

Taking action based on these reports completes the control loop, but only after deadening delays that often yield contrary results. We explore these aspects of conventional oversight and then the alternative: intensive management of processes and tracking of their direct-effect results.

Remote Control(s)

Senior executives keep a close eye on the bottom line (earnings)—top line, too (sales revenue). They also monitor other, closely related marks of business performance: market share, sales per employee, total inventory turnover, return on equity, earnings, and, if a publicly traded firm, stock prices. While required no more than quarterly (by the U.S. Securities and Exchange Commission), executives usually track several high-level indicators (sales, for example)

	COMMAND AND CONTROL	ECONOMY OF CONTROL
General Characteristics:		
Speed	Delayed	Quick
Cost	High	Low
Locus of responsibility	Staff/managerial levels	Front-line employee level
Data support	Indirect, aggregated, often contaminated by variety of influences	Direct, close to root causes
Effectiveness	Usually low	Generally high
Types of Application:	**Relies on ...**	**Employs ...**
Defined problem	*Staff intervention:* Inspectors, schedulers, expediters intervene intermittently	*Self-adjustment:* Front-line operatives employ simple, direct methods continuously
Fuzzy, undefined problem	*Professional, reactive response:* Professionals (quality engineers, buyers) conduct studies to address general deficiencies (lateness, rework, etc.)	*Data-based, operator-centered process improvement:* Operators collect and categorize mishap data, revealing root-cause deficiencies (such as an unnecessary approval), leading to solutions
Management oversight	*Aggregated financial metrics, or "balanced" scorecard:* Emphasis on stock prices, revenue, earnings; limited, "at arm's length" oversight of process activities and metrics	*Time-relevant performance metrics:* High reliance on self/team process management and improvement and tracking of results; aggregated metrics watched, not managed
Information support	*Transactions and reports:* Information system collects data and generates reports for professional/managerial corrective actions	*Transaction reduction:* Simple, direct, visual tracking of mishaps and delays provides grist for operator-level problem resolution

*Exhibit 7.1. Command and Control vs.
Economy of Control*

MIDDLE MANAGERS	SENIOR EXECUTIVES
Unit costs	Sales
Customer losses/retention	Market share
Lost-time accidents	Sales per employee
Inventory turnover partials	Total inventory turnover
Employee turnover	Return on equity
Labor productivity	Stock prices
Cost variance	Earnings

Exhibit 7.2. Performance Reports for Middle and Senior Managers

monthly. And they may check their company's common stock price daily—or more often.

But what can executives do about these performance measures on a monthly or quarterly basis, or even a yearly one? Typically, a series of quarterly increases in sales or earnings is owed to measures taken years before—new product lines, extensive plant modernization, and so on. Inasmuch as executives no longer with the company may have initiated those actions, these measures cannot fairly judge current executive performance.

To be sure, an executive, alarmed by declining sales, can get results more quickly. For example, direct the sales manager to slash prices, thereby causing sales revenue to jump and soon market share along with it; this could take place in a single quarter. Such actions, however, will erode profit margins and earnings, and prices may just have to be upped again. Such a sorry sequence is what the late Dr. W. Edwards Deming called "tampering." Short-term control of long-term results is ineffective.

Middle managers tamper, too, sometimes as often as weekly or monthly, which is how often their summaries of results come out. The reports typically cover unit costs, customer losses/retention, lost-time accidents, inventory turnover partials (turnover of purchased materials, work in process, or finished goods), employee turnover, labor productivity, cost variances, and other medium-term metrics. Tampering at this level was described in the previous chapter. The example was of a production manager, under the gun to meet an imposed cost-reduction target, who cuts back on employee training and equipment maintenance and eliminates overtime. Performance deteriorates, and some customers are lost forever. Here is another example:

A senior executive presses the vice president of purchasing to reduce investment in purchased materials. For the VP, no problem: just stop buying or, more realistically, buy less per period. This could meet the senior executive's target in as little as one month. The likely consequence, though, is missed shipments for lack of parts. But that is someone else's problem. The purchasing VP will have made his numbers.

From these examples it is clear that short-term control of medium-term results does not work, either, though it is standard practice.

Intensive Process Management, Direct-Effect Results

Until twenty or so years ago, companies relied almost totally on remote-control oversight. Then, under the guidance of Deming, Juran, Shingo, and several others, process management stepped forward. It has many key ingredients. They include statistical process control (SPC), seven basic tools, total quality, *kaizen,* fail-safing, source inspection, and quality function deployment. Other tools are kanban/queue limitation, reduced lot sizes, quick setup/changeover, multiskilling, self-directed teams, work cells, focused plants-in-a-plant, total preventive maintenance, 5S, process benchmarking, activity-based cost audits, and design for manufacture and assembly.

Notably, all the items are new—at least in Western business and industry—as of the 1980s. (SPC was previously known but had fallen into disuse.) Typically, processes were designed (poorly by today's standards), put in place, and left to deteriorate. Instead of SPC, source inspection, and fail-safing, it was large-lot inspection. Prior to visual kanban, production required purchase orders, work orders, and move tickets. Setups were not managed, lot sizes were on a growth path, operators were single-skilled and separated functionally, maintenance was mostly of the breakdown variety, and so on.

Bringing in the new, with all its features, requires high commitment to training and re-education. The entire workforce, including middle management and senior executives, needs to become process-management "literate." Absorbing the lessons includes casting off much of the conventional alternative: control-oriented, delayed-reaction management.

Visually Closing the Loop

With training at the front end and action in the middle, feedback on results closes the loop. But if the loop closing is delayed, it is for naught. It must be quick in order to re-energize effort and regenerate the cycle. "At its best," notes Gwendolyn Galsworth, it is "point-of-use information . . . so close to the process, it is virtually indistinguishable from the process itself."[9] In this high form of process management, feedback is quick, direct, and on display at or within the process. It may take a variety of forms, including quality charts showing declining nonconformities and defects; just-in-time charts tracking reductions in flow times, flow distances, setup times, inventories, stock rooms, and handling devices; and graphs displaying improved customer satisfaction, numbers of certified skills per operator, reductions in unsafe incidents, and improved warehouse fill rates, to name a few. How timely can these kinds of measures be? Here are four examples:

- At two-time Baldrige award winner Solectron, sales reps gather satisfaction assessments from customers *every week.*[10]

- At UpRight-Ireland, a maker of custom aluminum scaffolding, JIT suppliers make *daily* deliveries. In making a delivery, the supplier stops to look over a clipboard on which Upright has rated that supplier's *previous day's* performance.[11]

- Herman Miller, the office equipment manufacturer, does what UpRight does—provides daily ratings of supplier performance. The means, however, is its Web-based system that links with five hundred suppliers, for ordering as well as for feedback on supplier delivery and quality performance.[12]

- At Avery Labels, Maidenhead, U.K., operators time and plot *every changeover*—several per day—on its roll-to-print/cut/package lines. The large trend charts on nearby walls track average changeover times daily, weekly, and monthly. Timing and plotting every changeover make quick changes a habit, not just for onetime bragging rights.[13]

These are special kinds of feedback. Their subjects are what process team members themselves might have on their radar screens, since they concern the work itself. Some such kinds of feedback are readily seen by the workforce as what customers care most about: quality, flow times, fill rates, flexible response. Others are at the level of personal aggravations. High on operators' lists are machine breakdowns, double handling, and producing too much only to see it stacked up at the next process, awaiting a long setup. Irksome as well are inability to help out at the next process for lack of cross-training and standing by twiddling one's thumbs while someone from inspection or maintenance does what anyone could easily do, such as gauge the part or tighten the belt. We saw in chapter 6 the value of bringing performance management down to this personal aggravations level.

CONTRAST: DIRECT-EFFECT AND CONVENTIONAL PERFORMANCE METRICS

Exhibit 7.3 contrasts process management and its direct-effect metrics with conventional management and its reliance on periodic reports. The latter, periodic reports (exemplified in Exhibit 7.2), are neither customer-oriented nor dear to the hearts of the front-line workforce. A supervisor may browbeat—or bribe (as with a hamburger fry)—front-liners into worrying over a negative cost variance or reduced sales volume, but these are not natural concerns of the rank and file.

Intensively Manage	Everyone Watches	Okay to Watch—Don't Tamper!	
BASICS—SOURCES OF COMPETITIVENESS	KEY DIRECT-EFFECT METRICS (MONITOR CONTINUALLY)	SECOND-ORDER METRICS (WATCH YEARLY)	THIRD-ORDER METRICS (WATCH AS MULTIYEAR TRENDS)
Design for operations	Design-to-market time	Customer retention	Sales revenue
Customer-/product-focused organization	Customer satisfaction	Warranty costs	Market share
Supplier/customer partnerships	Certified suppliers	Labor productivity	Sales per employee
Process capability/SPC	Quality/yield	Unit costs	Total inventory turnover
Quick setup/small lots/queue limits/synchronized schedules	Cycle time/on-time/setup time/fill rate	Inventory turnover partials	Market share
Total preventive maintenance	Facilities availability	Cost variance	Earnings
Labor skills	Unsafe incidents	Overall equipment effectiveness	Stock price
Labor flexibility	Certified employees	Lost-time accidents	Accident insurance costs
		Employee turnover	

Exhibit 7.3. Time-Relevance of Performance Metrics

Third-, Second-, and First-Order Metrics

Exhibit 7.3 conveys, in capsule form, most of the points that have been made about economy of control as applied to management oversight. The over-arching message pertains to time relevance: The usual executive-level metrics are third-order. They are thrice removed from where value is added or directly supported: designing, producing, and selling; and purchasing, hiring, and so on. Though critical determinants of financial success, being so removed from the action, they reveal nothing specific about causes. Attempts to use these metrics as levers to steer the company often are counter-productive. Reacting to them monthly, quarterly, or even yearly is, as has been said, tampering. They are meaningful—strongly indicative of things going right or wrong—only as multiyear trends.

Favored middle-management metrics are second-order—twice removed from business process action. Since they reveal little or nothing about root causes, basing control actions on any of these indicators can have dubious results. If, over, say, twelve monthly or four quarterly periods, customer retention, unit costs, or lost-time accidents improve, it seems likely that processes have improved. For fewer periods those indicators are unreliable. They are too easily the result of a lucky break or short-term expediency. For example, a competitor dropped out, resulting in improved customer retention. Or all hiring and travel were canceled, thereby cutting expenses and unit costs.

Control via the second- and third-order metrics is costly. It demands the attentions of well-paid managers and professional and technical staff, and so often is ineffective. Until the last two decades, however, these controls were *all we had.*

Now we have columns one and two in Exhibit 7.3. They make up a full set of basic tools and direct-effect metrics for continually improving what cause cost and customer retention and, by extension, sales and earnings. Intensively managing the basics shows up quickly in the form of improvements in the first-order metrics. These indicators get at the wants and needs of customers. Moreover, they are behavior reinforcing to the workforce. That is because cause-effect linkages are uncontaminated; sources of a good effect are clear and beg for more of the same. These are the main mechanisms that allow us to think that first-line, self-directed teams can be effective. That, in turn, allows the organization to reduce management layers and frees senior management for more strategic pursuits.

The second column in Exhibit 7.3, labeled "Key Direct-Effect Metrics," may be summed up thus: The new system offers *to* process team members performance measures that are direct effects of improvement activities *of* the teams. Middle managers and senior executives may stand aside.

Actually, it is much more preferable that they not stand aside. Better that executives and middle managers become active advocates of process management. When they get out of offices to listen to team presentations, hand out recognition, and otherwise do "cheerleading," their companies win awards. Good examples are Robert Galvin (retired) of Motorola, David Kearns (retired) of Xerox, Roger Milliken of Milliken and Company, and Ronald Schmitt of Zytec. All were/are ardent advocates of the full process-management agenda and all CEOs of Baldrige award–winning companies.

But management traditions die hard. Executives who earned their spurs on management by periodic reports have been presented with a new way to preserve that. It is called "the balanced scorecard." The scorecard also may be seen as helping executives to become champions of process management.

The *Un*balanced Scorecard

The balanced scorecard concept recognizes the failings of bottom- and top-line management. The idea is also to look between the lines, so to speak: 1) see what's going on in innovation, customer relations, and internal business activities; 2) raise these key business factors to prominence alongside the financial numbers, with the same degree of systematic measurement against goals; 3) at the same time, help executives to become champions of process management.[14]

It is a fine idea on the surface: bring competitive factors such as throughput time, time to market, and quality into the executive suite. Intermixing them with the usual middle-management and executive-level numbers, however, creates an *un*balanced scorecard. We have already seen why: it is unbalanced in time relevance—gaping differences in degree of lag between cause and effect. As effects distance themselves from causes, what to do becomes increasingly blurry.

The ideal system of performance management, which perhaps does not exist, even among the world's best-managed firms, goes something like this: All employees dedicate to intensive, data-based management of processes. Direct results of those efforts show up as soon as weekly, daily, hourly, or, in some cases, real time. Those metrics, therefore, are tracked that often, displayed on visual signboards in all the work centers, and summarized in main trafficways. They constitute the workforce's *and management's* time-relevant scorecard.

Second- and third-order metrics cease to be the base for management actions. Some may be measured and watched but should not be managed. In team sports, point differentials and won-lost records are the same. They give the vital score and are cause for cheer or hand-wringing, but they are not effective as elements of the *managed* (time-relevant) scorecard.

Let us return to the conventional measures labeled in Exhibit 7.3 as second-order metrics. There is more to say about two of them, labor productivity and overall equipment effectiveness.

Labor Productivity

Second-order metrics such as unit costs and WIP (work-in-process) inventory turnover qualify as being okay to be measured and looked at now and then—but not managed. Direct-labor (DL) productivity, on the other hand, should no longer be measured at all. Yet so ingrained is this measure that most manufacturers still measure it religiously. Many also post it prominently, which we've already roundly faulted, here and in the previous chapter. What's wrong with measuring it? Direct labor no longer has meaning. Say that your plant measures DL productivity for the usual reason: to raise it, thereby lowering cost, thereby attracting more revenue and making more profits. Easy ways to raise it include the following: Take away responsibility for quality and give it back to rehired inspectors. Return responsibilities for machine setup and preventive maintenance to the maintenance department. Hire more people as materials handlers so that operators are free to just produce. Transfer data collection and all team-based process improvement back to quality engineering, production control, information technology, human resources, and other staff departments. We need not go on.

The righter we do the wrong things, the wronger we become.[15]

Direct labor may be a legal category (in the United States separate records must be kept for such a group, which is covered by special labor laws). Otherwise, DL is defunct. Direct labor employees do, or should do, much more than direct labor. Whole payroll productivity is a laudable metric. If DL productivity is still relevant in your company, it means that yours is still in the dark ages with regard to proper roles of people—and the management thereof.

Unlike labor productivity, overall equipment effectiveness (OEE) is a component of a worthy package of excellence tools. As such, it, too bears separate discussion.

OEE: Its Limited Value—An Example

Overall equipment effectiveness is, like the "balanced" scorecard, new and fast-growing in popularity. OEE is a spin-off metric from the thriving total preventive maintenance (TPM) movement. To digress briefly, TPM was listed in chapter 1 as one of the eleven standout management innovations from Japan. TPM's international home is the Japan Institute of Plant Maintenance (JIPM), headquartered in Tokyo (Web site: jipm.or.jp). It sponsors a newsletter[16] and other publications, hosts global and regional TPM conferences, and charters affiliates. At the 1999 global conference, 150 plants from around the world received various TPM awards. JIPM sponsored the fourth (year 2000) TPM conference in the United States. As part of the conference, an affiliate, TPM Initiative of North America, or TINA (jipm@mindspring. com), was established.

TPM is a collection of forceful tools for preventing equipment and plant downtime, raising standards of cleanliness and housekeeping, and improving safety. TPM blends with other elements of total process management—training, quick setup, kanban, 5S, quality, visual management, and others. Improving one generally improves them all. Regrettably, wrong notions about TPM are creeping in, as noted in the accompanying box.

OVERALL PERFORMANCE.
With all that blending, how about a blended performance metric? So one was developed: overall equipment effectiveness. Its formula: OEE = $A * B * C * 100$. A stands for equipment availability, B for process efficiency, and C for an index of quality. Availability, in turn, captures downtime losses from breakdowns and setups/adjustments. Efficiency nets speed losses from minor stop-

---

"We Did Our TPMs"

What's wrong with that statement (which one hears now and then)?

It's like saying "We did our JITs." Or ". . . our leans."

Before TPM, there was ordinary preventive maintenance—no "T." Saying, "We did our PMs," reflected good management. Total PM requires "doing PMs" and much more. Under TPM, operators have a voice in selecting equipment—and may be sent to the equipment maker's school to learn about maintaining it. Operators record causes of every equipment malfunction. They generally take over the job of changing over the equipment and maybe ordering parts for it. They make simple repairs and assist maintenance in more difficult ones. And more, though it takes time for these roles properly to be absorbed by operators.

Total quality requires shifting prime responsibility for quality from inspectors to operators. That is well-known. Total PM is similar. It requires transferring ownership of equipment from maintenance and engineering to the same front-line associates. That is the reason and meaning of the leading word: total.

pages and slowdowns. And quality accounts for rejected units and yield losses. OEE has been widely and quickly adopted, as part of the TPM package, by manufacturers globally. The many TPM consulting companies and TPM conferences encourage this.

But let's consider what OEE really is. It is a scorecard measure twice removed from the reality of breakdowns, setups/adjustments, stoppages, slowdowns, rejects, and yield losses. It is another middle-management metric that tells next to nothing about causes. Yet it goes up on signboards in plants from Osaka, Japan, to Toluca, Mexico. At Continental Teves, Morgantown, North Carolina, producer of automotive brake systems, an in-the-plant scoreboard is updated with the current OEE number every thirty seconds. Continental Teves is a fine facility that does many of the basics well. It trains employees extensively, rotates operators along production lines every hour, and makes *kaizen* projects a way of life.[17] But what could any operator, supervisor, engineer, or plant manager at Teves do with an OEE index? At best, there are just these two uses: 1) Raise alarm if, after a number of months (*not* after thirty seconds!), the OEE clearly has not been improving. At Teves, this would suggest deficiencies in basic processes for reducing capacity losses due to breakdowns, setups, rejects, and so forth. 2) Benchmark against other plants in its industry, worth doing, at best, no more than once a year. (Or do it for crowing purposes if invited to a TPM conference.)

The main criticism of OEE, however, is this: Instead of tracking OEE, why not keep score on each component? Pay heed to breakdowns (more important, their causes), setup-time losses (better yet, setup times themselves, and causes of losses), and so on. Each such OEE component is where the action—and real information content—is.

For all that, OEE does have one comparative advantage and one valid use. It is superior, at least, to the dominant measure of the past: machine utilization. Utilization—of machines, production lines, labor, or capacity—has no merit as a measure of performance. Clearly low utilization is not good. But raising it is only partially the responsibility of operations. It also requires sufficient demand. That comes from more popular products, better marketing, improved customer service, and so on. Very high utilization is bad. It ensures lengthened lead times and excessive stock-outs and back orders. Outside customers will defect; inside customers will wait and lose efficiency. Therefore, the utilization measure is useless, since there is no "right" degree of utilization. In contrast, the higher the OEE the better. That is because of OEE's three factors. The A factor in OEE is not utilization, but availability: Is the equipment available (and operable) when needed? If not, customers will be poorly served. The B and C factors, efficiency and quality, also get at the interests of customers. Utilization does not.

But back to the main point: OEE is too remote from root causes to be generally useful. Still, OEE's positive attributes give it validity as an alarm or trigger for major changes—as is explained next.

"IT'S THE EQUIPMENT, STUPID!"

Your plant is not doing well. Corporate executives have your plant manager on their short list, but not for advancement. The plant has made great strides in training, teaming, and temping. Timely delivery—in from suppliers and out to customers—is good on average but varies a lot around that average. (John Ettlie: "Most companies . . . deal in averages. Customers see variance.")[18] Costs and inventories are the big problems: they're stuck—on high.

From the sound of it, this plant needs strong medications: best medicines are the "hard sciences" of quality and process capability, TPM to cut equipment losses, both quality and TPM to cut wasteful just-in-case buffer stocks, and quick setups to drive down lot-size inventories. Finally, someone coaxes the plant manager and a couple of supervisors into attending a local TPM presentation. They hear about OEE for the first time (and TPM for the third, fourth, or fifth time), and they come away with OEE numbers that companies in their industry and others are achieving. Back at the plant, they get busy finding out their own OEE. They are suitably shaken—which triggers a mad effort to turn on to TPM, plus quality and quick setup.

Does this story sound familiar? In the early 1980s, when quality was abysmal in Western industry, cost of quality (COQ) was the trigger. High executives from Motorola, Ford, IBM, Milliken, Xerox, Baxter, and others among the well-knowns trooped to Philip Crosby's Quality College in Florida. They heard the Crosby team warn them that their quality losses as a percent of sales probably were double digit. The shock effect took. COQ became the hot new metric, and it helped set the quality movement in motion. Before long, quality norms had been elevated by orders of magnitude.

In industries where, as they say, quality is now a price of entry, the COQ metric no longer serves a purpose. (At a seminar a senior manager at Rainbird said cost of quality is "a waste of time." Someone asked why they did it at Rainbird then. He replied, "Because the president wants it.")[19] OEE is the same. Once TPM has been triggered, OEE may be retired. Caveat: Some companies have little continuity from regime to regime. A stellar quality or TPM program can be snuffed out at the whim of a new top executive. That might call again for another COQ or OEE trigger pull.

To sum up, if OEE has any value, it is just for infrequent benchmarking and as a rare signal of alarms. As such it belongs in a plant manager's office, not on the production floor. The same may be said for the other second-order metrics in Exhibit 7.2.

SUMMARY AND IMPLICATIONS

The theme of this chapter, stated at the outset, is that best control is fewest controls. We have seen how that can happen: school the workforce—including those in sales, product development, maintenance, and all others—in ways of fixing the processes, continuously.

Controls take root when processes are complex, incapable, failure-prone, and varying. Economy of control flourishes, on the other hand, in the organization bent on making processes simple, capable, rarely nonconforming, and consistent. First-line employee teams become trained in the new, economical tools of quality and simplicity, which become elements of the processes themselves. SPC, kanban/queue limitation, fail-safing, and source inspection are prominent examples usable especially under well-defined conditions. Less trenchant problems often require investigation employing simple problem-defining tools: process flow charts, check sheets, Pareto charts, and fishbone diagrams. By those and related means, processes acquire built-in simplicity and capability, with teams sifting data for further process improvement. As a result, various kinds of transactions and reports—the trappings of conventional heavy-handed control—may fall by the wayside. Finally, middle-managerial operational controls and executive-level financial controls prove to be redundant, except for scorekeeping purposes and long-term indicators of business health and success.

The pessimist might say that economy of control doesn't stand a chance—not with Wall Street, the City of London, other meccas of money, and the investment community pressing CEOs to increase earnings and make their numbers, quarterly. The evidence is otherwise. Process management is alive and by now standard practice in better-performing organizations. Executives, usually masters of ambiguity, may in effect be keeping two sets of books. One set responds to "can't wait" investors; the other set—consisting of first-order, close-to-the-action measures—keeps watch on the processes. Spending time on the conventional second set is itself not economical, but not easy to avoid.

Even best companies implement the four elements of economy of control (self-adjustment; time-relevant metrics; transaction reduction; and data-based, operator-centered improvement) piecemeal. That denies mutually reinforcing benefits of all four and slows the implementation. For example, most companies retain their cost-variance systems, and company bulletin boards still feature "how much did we produce last week?" measures. Yet I hear company managers—for example, at Milliken years ago and the Cryovac unit of Sealed Air Corp. recently—say that their cost-variance systems are largely ignored. Seeing these vestiges of conventional controls go away may have to await new blood in high places, since the current generation of managers got where they are by and through those kinds of controls.

Competitive enlightenment will, however, usher in economy of control, which is the alter ego of process management. Managers, executives, and ultimately Wall Street and the investor may profit from a better understanding of both.

8

Focused Form and Structure

What single idea best captures the industrial renewal mind-set? The answer is focus: focus on the customer and what the customer buys (or in some cases receives free of charge). This requires tearing down the walls around functions, departments, and shops. Doing so greases the flow. Information and products move more quickly through the processes. Moreover, focus opens eyes. Employees can see sources of revenue; changing customer needs; and root causes of bad quality, costs, delays, and inflexibilities. Such opening of eyes is a key to gaining broad commitment to the urgent need to renew or risk loss of competitiveness.

Becoming customer- or product-focused touches on most of the decision points of a manufacturer. Some of those points are broad, affecting the greater enterprise. These include organization structures, mergers and acquisitions, expansion into new markets, supply and customer chains, makeup of the product line, and mix of customers. Focus also affects decision points within the firm and its production facilities: physical layouts, choices of equipment, building sizes and shapes, internal staffing and training, modes of production, costing and pricing, and allocation of funds and human resources.

Treating the breadth of these decision points requires a pair of chapters. Next one looks at focus within the company. This chapter examines how focus bears on broader issues. One of the broadest, which is the concluding topic in this chapter, is how the benefits of focus extend even to geographical regions—Silicon Valley being only one of many examples of how a region may profitably zero in on a core competency.

THE FOCUSED ENTERPRISE

The old belief was that division by function is good for low-volume, high-mix activities, which characterizes most kinds of work. The alternative, focus, was for the special case of high-volume, low-mix.

The enlightened belief is single-minded: Push for focus—with all its advantages—and away from functional groupings. Where volumes are low and product mix high, gain focus by families of similar products, or families of customers. Many companies have grasped the business logic of this and acted accordingly. Many others seem to have a functional fixation. If stated, the rationale probably will revolve around the critical-mass idea. The unstated resistance to breaking up the functions surely is that people want to stick with "their own kind." It's an insular point of view—and selfish in that it is bad for business not to establish work-flow or information-flow relationships.

If that fixation is overcome, there may be a tendency toward relapse, which Brown and Hyer have labeled "functional drift."[1] This refers to a possible tendency for focused forms to revert back to the functional format. If Brown and Hyer's suspicion is correct, then the push for focus must be relentless and repeating.

Though focus in the abstract may sound good, some functions nearly always seem to be set up as unfocused specialties. Following are two examples, with comments on gaining focus anyway:

- *Public relations.* This function seems always to be a separate specialty—a department—because having each focused unit issue public pronouncements might get the company in trouble. Some companies will take that risk. Years ago Robert Townsend, as CEO of Avis, the car rental company, abolished the public relations department and conferred the responsibility on his department heads. When the news media wanted a quote, they got one fast from whoever was available. This earned Avis a good deal more free publicity than it had been getting.[2]

- *Human resources.* HR, as a separate function, is the norm because employees surely cannot be expected to manage their own benefits, training, grievances, and so on. But Hewlett-Packard's Singapore components business has partially achieved self-management of these kinds of actions. A small, central HR group still exists. Most HR activities, however, are dispersed to the product-focused production areas. Adjacent to each is an HR alcove. Within is a library of personnel action manuals and forms and a desk and telephone. Want to switch health benefits? Find the correct form, sit at the desk, and fill out the form. For questions, phone the staffer at HR central.[3]

These examples are just two of many. Considered next are examples of focus beyond the existing organization. Included are evolving strategies for gaining focus through mergers and acquisitions, value-chain outsourcing, the webbed organization, and multilocal global expansion.

Conglomerates

The conglomerate system—corporations made up of dissimilar businesses—is nearly dead in the United States, Canada, and Germany and losing its fizz in the United Kingdom and a few other countries. Forget about synergies. Mergers and acquisitions twenty-five years ago in the United States created corporate mishmash. Under Charles Bluhdorn, Gulf + Western's acquisitions in the 1960s included companies in sugar, cigars, steel, machine tools, cable TV, horse racing, zinc, meatpacking, baking, moneylending, paper making, phonograph records, automotive parts, and moviemaking. LTV, ITT, Textron, Litton, Teledyne, Boise Cascade, and United Technologies were doing much the same thing. Many others, not so well remembered, were, too (for example, Bangor Punta, Questor, Rapid-American, A-T-O). They had their comeuppance in the conglomerate crash of May 1970, when share prices of nearly all plunged. Sobel traces the movement in a book with the telling title *The Rise and Fall of the Conglomerate Kings.*"[4]

Conglomerates were always bad economics and usually poor management. Permissive financial regulations, strange tax codes, stock market anomalies,[5] corporate chutzpah, and follow the "leader" are reasons why odd assortments of businesses become allied in the first place.

Today's alliances (some, anyway) make more sense. Phone companies merge among themselves, pharmaceuticals with other pharmas, carmakers with their counterparts, and so on. Some of this is going on in order to consolidate and shrink industries having overcapacity and at the same time gain a global foothold.

Another of today's more rational acquisition formulas puts dozens of smaller manufacturers under a corporate umbrella in a few focused groupings. Dover Corp., more than tripling in sales in ten years (to about $4.5 billion), currently has four such groups: Dover Technologies (high tech), Dover Industries (metal-fabricated equipment), Dover Resources (energy industry equipment), and Dover Diversified (aerospace and industrial equipment). Dover has put together these groups by acquiring over one hundred small and medium-size manufacturers in the past decade.[6] Illinois Tool, Emerson Electric, and Swiss-based ABB have followed much the same pattern. All four companies have financed most of their rapid growth from cash flow—not by mortgaging their futures through debt equity. They rely on lean but enlightened corporate oversight to raise management standards in each acquired company.

The conglomerate system remains strong, with some signs of cracking, in Mexico, South America, Korea, India, and Japan. The mother companies may be named group, *groupe,* or *groupo;* or, in Japan, *keiretsu;* or, in Korea,

chaebol. In a few European countries, especially France and Italy, some of the groups are partly government owned. This tends to provide cover for under-performing sectors within the group and draw resources away from the stronger ones. Commonly, a group has strong family ties. Over the generations, as family members try to run the show, there may be little room to bring in good people and ideas from the outside. Examples:

- In Korea, the top thirty *chaebols* are in an average of 18.8 industries, and twenty-nine of the thirty have been managed by the founder-shareholders or their sons.[7] One of the largest *chaebols* is Hyundai, whose businesses include autos, electronics, construction, shipbuilding, petrochemicals, insurance, banking, finance, a cruise line, and more. Consultants at McKinsey & Company place blame on the *chaebols* for Korea's deep recession of the late 1990s. Their prescription: The *chaebols* must "focus on core businesses that have a chance of becoming internationally competitive, and sell, spin off, or close other businesses."[8] In other words, get focused.

- In Japan, "operating globally, integrated both vertically and horizontally, and organized around their own trading companies and banks, each major *keiretsu* is capable of controlling nearly every step of the economic chain in a variety of industrial, resource, and service sectors."[9] Typically, *keiretsu* members are bound by cross-holdings of one another's stocks. Following Japan's decade-long period of malaise, however, the *keiretsu* system is beginning to come unglued. Giving impetus, France-based Renault fashioned a merger in spring 1999 with Japanese automaker Nissan, which had lost money nearly every year of the 1990s. As noted in a report issued by the Organization for Economic Cooperation and Development (OECD), "A major highlight of [Renault's] 'revival plan' for Nissan is to reduce the number of *keiretsu* companies tied by cross stock-sharing from 1,400 to a mere four. The stock currently held by Nissan in these companies will be sold off to generate some much-needed cash."[10] Mitsubishi, another money loser and Japan's biggest *keiretsu,* is also coming apart: the Mitsubishi car company's new owner is Daimler-Chrysler; and Mitsubishi Heavy Industries, which lost nearly $1.4 billion in 1999, has been seeking an alliance with Boeing or Airbus Industries.[11] With these breakups, the sprawling *keiretsu* becomes transformed into multiple independent companies, large and small. Each is focused, minus *keiretsu* commitments, on its own products and customers.

- In India, the giant ($9 billion) Tata group (steel, auto- and truck-making, power generation, chemicals, hotels, computers, consulting, consumer goods, telecommunications) is in the throes of change after a decade of weak performance. Since its founding in 1868, the conglomerate has been headed by the Tata family, whose strategy is to refocus on a core of some fourteen or fifteen businesses instead of thirty-five to forty.[12] Chairman Ranan Tata, architect of the plan, also announced that within two years he would step aside; moreover, instead of the long-standing practice of naming his own successor—always a Tata—he would leave the matter of his succession to the board.[13]

- In Italy, the Fiat Group is responsible, by one Fiat manager's estimate, for some 10 percent of Italy's economy. Besides cars and trucks, Fiat's empire includes agriculture and construction equipment, metallurgical products, aerospace vehicles, trains, and production systems. Among its nonmanufacturing businesses are insurance, publishing and communications, and operating railroads.

- Mexican billionaire Carlos Slim Helu's sprawling empire, Grupo Carso, includes department stores, various other retailers, tobacco manufacturing, railroads, mining, chemicals, construction materials, and auto parts. When Slim suffered a heart attack in 1997, the group's stock price sank. He has since opened the firm to investors and has passed on its operations to his son Patrick Slim Domit.[14] (James Michener is not known as an authority on management. His novel *Caribbean*,[15] however, offers a plausible take on why Latin America has not enjoyed the economic success of its northern neighbors: The loyalties of the Spanish in their new countries followed the slogan, "*Dios, patria, familia*": "God first, country second, and family third." In actuality, so said the book, it was the reverse. In government and business, family came first, country second, and God last. In practice, then, business leaders in the southern Americas would make jobs for their competent-or-not relatives, while U.S. and Canadian companies sought talent.)

To Merge/Acquire/Divest—or Not

Bucking the bigger-is-boffo movement are Merck in pharmaceuticals and Honda in autos. Judging by how their stock prices are holding up, neither appears to be suffering for its resistance to merge. Analysts may be able to look past and see through the corporate puffery generally attending megamergers in oil, autos, pharmas, foods, and so on. Big mergers bring on plentiful troubles. Some that stand out are language and cultural mismatches, pay and perk differences, regulatory and currency issues, and, especially, hard-to-manage complexity that comes with great size. There may also be structural contradictions. For example, Mercedes-Benz, among the most vertically integrated of auto companies, merged with Chrysler, among the least. This may be a greater barrier to making the merger work than the cultural differences. In going it alone and staying focused, Merck and Honda may end up the winners.

For all its advantages, too much focus can carry a company to the grave. Persist in the same product line and mix too long and you end up like the proverbial buggy-whip maker at the advent of automobiles. To avoid this, most manufacturers, at some point, need to undergo a makeover: acquire or merge, while selling off the "buggy whip" assets. Emerson Electric, suffering angst in recent years over lack of rewards in the stock market, refocused its acquisition formula. Instead of adding more old-line industrial companies, it is bulking up on higher-tech manufacturers having greater profit and growth potential. Wall Street showed its approval by pushing up Emerson's share price.

Often the divested business gains a new lease on life. The AT&T breakup begat the Baby Bells, each a large, mostly successful business. The AT&T development and production arm, Western Electric, became telecom powerhouse Lucent Technologies. Though Lucent badly stubbed its toe in 2000, that takes away only some of the luster: Lucent grew from $24 billion revenue on its inception in 1996 to around $40 billion in 2000.

It took antitrust action for AT&T to do the wise thing. IBM and Hewlett-Packard were able to figure out on their own that they had become too large and unfocused. IBM's once dominant typewriter business no longer made sense for IBM or for the business itself. Spun off in 1991, it emerged as Lexmark, now the world's number two producer of computer printers and giving leader H-P serious competition. IBM also divested what became Celestica, a global producer of electronic components from circuit boards to routers. Out from under Big Blue's thumb, Celestica has grown to become the world's third largest electronics manufacturing services company with twenty-three thousand employees.

Hewlett-Packard startled the investment community in 1999 by splitting itself into two reasonably sized and focused independent companies: its computer and computer peripherals business retains the H-P name. Agilent, a new name, houses H-P's former life science and health care, electronic test, and communications business units. So far, there has been no stampede of other business giants following H-P's bold and perhaps brilliant move. Rather, we see the opposite: merger upon merger. And Microsoft waits for the government to force its breakup.

Sometimes opportunity calls, and a more complete transformation is the answer. Corning, long known for its glass casserole dishes, has become the world's leading producer of optical fiber. To make room, Corning has jettisoned products making up half its sales since 1995, including the cooking glassware. Liss Bogaty, analyst at Salomon Smith Barney, says, "Corning has really transformed itself into a focused telecom company," and, riding on the Internet, that market "has exploded." Related products include liquid crystal display screens along with more conventional TV tubes. Within its old science products business—Pyrex beakers, flasks, and so on—Corning has added lucrative, fast-growth products, such as small plastic plates used by biotechnology labs for growing human cells.[16]

Transitions, though, are risky. They require bringing in new technical skills, managers, equipment, suppliers, logistics, and customers. And in transformation, the company goes from focused (on the former) to unfocused (outgoing old mashed with incoming new) to refocused (the new). The travails of many old-line companies trying to establish on-line selling testify to the risks and problems in these transitions.

Value-Chain Outsourcing

Further accelerating the pace toward focus are broad-based strategic shifts among value-chain members. Automakers offload not only production but also design responsibilities to first-tier manufacturers. They, in turn, may extend the downloading to the third tier. In electronics, end producers are triggering the same cascading pattern of outsourcing. One result is emergence of the electronic manufacturing services sector as a massive growth engine. The scenario repeats in one industry after another, not only in manufacturing but also retailing, human services, and government.

Value chains had long been bimodal. Big companies were concentrated in basic materials at one end and final products at the other, but many small, fractionated players were in between. Outsourcing grows the middle group— in average company size, financial strength, and stability—while shrinking its numbers. The end-product outsourcers, formerly trying, with some futility, to "do it all," become focused on expertly doing just a few things—their core competencies, they hope. (Michael Paris suggests, however, that core competency is too often "a legacy of past success . . . what's left after the apple has been eaten—and competency becomes complacency.")[17] For their part, the enlarged middle-tier producers become focused on fewer customers.

Where will it end? That is, where lies the true core of competency? Charles Fine suggests that an organization's solid core is the capability to design its supply chain. This, he says, is one competency that cannot be bought.[18] His point seems well taken for the final-product manufacturer. It also makes some sense for those earlier in the supply chain, for each entity in the chain is at the mercy of preceding echelons. Failure to probe the echelons—to design the supply chain, as Fine puts it—is myopic.

By much the same token, however, every supplier's fortunes are linked to its customer chains. Design of those chains is another leverage point. In both directions, supply chain and customer chain, one objective must be to aim for focus. Your business cannot be all things to all customers, or all to all suppliers. Supplier reduction has been popular sport in the past twenty years. Customer reduction needs attention, too.

The Webbed Organization

But is focus opposed by the Internet? Does the Net encourage rapid shifts from one supplier to another and from this customer to that—with focused loyalties the loser? Not necessarily. Scattered members of an Internet-linked enterprise may stick with each other simply because results improve with familiarity. With or without the Web, strong and sticky strands beat short, fleeting connections.

Still, the linked-up manufacturing world generates new issues. Take Dell Computer, for example. Dell was the first manufacturer to gain magnitude advantages from the Internet on both the supplier and the customer sides. With up-to-the-minute inventory and capacity information on their screens, Dell order takers are able to shape demand. Knowing what's in their own warehouses and supply chains and what isn't, they aim at steering customers away from shortages and toward what is plentiful. Tell the order taker you want the PC on catalog page 12, the one priced at $2,495; she may immediately suggest instead the one on page 13 with a big, flat-screen monitor, catalog priced at $2,795—but for you the same price as the one on page 12: $2,495. What a deal for the customer! And what a deal for Dell and its supply system, which is overstocked on the larger monitor and approaching back order on the smaller one.

DELL DILEMMA.

But here is, we might say, the Dell dilemma: If one of Dell's supplier-partners—in our example, the supplier of the superior monitor—keeps plenty of inventory and extra capacity on hand, Dell's order takers will tend to steer orders toward that supplier. But, with all its excesses, that supplier becomes a high-cost, non-JIT producer. It learns that fattening up on inventory brings more orders. So it slides more deeply into the batch-and-queue mode. If, on the other hand, that supplier becomes leaner—on both inventory and capacity—fewer orders will be guided its way. Thus, unlean suppliers will progressively gain business with Dell. And Dell's supplier base goes downhill. (In extension of the Brown/Hyer idea, functional drift, how about another syndrome: batch drift? Ken Doerr and others did field research in a fish-processing plant. One of their conclusions: Pull systems are not in keeping with human nature.)[19]

What can be done about the Dell dilemma? Best answers lie in purchasing organizations. They must adopt more sophisticated ways of selecting, rating, and developing suppliers.

Let us say, hypothetically, that central purchasing at Dell presently sizes up suppliers based mainly on these factors: price, on-time delivery, and quality. That sounds good. It is two steps up from a fixation on just price, the norm in by-the-numbers, short-term-results companies. A supplier with low price, great delivery, and excellent quality, however, may actually be a poor partner. It just masks its weaknesses. It can show up as best on price simply by bidding low—perhaps below its own costs to "buy" the contract. Its high costs will, sooner or later, force price increases or inability to perform. To get high marks for its delivered quality, the supplier may simply resort to legions of inspectors, a high-cost way to look good when process quality actually is not good. To achieve high on-time deliveries, it may just bulk up on inventory, the costly, unlean, ineffective way of the past.

In competing for a chance to get a contact with the Dells of the world, what is a maker to do? The strong temptation is to bid precariously low and slide backward into inspection-based quality and high-inventory-based delivery. The watchful customer, using advanced sourcing methods, can ensure that this does not happen to its suppliers.

ADVANCED SOURCING—INTO THE SUPPLY CHAIN.
A simple, two-factor way of assessing suppliers presents itself. The two factors are 1) units on hand, and 2) lot-replenishment time. (A third factor, variation in lot-replenishment time, may be necessary for suppliers with shaky processes.) Because of the masking effect noted above, these two factors can say more about cost/price, on-time, and quality than do price, on-time, and quality themselves. By this assessment method, best suppliers are those that are lean on inventory—low units on hand—and have short replenishment times. The *lean* component of the lean/quick combination is a good marker as well for low cost. The *quick* component indicates high likelihood of making on-time deliveries—dependably. As for quality, a supplier that is both lean and quick surely must have excellent process quality, which is true quality. Poor quality, on the other hand, bogs down the processes, ties up inventory, and injects uncertainty into the timing of deliveries.

This advanced sourcing formula, while simple, requires an information system. Purchasing needs current, accurate information from suppliers on how many units they have on hand and what their lot-replenishment times are. This information will differ for each part number. The supplier is obliged to make the two factors dominant in its internal performance management system, since its customer will grade it over and over on the two factors.

As for communicating this information, the Internet, or an intranet, is a natural. Say that Celestica has a contract to deliver fifteen different mother boards to Dell Computer. Celestica's inventory master file, showing up-to-the-minute units on hand, links to Dell's. It is a mouse click away for Dell's supplier-development people. Besides inventory information, Celestica provides frequently updated information on its lot-replenishment times. In the high-tech world, lot-replenishment times can be unstable, varying with process yields and component shortages. (The third factor, variation in replenishment time, might be a fitting addition in this example.)

Mathematically combining the two factors would give Dell supplier-development a *flexible responsiveness index*. For each purchased mother board, the Dell system recomputes the index number simply by dividing units—better yet, lots—on hand by current replenishment time. For example, if Celestica has forty lots of mother boards on hand and can replenish a lot in twenty hours, its flexible-responsiveness index is 2. If forty lots and ten hours, the index is 4. If only ten lots, replenishable in just one hour, the index is 10. The higher the index, the better. An index of 2 might be considered as very poor, an indicator that the supplier is fat/slow, at least for that part number. An index of 10: lean/very quick. The number of units in a standard lot would be whatever is normal and acceptable for Celestica's production process and for shipping to Dell.

This example of a flexible response index is simplified. The inventory data available to Dell over its intranet actually should include not just the fifteen mother boards, but also semifinished components and raw materials that go into the mother boards. A full supply-chain management system extends the inventory status information beyond that—to Celestica's suppliers of board components. Supplier-development people at Dell would hope to see falling stock levels throughout the supply chain, along with speedier lot-replenishment times.

Effective execution requires follow-through. Under advanced sourcing, Dell's supplier-development teams would conduct random visits to supplier-partners. One purpose is to check on the accuracy of the inventory and replenishment time data. The visiting Dell teams should also become familiar with Celestica's means of being lean and quick—cross-training, cells, TPM, quick changeover, and so forth. Having good knowledge of Celestica's processes enables supplier development at Dell to offer advice and assistance. Equally important are helping to remove obstacles interfering with Celestica's ability to cut stock and become more flexibly responsive. Dell-specified boards in nonstandard sizes may be a large impediment, and perhaps Dell's paperwork or physical delivery system is a problem.

Though hypothetical, this example of supplier-development issues at Dell is realistic. Besides many newspaper and journal articles about Dell, a source for this example is a presentation at an academic conference. Jan Salsgiver of Arrow Electronics, a Dell supplier, and Stuart Smith of Dell Computer spoke on their supplier-customer partnership. John Buzacott, a professor in attendance, wrote a review of their talk. Buzacott's piece raised the issue "What happens if a customer like Dell 'tries to modify demand based on supplier inventory levels?'" He partially answers the question, suggesting that "the part with the lowest inventory may start to influence final demand. . . ."[20] Our example of Dell and Celestica probes that issue. We've considered how supply-chain partners must work together to keep demand, quality, and costs/prices pure, thereby to build up rather than weaken the supplier base. (Note: Paul Ericksen, manager of materials resources for John Deere's Horicon, Wisconsin, Works, has led implementation of a supplier-development program similar to that described above, but without the Internet as an explicit component.)[21]

We've considered how supply chains and information technology can aid or impede focus. Our next topic enlarges the issue: how to maintain focus while adding plant sites and expanding globally.

EXPANSION BY ADDITION

Sometime last century, when the West first began to study the Toyota system, it learned that one of Toyota's advantages lay in a preference for standardized machines. (My own 1982 book contrasted that idea with the Western tendency to pick new machines based on low bids—and never mind if they match.)[22]

Now the idea of standardization has been upped a peg. More than like machines, it's like factories. That is, in a multiplant company, make each factory about the same as others. This removes sources of variation that interfere with focused attention to the family of products made in those factories.

Focus in Multiplant Companies

The origin of this idea is not Japan. Partial credit goes to the giant chipmaker Intel, which has named the concept "Copy Exactly!". Intel includes the exclamation point because the idea is surprising, especially for a semiconductor manufacturer. How, we might ask, can a fast-changing and fast-growing manufacturer such as Intel maintain any semblance of sameness from one plant to the next? An Intel notice to its also fast-growing chip suppliers helps with the answer. (Besides producing in its own plants, Intel contracts considerably with outside fabricators, or "fabs," for chips.) The advisory, on Intel preferences for its supplier plants, includes the following:

> Copy Exactly! is a design philosophy utilized by Intel in the details of fab construction and operation. The intent . . . is to duplicate the same design from one factory to the next. As a supplier to Intel, you will be asked to adhere to past standards of design in order to achieve repeatable results. This methodology allows both parties to maximize learning efforts and to make changes relative to a baseline of construction techniques. As supplier to Intel, you will still be encouraged to lower the cost of facilities and/or improve productivity; however, these types of changes will require formal review.
>
> Copy Exactly! is not intended to limit innovation but . . . to control deviations in process in order to avoid unplanned consequences. As a supplier, you should understand the importance of Copy Exactly! and plan accordingly. The Intel project team is committed to ensuring the Copy Exactly! is timely and well organized so that both parties can work towards a successful outcome.[23]

In semiconductors, processes are temperamental and yields highly variable. Copy exactly puts a floor of stability under the processes. This shrinks the large number of variables that determine process yields.

Copy exactly has caught the eye of various other manufacturers large enough to have multiple factories. One is Nypro, which has some twenty-five injection-molding plants around North America and elsewhere, most either product-focused or customer-focused. For Nypro, greater standardization of plants and processes should lower its unit costs. At the same time, copy exactly should help the company maintain its chief competitive advantage—ultrahigh quality.

Exxon Chemical, with thirty-one petrochemical plants worldwide, is another fan. In this unit of ExxonMobil—with plants already built and affixed with hard "plumbing"—copy exactly would entail extensive plant conversions. The feasibility of doing so is under investigation at the company.[24] Honda automotive also has begun to embrace standardized facilities. President Hiroyuki Yoshino states that Honda is "aiming to largely eliminate the need to retool assembly lines around the world by making them nearly identical."[25]

While Intel gets the glory for copy exactly, there is precedent for the concept in other industries: one is nuclear power generation. Nuclear, like semiconductors, depends highly on control of large numbers of complex interacting variables. We all shiver occasionally at the thought of another Chernobyl, for any nuclear power accident can spread death globally. The French take pride in their extensive nuclear power industry, which quietly and reliably keeps the country lit year after year. Is it luck? *Non,* as almost any Frenchman or woman will explain. The high standards of safe operation come from standardization. Unlike those in the United States, United Kingdom, former Soviet Union, and various other countries, the plants in France all use a tried-and-true design and basic standards of operation.

Industries with far fewer interacting variables are also profiting from their own versions of copy exactly. Chain retailers, hotels, and fast-food restaurants are good examples. Whatever the industry, companies bent on expanding into new locales need to be aware of the advantages of focus on a larger scale than plants and restaurants. Focused regions, the next topic, concludes this chapter.

Multilocal Global Expansion

As global trade mushrooms, brand-name companies restlessly move operations from one low-wage region to another. Ever larger ships and planes move goods over ever longer supply lines. It won't last. Shipping distances for many kinds of goods are sure to shrink. The reason is that have-not countries and regions are gradually beginning to have. Southeast Asia's Four Tigers—Korea, Taiwan, Singapore, and Hong Kong—have strong new rivals. Thailand, Malaysia, Mexico, Brazil, and Argentina, to name a few, can claim first world expertise in making cars or TVs, athletic equipment or infotech routers, high-fashion clothing or cellular phones. Add China and India, if you will.

Countries on this growing list often develop focused manufacturing centers. Taiwan's specialty is electronic components. In Malaysia's Penang Island, it's semiconductors and finished electronic assemblies. In southern Brazil the Curitiba area is that country's second major auto-manufacturing center. And in Mexico there are several industrial centers, each with its own focus: Tijuana has become the world's largest center for production of TVs. Ciudad Juárez enjoys the same distinction regarding wiring harnesses for cars and trucks. Monterrey is brimming with top-notch metal-forming producers. And Guadalajara is a high-tech mecca. The outputs of these Mexican plants nicely serve the North American market without necessarily raising balance-of-payments alarms. (See box for commentary on how exports from countries like Mexico can actually benefit payments accounts of trading partners.)

In an older strategy, the output of these industrial centers was for export to markets anywhere in the world. The trouble is, though a center achieves high focus on a type of manufacturing, it loses out on focus with its remote customers and their countries' cultures, regulatory agencies, and so on.

In a newer strategy, the problem corrects itself. Instead of ever greater exports, many manufacturers are setting up sister plants in Asia and Australia, western and central Europe, and South America and South Africa. For the companies involved, it is a *multilocal strategy*.[26] With manufacturing in each foreign market, the company gains focused suppliers, customers, and intangibles related to local cultures.

Flextronics International's EMS (electronics manufacturing services) plant

---

Trading with Mexico: The Trampoline Effect[27]

Rich countries are often criticized for not trading more with poorer ones. Why don't they do more? Too much importing from lower-wage countries is thought to produce trade deficits for the richer country. But let's look more closely, using Mexico as an example.

In 1999 the United States ran an apparent $15 billion trade deficit with Mexico. Looking behind that number tells a different story. Much of Mexico's production—of electronic, automotive, health care, and other items—are assemblies whose components come from the United States. The difference in value between the components to Mexico and the end products from Mexico still favors Mexico's accounts. But a significant portion of Mexico's output is then exported to countries around the world. As one example, of some $3 billion of goods exported from IBM's plant in El Salto, around 25 percent went to countries other than the United States. That 25 percent improves the U.S. balance of trade with those other countries—but critics tend to fixate only the one-to-one trade numbers with Mexico. Economists call this hidden benefit the "trampoline effect."

The trampoline bounces still higher as Mexico inks free trade deals with Europe and South America, since Mexico's trade pacts raise its total exports, including those containing U.S.-made components. But the trampoline effect is not just for the United States. Volkswagen's plant in Puebla, Mexico, will export, to VW assembly plants in various countries, over five hundred thosuand engines this year. Many components for those engines come from Germany and the United States, which benefits both countries' trade balances. Japan has a large TV assembly presence in Tijuana, Mexico, much of the components coming from Japan and much of the finished TVs shipped to various countries; Japan's balance of trade benefits.

Multilocal expansion, which increases trade with less developed countries, has more advantages than meet the eye.

in Guadalajara, Mexico, is illustrative. Its one-million-square-foot facility opened in 1997 produces Web TVs for Sony, personal data assistants for PalmPilot, printers for Hewlett-Packard, and blood-glucose monitors for Johnson & Johnson.[28] While Flextronics could export these products to (besides the United States and Canada) Europe and Asia, it has a better idea: Have its European (for instance, Irish) plants produce for Europe, and its Southeast Asian plants for the Asian markets.

Or maybe Solectron's EMS plants around the world will grab those markets. Alejandro Gomez, general manager of Solectron's plant in Guadalajara, comments on the emergent competitive strategy: "Chinese labor is cheaper, but the real issue now is speed. . . . The faster you get something through the production chain, the longer it will be on the market."[29] Long chains are slow chains. Short ones—making in the same region you sell in—are fast and more focused.

There is much more to say about focus—and speed. From the broad view in this chapter we go to focus within the plant in the next.

9

Focus Within

The previous chapter—in this two-part set on focus—ended by noting the need for speed throughout the supply and customer system. It's the same within the facility. Fast flows are vital. They are the main purpose behind just-in-time and lean manufacturing. Quick throughput is far easier in focused plants, production lines, cells, and equipment than in old-style plants chopped up into shops and functional departments.

Focus comes in various forms. One form, presented in the previous chapter's discussion of copy exactly points to a general truth: Standardization—whether in designs of plants, products, or processes—freezes large numbers of variables. This enables designers to focus improvement on a manageably small number. Standardization, then, does not inhibit innovation, it allows innovation to be successful. The point about standards holds, too, for the design of single plants, our next topic. Following that, the discussion narrows further, to design of cells and production lines, which concludes the chapter.

FOCUSED PLANT DESIGN

Multipairs of chess players hunch over small wooden tables in one of the open-air, sit-and-play street alcoves in downtown Santiago, Chile. A ten-year-old aficionado licking an ice-cream cone walks by, pauses at the corner table, and after a quick glance says, "*El blanco ganará*" ("White will win"). How does she know? Because white's bishops have taken command of the longest diagonals, and its pawns and pieces sit so as to carefully guard each other. In its fifteen-hundred-year existence, this game's complexities have been thoroughly steamed, stirred, and strained. A casual student of the game will know this strategic truth: Chess is positional.

Manufacturing is positional, too. World-class manufacturing, at a young age, is still evolving. It is hard to find documentation on its strategic positional norms. However, a competitive plant is like a competitive chessboard. Experience teaches right positioning. Plants should be neither too big with too many people and part numbers nor too small with too few. Plant shapes and flow patterns, and nearness to other facilities, make up further positional rules of thumb.

Size

Acme, Inc's., three-year-old factory houses seven hundred employees in 350,000 square feet (32,500 square meters). It fabricates and assembles several related product lines. I've been invited for a tour. After a briefing, we enter the production floor. I take a quick look around and see that my negative impressions, from the briefing, are confirmed. The plant cannot be efficient. I see conveyors overhead and wide aisles teeming with forklifts in fabrication and in the stockroom just in view. I had already learned that half of the seven hundred employees are nonproduction. Half of those are in essential roles such as product development and customer service. The rest, though, are in production support—mostly scheduling, stock picking, material handling, putting away and keeping track of parts by computer, and so on. Non-value-adding functions.

The plant's management is up-to-date. The plant is focused on a family of related products, employees are well trained, maintenance is "total preventive," and signs of visual management, SPC, and other best practices are widely in evidence. So what's wrong? The plant is too big.

Though the Acme, Inc., example is hypothetical, plenty of factories are like it. When a plant is too large, there is no way to get incoming parts to action zones or finished products to outbound docks simply and efficiently. When you already are stuck with an outsize plant, *internal flows*—fabrication to assembly to pack-out—can be made simple and efficient. Multiple focused plants-in-a-plant and multiple work cells provide the means. There is still, however, the problem of long distances to and from outbound and inbound docks.

Large plants have another problem. They hold too many people. Small plants can "feel like family," not a minor consideration. Carving a building into focused factories and work cells can help bring back a family feel, but only if the units are well zoned off. In a 1990 book, I described what compressor manufacturer Copeland Corp. did about a too large plant.[1] Its six-hundred-thousand-square-foot facility, in Sidney, Ohio, was not only too big, it was also stuck with thirteen diverse, lower-volume compressor lines. Copeland had moved other higher-volume lines to new, focused plants in lower-wage areas of the country. The solution to the triple hex (too big, too many people, too many product lines): They moved all the machines and people to form two factories-within-the-factory. One focused on compressor lines with high welding content, the other on machining-intensive product lines. Further, to gain some semblance of "family," the two plants-in-a-plant were separated by a brick wall and served by separate plant managers, parking lots, and labor bargaining units. Still, the plant remained too big, requiring long to-from dock distances.

WHY SO BIG?

Why do so many manufacturers persist in responding to sales growth with enlarged plants? Reason one is blind adherence to the economy-of-scale concept. But diseconomies of complexity come with size, soon washing out the hoped-for scale economies. A plant small in size with few people and items is simple; a large one with many people and items is complex.

Reason two is that growth is often by acquisition. That usually brings in new and different products lines. At the same time, to meet tough sales targets, marketers and product developers extend, expand, and add to the product mix. The plant becomes unfocused, and the enlarged mix with its many components and purchased materials push out the walls.

Managers should know better. Becoming unfocused invites rippling inefficiencies. Trying to cram the mix into a single building makes things worse. A few well-regarded companies have it right. The admired expansion formula at 3M, Solectron, ABB, and Nypro is to keep adding new plants, each reasonably small. That recipe dovetails with those companies' multilocal siting strategies.

What is "reasonably small"? There can be no definite answer, but experience does at least suggest some upper limits. My own opinion is that for the dominant kind of manufacturing—fabrication and assembly—the following upper size limits hold rather well:

- Maximum area: 200,000 square feet (18,600 square meters)

- Maximum number of people: 500

- Maximum number of parts or stockkeeping units (SKUs): 2,000

These are upper limits. To get something approaching optimum, for a fab/assembly plant, cut all the numbers by four. The hundreds of small but successful manufacturers in northern Italy, including makers of some of the world's best machine tools, testify to the "small is good" point of view. Similarly, the German industrial success story is less attributable to the massive factories of the well-knowns, such as Mercedes and Hoechst, than to the modest-size facilities of the hundreds of *mittelstand*—middle-size—manufacturers.[2]

There are, of course, exceptions. In some industries, such as capital-intensive petroleum, ores, and grains, technology tends to dictate larger plants with rather few people and SKUs. This statement does not apply to steel mills. Though steel complexes are massive, they are usually made up of many not-too-large manufacturing buildings: a few electric arc furnaces in one (or two) buildings, rolling mills in another, continuous casters in still another, and so on.

Until recently, the auto industry looked to be an exception to "small is good." Auto assembly plants of 500,000, 750,000, and even 1 million square feet (93,000 square meters) are common. Discussion in chapter 4 on modular plants, however, points in a different direction. The trend is to much smaller assembly plants for joining together small numbers of multipart sub-assemblies delivered from modular suppliers. David Cole, director of the University of Michigan's Office for the Study of Automotive Transportation, says the new plants may cost automakers only about one-third of the $1 billion–plus that they have been spending.[3]

HOW SMALL?

There is less to say about minimum effective plant sizes. As mentioned, technology sometimes sets a lower limit. A microchip plant has to be big enough to hold a large network of vessels, pipes, and transmission facilities, along with the production equipment they support.

On the other hand, in machining, stamping, welding, molding, dyeing, sewing, printing, assembly, and many other common processes, there might seem to be no lower limit. Plenty of competent fabricators, in fact, started out in the home garage and haven't grown much from that. Such a small business, though, leads a precarious existence. To survive, it must grow certain competencies. It will need to beef up its capability to design competitive products and processes, buy wisely, deal with information technology, and market itself adequately. Supporting the costs of these specialties requires a lot more sales revenue than can come from the home garage. Hiring out these functions—the virtual company route—is a possibility; that, however, requires enough understanding of the functions to find and manage one's virtual provider. To possess the required expertise, such a business needs to reach, say, one hundred employees and fifty thousand square feet. Moreover, it needs to expand product offerings enough to withstand loss of a critical account. The minimum number of SKUs—end products plus components—might be around one hundred, and the optimum a few hundred.

Shape and Flow

Let's extend the chessboard analogy. Shape? An oblong chessboard would ruin the game: too few options for moving pieces and pawns. The square shape of a chessboard allows an enormous number of combinations of ways to move about the sixty-four red and black squares.

The same is true of factories. Long and narrow doesn't work. Such shape is a nightmare to equip. No layout makes sense. In 1988 a business unit of pressure-products maker Rosemount, Inc., Chanhassen, Minnesota, was shoehorned into a leased facility that snaked through the edges of a building; other lessees had the rest of the building. The Rosemount team was tearing its hair out trying to find space for setting up focused cells while still allowing passage for material flows. Fortunately the business unit found a new, better-shaped home before long.

May we conclude that square-shaped plants are ideal? I think not. Slightly elongated, about sixty-forty, is better, offering more layout options. A square may not offer enough side-to-side distance for some purposes and too much for others. Of course, if the plant is half a million square feet or more, square or oblong doesn't matter. With such expanse, most processes will be too far from certain sister processes or support services.

Assuming the factory is not too big and is somewhat oblong, the next issue is placement of facilities for efficient flows. Here the rarely seen ideal is for each U-shaped cell or line to have its own ship and receive docks. In other words, locate each cell/line on one of the four walls or building corners. Conventional layout, receiving at one end of the building and shipping at the other, has no merit. With or without cells, it is better to cut holes in outer walls so that different direct materials can arrive near to where they are used. Bulky packing material should arrive close to packing, maintenance materials by maintenance stores, and so forth. In the early 1980s some Western auto-assembly plants retrofitted their receiving configurations in that way. Instead of docks on just one side, they were dispersed around the building for receiving at points of use. One of the first to adopt this idea, borrowed from Japan, was Ford Motor Company's Wixom, Michigan, facility. Ever since, the Wixom plant, assembling high-end Ford and Lincoln models, has been on lists of most profitable of the world's assembly plants (though not just because of where the docks are).

The Ford-Wixom example is one of making the best of a much too large and complex assembly plant. It is one destined to be made obsolete by next generation's compact, modular-system plants. A more extensive example, next, wraps up and ties together several points that have been made about plant design.

One Manufacturer's Journey

One of Cutler-Hammer's plants, in Beaver, Pennsylvania, produces assorted circuit breakers and electric transfer switches. The massive plant, originally for aircraft assembly, was sold to Westinghouse in 1942. By the 1960s it had become headquarters for the components division and a cash cow. But as Westinghouse's fortunes slid downhill, so did the Beaver facility's. By the 1990s, when Cutler-Hammer (now a subsidiary of Eaton Corp.) took over, Beaver was in poor shape.

It is easy to see why. The numbers all exceed the maximums suggested earlier: 976,000 square feet, 700 employees, and over 20,000 part numbers (versus 200,000, 500, and 2,000). But division chief Spencer Duin and right-hand man Vinod Kapoor, who had brilliantly managed transitions to "world class" while still with Westinghouse, made the best of it. With new plant manager Asim Kokan coaxing and cajoling, the plant was relaid out, first into seven giant cells, later subdivided into thirteen still large cells, and finally chopped into thirty-two cells. Every machine was moved, most more than once. Work-in-process stockrooms were eliminated. Operators were cross-trained and job classifications cut from seventy-two to fifteen. Piece rates were abolished, and everyone was trained in JIT, process mapping, and process control. These and many other changes drove throughput times from three to four weeks to three to four days. The plant became profitable.[4]

And what about all that space? Only about half is occupied, even though three suppliers were moved into the building—supplier partnership up close. The in-house suppliers pay rent, maintain inventory, and deliver to production lines. With the reduced space and cellular efficiencies, forklift trucks were reduced from around thirty-five to eleven. That is still too many, but plants with hundreds of thousands of square feet too many have long distances to traverse.

In retrospect, it might have been better for Cutler-Hammer to bulldoze most of the factory and rebuild and resettle into two or three reasonably sized and focused buildings on the site. That—the bulldoze option—is extreme but sometimes is the best solution to a grossly oversize plant.

Best way to deal with the big, big plant problem is avoidance. Quit the widespread practice of adding on and adding on again. Stop at fifty thousand or one hundred thousand square feet and build another plant. Don't work on bringing suppliers' stockrooms or production into your building (but do welcome suppliers' facilities on-site in another building); it is hard enough to maintain focus with your own products and people without adding those of suppliers.

I was an invited speaker for the grand opening of an Invensys factory in Tijuana, Mexico. It is a beautiful facility, designed to dazzle employees with, for example, the best—and best maintained—rest rooms they have ever seen. The designers believe such a fine place to work in will do much to solve the area's high employee turnover problem.[5] (The plant has many other positive features, such as work cells with kanban flow control and point-of-use stocking.) But the 173,000-square-foot plant was built with a "soft wall" on one side. Executives had planned ahead, expecting to expand through the soft wall when sales growth pushes on the present space. Bad idea. Instead, harden the soft wall and erect a second plant on the site. Give each building its own focused family of products and family-size workforce.

CELL/LINE DESIGN

Shifting from broad to narrow, we come to the matter of facilities within the plant—specifically, design of cells and lines. Issues to be taken up include shape, length, number of stations, number of people, work content per station, whether to sit or stand, and output rate.

Shape

From shape of plants we home in on shape of cells and production lines. The newer wisdom, now well-known, is this: Strive for U-shaped or serpentine wherever feasible. Advantages include the following:

- *Flexibility.* One person can run an entire cell with little walking, or load the cell with a person at each station.

- *Closeness.* A linear production line stretches people out: no team sense. A U shape brings operatives in close, facilitating cross-learning, job rotation, mutual assistance, joint problem solving, and peer pressure—as well as social interaction.

- *Passage.* Straight lines inhibit transit of materials, people, and tools. Bending long lines around themselves compacts it all, which opens up passage and offers accessibility around the perimeter.

- *Linkages.* U/serpentine shapes offer many options for linking to other cells or lines, storage, and docks. When modest-size buildings have docks opening on all sides, the factory may resemble Exhibit 9.1: cell end points are receiving and shipping docks.

- *Rework.* A tenet of quality management is to retain and process rework at the source. With bent lines, discovered defectives pass back across short distances to the offending station.

- *Configuration.* With U/serpentine shapes, adding or deleting work stations just requires increasing or shrinking the arc, as illustrated in Exhibit 9.2. The exhibit also shows a common elaboration of a cell: a subassembly or fabrication stem, which reduces flow time: positioning work on a stem permits parallel processing, whereas positioning within the cell—serial processing—adds its own increments of flow time.

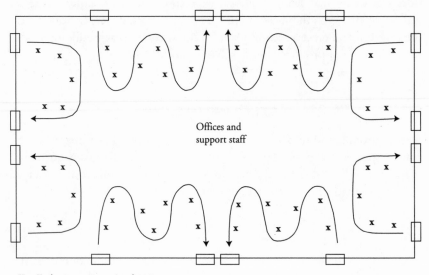

Offices and
support staff

Key: Each x is an operator/workstation.
   Sixteen receive and ship docks are on the perimeter

Exhibit 9.1. Cell Configurations

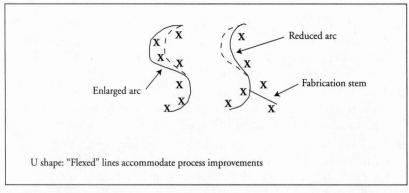

Reduced arc

Enlarged arc

Fabrication stem

U shape: "Flexed" lines accommodate process improvements

Key: Each X is an operator/workstation.

Exhibit 9.2. Configuration Flexibility in U- or Serpentine-Shaped Cells

People

Five to ten associates per cell or line is good, though cells of one or fifteen sometimes fit the situation. In machining, the trend is toward fewer operators per cell. For example, a single multiskilled machinist may operate three, four, five, or more machines in a U. Or those three or more machines may be replaced by a single stand-alone CNC machining center with multiple spindles and turrets for performing simultaneous operations. Machine-tool maker Giddings & Lewis sees customers increasingly asking for a pair of such machines to be run by a single operator.[6] Disadvantages of just one operator per cell include lack of peer learning, peer pressure, checking each other's work, and socialization. Advantages, though, sometimes outweigh the disadvantages.

People are limited in how many skills they can master and keep current. That, in turn, recommends upper limits on number of people per cell. In high-skill work, such as machining and welding, an operator may be able to become and stay proficient in no more than about five skill sets. In light manufacturing—assembly/test/pack—up to ten people in a cell can work, because a cell member may be able to become certified and maintain certification in that many skill sets. With as many as ten people in a cell, other negatives crop up. Sense of family tends to fade, cliques and feuding factions to form, cooperation and agreement to become problematic, and peer pressure to fizzle. The latter factor, peer pressure, is no small thing, as noted in the box on the next page.

What of the many cases in the world of thirty, fifty, or seventy people per line (no longer to be thought of as a cell)? These numbers are common in assembly-oriented factories in lower-wage countries. Lines with that many people are producing TVs and VCRs, circuit boards and modems, cameras and telephones, wiring harnesses and medical devices, and all manner of toys and games. Producing these products entails many steps, and designers of the process choose to assign those many steps to many operators.

The bad effects of such designs multiply. Chapter 6 detailed such effects in the section entitled "Cycle of Woe." Each person's job has little work content. This keeps the workforce from learning and growing in skill, value, confidence, and pride. A system that holds back growth of employees holds back the companies and inhibits the economic development of the resident countries. Job rotation helps but cannot include twenty, fifty, or seventy jobs. Rotation through just a few of them, all narrow tasks, provides small learning compared with rotating through the stations in a well-designed cell with high work content per station.

Peer Pressure at NUMMI

Jamie Hresko, a Buick City supervisor, was a comer. His employer, General Motors, had designated him as a high-potential manager. That honor included GM's assigning him to spend a year in an accelerated master's program at Stanford's Graduate School of Business.

To make the experience more meaningful, Hresko came up with an audacious plan. Prior to start of the term, he would arrange to be hired as a production associate at NUMMI (New United Motors Manufacturing, Inc.), the Toyota-GM joint-venture car plant across the bay from Stanford's Palo Alto, California, campus. He wanted to really understand the essence of the Toyota system—to be able to separate truth from legend. Hresko duly documented his experiences and worked them into class studies, some of which are reported in a book by two Stanford professors. After an exacting training period, Hresko was assigned to a team of four building radiator supports, with job rotation every couple of hours. His comments about the experience, as transcribed by the professors, include the following:

> The peer pressure is intense. Most people were willing to stay after their shift to finish their job if necessary. I wasn't accustomed to this type of attitude. People at NUMMI just go do it. They believe that their job is to protect the customer by never shipping a bad product.... During my first few days when I would get behind, other team members would come over and help me catch up. In fact, the team really handled not just the work but also the discipline. When one team member came to work late a couple of times, he was strong-armed by the entire group. The peer pressure is really big-time. Teams can really impact the decision to keep a person or let them go.[7]

Moreover, vision is impaired. If I am one of thirty-plus people on a single line, I lack the whole-product visibility that comes to members of five-to-ten-person work cells. (Studs Terkel comments on the matter in the accompanying box.) With no sense of product and its uses and misuses, and therefore no sense of customer, my motivation to perform perfectly every time is missing. I do not see my role as one of service to real customers.

No Visibility

In his book *My American Century*,[8] Studs Terkel includes an interview with steelworker Mike Lefevre, who says, "You can't take pride any more.... You're mass-producing things and you never see the end result of it. I worked for a trucker one time. And I got this tiny satisfaction when I loaded a truck. At least I could see the truck depart loaded. In a steel mill, forget it. You don't see where nothing goes."

Work Stations and Work Content

Often an apt alternative to the many-person production line is subdivision. For example, replace one 40-person line with four 10-person cells. If average work content for each of the 40 had been 10 seconds, the average in the 10-person cells will be 40 seconds. In a work shift of 420 minutes a 10-second task repeats 2,520 times, compared with 630 times per shift for a 40-second average work content. Even 630 repetitions is a lot; 2,520 repetitions is, for most people, intolerable unless better jobs are out of reach.

TYRANNY OF THE TEN-SECOND WORK CYCLE.
Ten-second station cycle times are not at all uncommon. My guess is that average work content per person is ten seconds or less in *most* manual assembly lines in the aforementioned regions. In TV manufacturing plants in Tijuana and wiring harness facilities in Ciudad Juárez, ten- and eight-second work content per person is fairly common. At eight seconds a task repeats three thousand times per shift—day after day. It is no wonder that, as pointed out in chapter 6, average employee turnover in these plants is over 100 percent per year.

Why does this happen? The companies responsible for these numbers aim, of course, for efficiency and effectiveness. Looking only at the short-term, obvious factors, they see minimal training expenses for simple, short-cycle tasks. So if can't-stand-it-anymore employees quit after only weeks, a few months, or a year, the cost to train replacements is affordable. This is the main rationale for extreme division of labor, as it was in the time of Henry Ford I, the father of the assembly line: hire low-wage people and have them quickly up to speed on a very small task.

In the 1960s and 1970s, most college students in business, industrial psychology, and industrial engineering studied reports on the "heartless" assembly line. The 1952 exposé *The Man on the Assembly Line*[9] was standard fare. It did no good. The students, myself included, graduated and went to work designing production lines the same old way.

THE CELLULAR ALTERNATIVE.
A main reason: No clearly good alternative. That reason, or excuse, should have died with discovery of cellular manufacturing and the high payoff for a well-trained, multiskilled, highly flexible workforce. In industrialized countries the line without a heart has all but died. An intelligent manager goes to the Dominican Republic or the Philippines, however, and sees only a plentiful, undereducated, low-wage labor pool. So bring it in cheaply, train it narrowly, and enforce tight controls. On the surface it works. Quality is high, and costs are low. Quality is nearly always higher and costs lower, however, in cellular manufacturing with high-flex employees. And the payoff is quick.

Five production lines, forty assemblers/testers/packers per line, 10-second work content per person

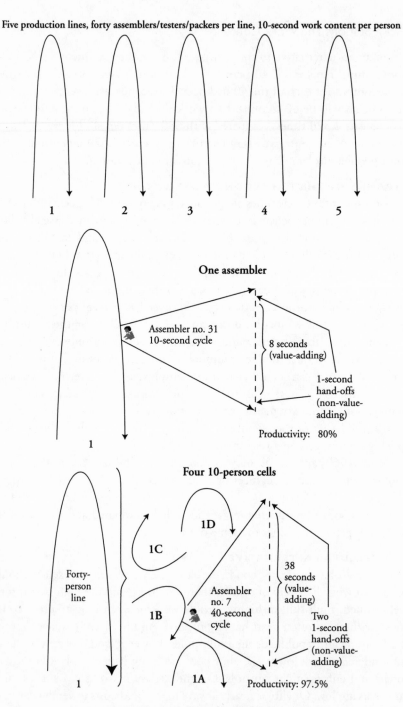

One assembler

Assembler no. 31
10-second cycle

8 seconds
(value-adding)

1-second
hand-offs
(non-value-
adding)

Productivity: 80%

Four 10-person cells

Forty-
person
line

1D

1C

Assembler
no. 7
40-second
cycle

1B

1A

38
seconds
(value-
adding)

Two
1-second
hand-offs
(non-value-
adding)

Productivity: 97.5%

Exhibit 9.3. TV Assembly Plant

Around ten years ago, engineers at Sony's division headquarters in San Diego questioned the design of production lines in the company's large TV-manufacturing complex across the Mexican border. Using careful time studies, they proved to themselves that the conventional ten-second job cycle was inefficient. Exhibit 9.3 illustrates. The first panel is a bare-bones schematic of a plant with five production lines, each with forty assemblers/testers/packers and a ten-second work cycle. Each line produces a different-size television model.

The Sony time-study results are a revelation, as shown in the second panel of the exhibit: in a typical ten-second cycle, eight seconds are value-adding work, but one second on each end are for hand-offs from and to adjacent operators. That adds up to two seconds out of ten in a non-value-adding state. Division of labor, esteemed in economic theory as a way of increasing productivity, does the opposite when taken to this ten-second extreme: with 20 percent lost to hand-offs, labor productivity is reduced to 80 percent.

What to do? The cellular solution is to break up the forty-person line into, say, four 10-person cells, labeled in the third panel as 1A, 1B, 1C, and 1D. The work content of each assembler in a cell expands from ten seconds to forty seconds. Now, with the two seconds lost to hand-offs over a forty-second cycle, labor productivity is up from 80 percent to 95.7 percent. But the productivity increase is minor compared with the benefits of a humane job. Chapter 6 fully discussed the matter in the "Cycle of Woe" section.

Can work content actually be increased by a factor of four? Often, yes. For example, combine, as one station in a cell, the following four adjacent production-line stations: 1) cut off two wires; 2) remove insulation from wire ends; 3) ultrasonically weld the wires to a connector; and 4) check the assembly with a gauge. The four stations, in becoming one, will require less side-to-side space. (Cells generally are space-saving.) Moreover, the new, combined station will entail a step or two of roaming room for the assembler. That may allow the job to become a stand-up, walk-a-bit operation. A stool may be there to lean against, but basically this is a healthful standing job with variety of motion. Elimination of chairs in production is a movement in its own right; see box.

Getting Around

"At Delphi Automotive Systems Corp. [Rochester, New York], . . . UAW Local 1097 . . . agreed to work with Delphi to introduce lean-production techniques to boost productivity. Among the changes was the elimination of chairs on the shop floor as workers were forced to move from station to station instead of waiting for material to come to them."[10]

One limiting factor in breaking a multiperson line into cells is the cost of extra pieces of equipment. In our example, the cells would each require four sets of small tools, tabletop ultrasound welders, and gauges, along with extra parts trays. Usually in assembly work, such equipment is relatively inexpensive. At one of Mallinckrodt's plants in the Los Angeles area, a manager reckoned that eliminating chairs, which were costing around $300 each, might pay for whatever extra equipment might be needed in converting to cells.[11]

DESIGN FOR CONTINUOUS IMPROVEMENT—AND BETTER HEALTH.
Besides the immediate benefits of cells instead of production lines, there are plentiful longer-term payoffs. Cell teams gain whole-process vision that fosters continuous improvement. When an assembler's work content grows from ten or fifteen seconds to thirty or forty-five, there is time to collect and record data, to think about task and process problems, and to develop better ideas. Higher work content and job variety stabilizes the workforce and cuts labor turnover. Not having to repeat the same motions two to three thousand times per day removes a main source of repetitive-motion injuries. That stems growing costs of errors and missed cycles, absenteeism, medical care, unemployment insurance, and rehiring. Going from a sit-all-day, backache-prone job to stand-up and move around work is a further nod to better health.

One industry undergoing transformation to the system just described is cut-and-sew. In that industry, cellular is called "modular," or the "Toyota sewing system" (TSS) method. Videotaped interviews with employees in plants that have converted to TSS highlight many changes in their work lives, notably health improvements. Transcriptions of some of the taped replies to a question on how they like TSS follow:

Person 1. "The thing I like about TSS is the freedom to move around—not have to do one job all day, so you don't get as bored."

Person 2. "Well, . . . sitting down, you have a lot of neck trouble and back trouble. And standing up, about the only problem you have is getting your legs used to standing. But when you get to move around a lot, it kind of relaxes them. Feels better."

Person 3. "I get more sore sitting down than I do standing up. My body is mostly moving when I'm standing up and I'm working from machine to machine. And then when I was sitting down I was doing one operation; now I'm doing three or four operations, and it's a whole lot better for me."

Person 4. "It's not boring. And I've learned how to just about put a whole shirt together."

Person 5. "You're getting to work with other ladies. And you can talk and work at the same time. But it's—the day just goes by faster and you're not just sitting and getting bored."

Several dozen more interviews, from three plants—making caps, jackets, and shirts—are in the same vein.[12]

QUALITY: MIGHT CELLS HAVE MADE THE DIFFERENCE AT BRIDGESTONE/FIRESTONE?

Besides quality of work life, cells stitching garments or other fabric items are happy homes for quality itself. It is well established: within cells there is station-to-station visibility of the many kinds of root causes that are not buried in technology. When in 2000 Bridgestone/Firestone was forced into a massive recall of radial tires for Ford Explorers, I could not help but recall my own experience in 1984 at a Firestone radial tire plant in Albany, Georgia. I had been invited to conduct a one-day seminar for fifty-six managers on a Saturday in June. It was a typical batch-and-queue factory, in which quality problems are mostly invisible to the workforce.

On arrival midday on Friday, I was given a thorough tour, which provided ammunition for devising a cellular plan for most of the tire-making processes. (Tire making is discrete production, which is fed by batch production of the rubber itself—done in earlier production stages in the same plant.) I found that the plant built tires in four steps, each a "department": first stage, third stage, press-cure, and final finish. (A second stage had been eliminated when the plant converted to radial tires.) About twenty first-stage machines produced carcasses that went into racks holding, typically, twelve thousand units. From there forty third-stage machines converted carcasses to "green" tires, which went directly to racks awaiting next processing in two hundred press-cure machines. Those racks held ten thousand to twelve thousand green tires.

For someone like myself—predisposed to see manufacturing through JIT eyes—twelve thousand carcasses and ten to twelve thousand green tires were a fantastic opportunity for improvement. My Saturday presentation included sketches on acetate of conversion to multiple cells. For good balance, each would have two first-stage machines feeding one second-stage machine, feeding four press-cure machines, feeding one final-finish station. Later, with the help, of plant manager Dick Clarke by mail and phone, the plan was refined and became part of a case study published in my 1987 casebook on implementation of JIT and TQC.[13] The instructor's manual for the casebook includes a sketch of the cells, with estimates of benefits. Did Firestone implement the plan? They did not. In checking with Clarke a year or so later, I learned what happened. Corporate pumped in some $20 million for automation, then shuttered the plant a year after I had visited, idling around two thousand people. (Finally, this new century is bringing forth the cellular mode of building tires. Most tire makers are experimenting with small-plant designs made up of compact cells, plus new automated equipment that largely avoids in-process fork trucking in and out of storage racks.)[14]

Whether the cellular plan would have saved the plant from extinction is not the reason for this discussion. Rather, it is this: Work cells give operators, supervisors, technicians, and engineers whole-process visibility and reveal quality causes while trails are still fresh. By rejecting the cellular formula, this and many other plants in the industry seem to have set themselves up for the kind of debacle that Bridgestone/Firestone experienced with its radial tires fifteen years later.

PILOT PROJECT.
Sometimes I've found managers in agreement with all the points made about bad jobs and plant design and how to fix them. Yet they hesitate. It takes boldness to switch to an entirely different blueprint for the facility. It takes only a little boldness to do a pilot project. Most of these plants have multiple production lines. The pilot approach is to overhaul just one of them. Set it up as several small cells with small teams and all the trimmings. Make a big deal out of it: new paint, logoed shirts, color coding, visual displays. It will outshine the other lines, and the rest is easy.

Benchmarks of Good Cell and Production-Line Design

We have considered examples of why and how plants should subdivide large, unfocused productive units into smaller, focused ones. To be more specific, in designing plant interiors, what are the guidelines for shapes and quantities? Given the many modes of manufacture, there can be no hard rules. For mainstream piece-goods manufacturing and office cells (for example, for order entry), however, the following will hold up rather well:

- *Best shapes:* U or serpentine; also circular with work stations on the outside perimeter, L shape, or two short, parallel line segments.
- *Maximum number of people:* fifteen, through five is often best.
- *Number of work stations:*
  - *Minimum:* two—for example, extrude and slit, print and fold; test and pack, flame-cut and punch, card and draft; it takes only two to make a cell.
  - *Maximum:* thirty—for example, three machines for each of ten cell members, as in the modular (cellular) method in cloth and leather goods manufacturing.

- *Distance between stations:* arm's length in manual assembly; machine's "footprint" in machine-intensive production; any longer invites non-value-adding conveyors.

- *Work content or station cycle time:* thirty seconds to five minutes in labor-intensive work; otherwise dictated by machine cycles.

- *Output rate:*

  ▶ In the case of mostly repetitive or continuous production, equal to the customers' recent average usage rate (reciprocal of the *takt* time); if sales increase beyond the capacity of one cell or line, add another.

  ▶ In an up-and-down, make-to-order business, there is no rate; however, there often are simplifying, cost-reducing advantages in striving to smooth production of components in such a business—getting them on a rate equal to a recent average of the end-products' jumping-bean order pattern.

AUTOMOTIVE ASSEMBLY AT TOYOTA.

Toyota's automotive assembly system, much revised for the 1990s, contains most of these guidelines. Takahiro Fujimoto's 1999 book on the evolution of the Toyota system provides carefully researched data:[15] The pre-1990s plant design featured continuously moving assembly lines, some nine thousand feet long, subdivided into trim, chassis, and final. The 1990s plan further divided the latter three elements into five to twelve segments. Each segment averages around three hundred feet and contains around twenty work stations. The segments wind back and forth serpentine-like, and the work cycle is usually one to three minutes. These numbers fall well within the above guidelines.

In this design, three points not covered by the guidelines are notable. They relate to effects on people, a matter emphasized repeatedly in this book. One is that the new Toyota system has each group of operators working on a set of related tasks. Earlier descriptions of the Toyota system reflected more of a labor productivity mind-set. A production associate with, say, twenty-five spare seconds per cycle would often be assigned to do a 180-degree turn and spend that twenty-five seconds on an unrelated task. That old way, which spread to other Japanese companies,[16] violates a concept of good cell/line design: Give each group a view of and responsibility for a whole component or product or product family; pass the responsibility around the group through frequent job rotation.

Additionally, the old Toyota practice had a number of automated steps done off the moving line, whereas the new way is to integrate those steps into the process. This, too, enhances employee visibility of whole processes.

Finally, the old system placed line-stop devices everywhere for operators to actuate to prevent bad quality from moving on. But since pulling the stop cord put the whole line out of business, people were reluctant to do it. In the new system, about five car bodies buffer each segment from the next one. The result is that each segment is more like a separate business unit. Operators in the new system are stopping their line segments more often, which isolates troubles more often and more quickly than under the old, more monolithic line design. Toyota's improved concept is, at the same time, more customer-focused—in the sense of next process visibility—and more operator-friendly.

Within, say, ten years, however, Toyota's current, improved system may seem archaic. As discussed in chapter 4, success in the industry seems likely to require adoption of whole-module deliveries from suppliers. With magnitude reductions in numbers of parts in the assembly plants, nine-thousand-foot conveyor lines should disappear. Their replacement may look something like the schematic in Exhibit 9.1: several smaller, largely self-contained, cell-like assembly units, each putting together small numbers of large modules.

PROCESS INDUSTRIES—AND PACKAGED GOODS.

What about industries making liquids, gases, grains, powders, and pellets—the process industries? Here, technologies set some of the guidelines. Still, there are management decision points that can make the difference, and the guidelines above can apply well to some or most of those decision points.

Take distance, for example. The packaging side of the process industries, and the packaged goods sector in general, is notorious for excessive, non-value-adding conveyors and accumulators that put distance between machines' footprints. That distances operators as well, to the point where they hardly seem or feel like a team. Why all the conveyors and accumulators? Because the machines jam up often and unpredictably. Absent material-handling equipment full of stock, when a filling machine jams, the entire line shuts down. Same thing when a filling machine runs out of fill, which should never happen in these plants where capital investment is tens or hundreds of millions of dollars. (The cycle labeled "total continuous improvement" from chapter 6 is the pathway to stamping out such mishaps.) Why do the machines jam so often? Because to meet ever more aggressive productivity targets set by remote management, the lines are run faster than their capability. (Time-relevant performance metrics, discussed in chapters 6 and 7, can drive out this kind of perverse-result goal setting.)

Brewing plants are good examples. Line stops were a problem at Miller Brewing's Eden, North Carolina, facility. But the seven-hundred-foot packaging lines "kept operators from seeing what was wrong, slowing fixes." So, did management aim at root causes, starting with removal of six hundred feet of just-in-case conveyor on each line? They did not. They added more costly technology to go wrong. They installed a computer on each line "to tap data about machinery operations. Info is dashed to a server in the plant's computer room, which transforms the information into easy-to-understand diagrams. They're posted immediately on the intranet, where they can be read quickly on computer monitors by line operators."[17]

In defense of the Miller-Eden management team, it would be expensive to tear the lines apart and reengineer them. Moreover it would take real boldness, since they were given the plant's design by the parent corporation. Still, the computers and intranet are a poor solution. Better that they had taken a lesson from another Miller brewery. Management at the Miller plant in Trenton, Ohio, was also stuck with thousands of feet of non-value-adding conveyor in its fill-and-pack lines. They, too, were not daring enough to take apart and shrink the lines. They had, however, a good "live with it" solution. They applied the star-point system in a way that converted line operators into empowered, self-directed work teams. How this was done and the remarkable success the teams have had in solving root-cause problems (such as the causes of stoppages) is documented in a previous book.[18] Miller-Trenton has become a popular site for other companies to visit for benchmarking.

CONCLUDING REMARKS

There is no point in consuming dozens more pages on details of plant design. That is for specialty books on the subject. Surprisingly, they are few in number, unless we go back twenty-plus years to the time before JIT, cells, U lines, process management, and focused manufacturing. (One specialty book that does delve into details, and mostly does not conflict with points made in this chapter, is Harmon and Peterson's 1990 book, *Reinventing the Factory*.)[19] Thus, the purpose of this chapter has been to present broad guidelines, all in tune with the focus imperative. With right guidelines, designing the details will fall rightly into place.

In the World Class *by* Principles benchmarking project, the fifteenth principle is the one most closely allied with the message of this chapter. The abbreviated name for Principle 15 is "Seek Simple, Movable, Scalable, Low-Cost, Focused Equipment." (See appendix 3 for the five-step assessment criteria under this principle.) The story behind those words gets at the message of this chapter.

10

Strategy of Global Proportions

In the past, strategic management was played close to the vest. It was local, resource-static, functional, and company-specific. It was also top-down. Planet-wide sight lines, continuous process improvement, some new technology, and employee empowerment change all that. Effective strategy has become global, resource-dynamic, and integrated. It remains company-specific in matters of architecture (design of the enterprise) at turning points. Otherwise strategy is tending toward universal. In addition, with little realization of it, executives are no longer the sole owners of strategy. This new, holistic approach to strategic management sees its target as the greater enterprise in a competitive environment spanning the continents (and, with the aid of rocket science, even reaching into the firmament).

The chapter takes up the four aspects of wide-vision strategy in the order mentioned above: broadened ownership plus integrated and universal features make up the latter part of the chapter; this part begins with reaching out globally and dynamically. Dynamism, though, can go too far. Without preservation of core proficiencies, a global strategy is reckless and destructive. While the core may be products or processes, a step up from that features proficiency in *generating and managing* products and processes. The following discussion offers a model that seems right for the times.

GENERATE, SIMPLIFY, STANDARDIZE, MIGRATE

Paul Goll, Boston Scientific Corporation (BSC) general manager at the Northwest Technology Center (NWTC) in Redmond, Washington, had this to say about shareholder value: It doesn't come from manufacturing. It's from the intellectual side of the business: generating streams of worthy new products.

Goll was explaining why his tech center was being shut down. One reason was the aging of the product line (rotational angioplasty devices for treating

atherosclerosis) along with perceived improvements in profitability by transferring this product to a low-tax country. Another was the related difficulty
for the seventy-five-person R&D staff to get management approval to work
on promising R&D programs in cardiovascular health care other than rotational atherectomy. I was at Goll's plant along with University of Washington
professors Karen Brown and Tom Schmitt. We were doing research on plant
closures/consolidations. The more we investigated, the more this particular
closure impressed us as being ripe with strategic issues. One, of expansive proportions, is this: How can a manufacturer maintain stability in this dynamic
era of global opportunities plagued with chronic overcapacity?

There is a way. It is a strategy little used in the past but likely to attract increasing attention as the calendar turns. The starting point is one or more
technology centers much like BSC's in Redmond: staffed and equipped for
both R&D and production. The strategy for each center shifts forward
through four stages, then repeats. The basic cycle, shown in the Exhibit 10.1
graphic, is as follows:

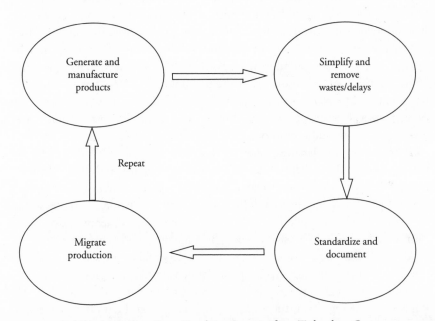

Exhibit 10.1. Four-Stage Revolving Strategy for a Technology Center

1. Generate and manufacture new products.

2. Simplify products and processes and remove wastes and delays.

3. Standardize and document product and process.

4. Migrate production to sites offering global competitive advantage.

5. Repeat steps one through four.

Stability Plus

I saw this strategy firsthand in my second trip to Japan in 1983. It was on a visit to Canon's Kanagawa development plant south and a bit west of Tokyo. Canon operated the facility following the four-stage strategy. By the date of my visit, its production line making Sure-Shot range-finder cameras had been perfected to the point of phased transfer. Production was moving to a Canon plant well to the north of Tokyo. There it would tap a hardworking, lower-wage, rural workforce for high-volume production. Kanagawa would then move on to develop, simplify, standardize, and migrate the next camera model. It could retain some production just for the purpose of sustaining engineering.

That strategy made sense for Canon then. With modification, it may be fitting for many manufacturers now. For Canon, a clear advantage was stabilizing the mission and resources of the technology center—a revolving kind of stability. Moreover, Canon's high-volume production sites gained stability as recipients of streams of new products from the tech centers: stability plus. That is, revolving stability in development, plus in production.

These days, even Japanese manufacturers have been forced to consider the world as potential production sites. Jobs for life are a luxury of the past. Plentiful outside-the-firm options are available, not only for production but also for product and process design, order fulfillment, and other functions. Cisco Systems, Inc., for example, is a collection of many acquired small companies. The stated purpose each time is to capture the bought company's innovative server/Internet products. The biotech industry is the same: a few majors grow by buying one start-up company after another for their hot new products or processes.

The full strategy is to keep bringing new products into the fold, developing and marketing them, then, as they age, sloughing them off. For the Ciscos of the world, ability to execute this strategy well may constitute their center-most competency. For an alternate, supply-chain development view, see the accompanying box.

The acquisition approach is an exception. Buying into product development plays well enough for a few industries sizzling with technological ferment and growth. For the bulk of manufacturing, the Canon formula, with

---

Designing/Developing the Supply Chain

Charles Fine suggests this about supply chains (as was also noted in chapter 8): Capability to design them is, these days, the most important core competency.[1] This is different from buying into the supplier chain but is in agreement that success and stability no longer can come from looking inward.

At Honda U.S.A. the term might be "developing," rather than "designing." A good share of the book *Powered by Honda* presents the company's Best Partners system for upgrading (not acquiring) its suppliers. The Honda approach is to help develop, at the supplier, strong, all-company improvement teams.[2] In effect, the Honda outreach effort aims at building supplier capabilities something along the lines of steps two and three of the four-stage cycle: Simplify and remove wastes and delays. Standardize and document.

---

modification, looks to be a better fit. We return to the Boston Scientific example to illustrate. (Note: BSC had extra, privileged reasons for closing the Northwest Technology Center. The example works well to demonstrate a strategy that may become attractive in many companies. The following discussion does not include all the pros and cons of BSC's closure decision and thus is not a judgment of the merits of the company's decision.)

Dynamic Tech Centers

The four-stage strategy, if put into effect some years ago, might have saved and stabilized the Northwest Technology Center. Of greater overall import are the competitive benefits for the parent, Boston Scientific Corp. The cycle, updated for the times, is illustrated below with NWTC as foil.

GENERATE.
First to consider is the role of the research and development group at NWTC. As it was, R&D developed, improved, and multiply patented the rotational angioplasty product. That's it. Without expansion of mission, its redundancy was assured.

Going beyond rotational artery cleaning, the R&D mission might have grown as follows: Develop and seek out vascular-protection technologies of any kind. Some of the R&D engineers at NWTC, for example, wanted to work on ways of using their catheter and guidewire expertise to precisely deliver medications within the blood system. The mission might be stretched to include contracting with outside laboratories and seeking to acquire or license others' patents. BSC might even give R&D at NWTC rein to (with corporate assistance) pursue the Cisco method: look for start-ups to acquire for their innovations—in this case vascular-protection products. (BSC already has an acquisition staff at headquarters; thus, for NWTC to also seek start-ups might be redundant. The strategy should be attractive, however, for other companies' tech centers.) Still another strength to exploit is R&D's patented expertise in miniature diamond-tipped abrasive burrs, which are at the business end of the rotational reaming devices. That is, seek other uses besides vascular care. Timely exits from aging products and technologies rounds off the enlarged R&D strategy. All told, for R&D at NWTC, this leg of the four-legged strategy might have offered *dynamic stability.*

SIMPLIFY.

Manufacturing processes at NWTC were greatly simplified and improved between 1995 and 2000 (see box). As it turns out, such simplification has made production that much more transportable. It facilitates Boston Scientific's decision to close Redmond and move production to Florida and Ireland for purposes of cost savings. In effect, NWTC improved itself right out of business.

Northwest Technology Center—
Record of Improvements, 1995–2000

Conversion from work-order system to pull manufacturing reduced

- ten-day flow time to forty-six minutes.
- MRP (later ERP) transactions from 172,000 to 10,000 per month.
- flow distance from 196 feet to 75 or less.

Implementation of cellular production.

Frequent line rebalancing facilitated by cross-trained labor.

Systematic supplier auditing/rating.

Heavy use of fail-safing fixtures for laser welding.

Miniaturization of former "monument" processes—for instance, small curing ovens located in each cell, allowing them to handle one burr at a time.

Elimination of curing time by replacement with simple snap-ins and welds.

Production employees doing their own time studies.

(This is not to say that NWTC has "done it all." Its kanban system is on PC screens—red for stop production, and green for go—rather than on simple cards or signboards.[3] And it accepts from its distribution-center customer an erratic stop-and-go schedule for demand that could be converted, for the benefit of NWTC and its suppliers, to a daily rate more in keeping with actual usage in medical centers.)

STANDARDIZE.

Processes that have been simplified are that much easier to standardize—everything characterized, validated, documented, reduced to templates and digital formats, and so on. The elements of standardization constitute a training package. With that, production is readily transferable to other plants.

The pity is, in transferring production, BSC loses the very people who have demonstrated mastery of how to simplify, rapidly improve, and standardize production processes: three-hundred-plus managers, professionals, technicians, and front-line operators. That few would want to transfer to Miami or Cork was fully predictable. That loss (gain for their new employers in the Pacific Northwest) may exceed the cost advantages accruing to BSC from relocation to Florida and Ireland. The loss is in good people as individuals, but the more so as a well-oiled improvement *team*. In our estimate (as the three researchers), only a small percentage of manufacturing sites around the planet have an improvement team as accomplished as that being phased out at the Northwest Technology Center.

MIGRATE.

The relocations dissolve the NWTC. Under the four-stage strategy, there would be no dissolution. Instead, NWTC would develop and maintain a group of experts in locating and validating new production sites and transferring production thereto. It would, of course, also maintain its large process-improvement team. Its continuing challenge would be reducing to a routine the production—and its simplification—of each new product coming from R&D. For the workforce as a whole, dynamic stability would generate high levels of intrinsic motivation from successively working its improvement magic on a parade of new products.

Such motivation among the NWTC group was apparent even without the generate-simplify-standardize-migrate mission. This is a finding of the closure research team, based on employee interviews and surveys. Though we may question BSC's closure decision, our study team has high admiration for the way BSC/NWTC management handled the closure. The two main concerns were to 1) ensure honesty, dignity, and respect for the people involved; and 2) do no harm to patients whose lives are saved by NWTC's line of health care products.

Enhanced Four-Stage Strategy

Let's review what is exceptional about the generate-simplify-standardize-migrate strategy:

1. *Global horizon.* The migration team may consider any production site anywhere. In contrast, Canon in 1983 gave no thought to sending production from its tech center to other than a Canon plant. Today's environment does not allow such restriction. For one thing, commerce in the twenty-first century is wide open. For another, much elevated performance standards, in which costs keep dropping, require scanning a wide set of alternatives. Outsourcing production is becoming common in low tech and high. For example, Intel, the world's premier semiconductor producer, sends much of its production to subcontractors, the so-called chip foundries.

   The global landscape also greatly expands potential sources of new products for investigation by the tech center's expanded R&D group.

2. *Improvement know-how.* Canon in the early 1980s possessed some level of skills in Toyota-like continuous improvement. Few other manufacturers globally had any such skills. Today they are common knowledge—though surely not widely and well executed.

   At NWTC, the skills were well honed and applied, though not for a succession of products. With a flow of products, the team's improvement skills should themselves improve. The team should become more skilled at simplifying and driving out waste at faster rates. Characterizing and documenting improved processes should become a routine. If rivals are less adept, they lose ground—and become acquisition possibilities. That scenario would have appeal at acquisition-minded Boston Scientific.

3. *Product-process synergies.* A tech center with co-located product development and manufacturing is poised for beneficial give-and-take. With R&D people steeped in the lore of DFMA (design for manufacture and assembly), they may do more to improve manufacturing than production people ever can.

   Manufacturing, in turn, can do much to enhance R&D performance. At NWTC, for example, slashing production flow times (ten days to forty-six minutes) meant that manufacturing could quickly discern and feed design problems back to R&D. Quality tools such as control charts and process capability studies provide other, valued kinds of feedback to R&D.

The last fifteen years or so have seen steady growth in industry of a function called "sustaining engineering." Its role, employed well at NWTC, is to keep product and process improvement alive after release to production.

Also at NWTC, R&D employed a concept called "frosting." Applied late in product development, frosting allows small, detailed changes that retain the main constituents of the design. This contrasts with the usual early design-freeze mind-set.

Dynamic Low-Tech Centers

The four-stage sequence described for NWTC may apply well in other industries with fast-changing technologies. For a manufacturer of more stable products, a slightly different version may work better. Two examples—oil seals and gas-delivery connectors—demonstrate the low-tech version.

MIGRATING DESIGN.

The LaGrange, Georgia, plant of Freudenberg-NOK (FNOK) produces a line of oil seals. A recipient of a year 2000 Shingo Prize, FNOK has a success story something like that of the Northwest Technology Center. The plant's twenty-year, stutter-step journey toward excellence has been documented by Robert Hall.[4] Suffice here to note that FNOK now functions as a self-sustaining continuous-improvement system. The focused factory and staff are subdivided, first, into "model cells," each concentrating on its own family of oil-seal models. Each of those is fully equipped for production and also has a full complement of salaried support staff, including design engineers. Each model cell is further divided into U-shaped subcells, each dedicated to a specific customer. Under this structure, Hall explains, "Each engineer is expected to thoroughly learn the applications of only a handful of customers." Thus, "Human response is much quicker and on the mark. The 1999 customer survey rates LaGrange 9.2 on the 10 scale." In effect, each cell is like a small business—not an average, but a highly effective, customer-centered small business. Is this capability—to set up such oil-seal mini–business units—migratable? Why not? As Hall puts it, "maybe even [to] Patagonia if a customer wanted service there."

What this example suggests is a modified four-stage application. Instead of a home base for generating the product and improving the process, the home business unit sets up remote small business units in its own image. Each has its own design engineering, other professional staff, and productive resources. The FNOK team has the know-how and should be able to apply it at other sites.

MIGRATING SIMPLICITY AND COMMON SENSE.

Still another low-tech version of the four-stage model could work for R. W. Lyall, a small, privately held company in Corona, California. Lyall produces plastic and metal connectors, meter boxes, and risers that marry up with natural-gas delivery devices at home residences. The thirty-year-old business was barely breaking even in 1996. Still owned by the founding family, Lyall had not embraced lean/world-class management. That changed when Jon Slaughterback, a battle-seasoned manager from the General Motors Allison division, hired on as general manager (now chief operating officer) in January 1997. Since then, Lyall has upped its inventory turnover from 4.7 to 17, lowered employee turnover from 80 percent (in 1996, its worst year) to 2 percent, and cut absenteeism from 13.1 percent to 1.7 percent. R. W. Lyall receives a steady parade of visiting groups from other companies and professional organizations. They go away as impressed as I was.[5] A few remarks on the company's transformation follow in order to show the possibilities for another version of the four-stage model of growth.

There was a forty-two-person layoff shortly after Slaughterback's arrival, but a guarantee of no more as a result of productivity improvements. Instead Slaughterback announced to all that the fruits of success (savings from waste elimination and process improvement) would be invested in training the people, installing better equipment, and increasing revenue by bringing in new products and lowering prices. The 165-person, mostly Spanish-speaking workforce has been rewarded. Pay is up 55 percent (four raises in the first year). Under the Christmas bonus program, payouts have increased three years in a row. The profit-sharing payouts, providing tax-deferred retirement savings for the entire workforce, have also increased three years in a row.

All this, and more, attention to the employees coincided with application-based training in lean manufacturing. Trainers from the California Manufacturing Technology Center (CMTC) ran a series of weekly classes on-site over twelve-week spans. (CMTC is one of the nation's government-supported Manufacturing Extension Partnership organizations.) One of the trainers, Eduardo Freiwald, teaching in Spanish, wasn't eager to leave after the training sessions. He and his trainees would march right to the shop floor and start moving equipment (where it did not require electrical or plumbing changes). Three weeks into the classes and applications, according to Slaughterback, the training had paid for itself. The plant is cellular, many machines are on wheels, kanban and quick-change apparatus are everywhere, and dozens of simple, homemade, low-cost innovations pepper the plant.

Front-line associates are heavy contributors to these innovations, and a few key managers are their inspiration. Two of the latter are Moises "Mo" Vasquez, plant manager, and Gerry Vargas, lean manufacturing coordinator. Neither is college educated, but both have skills and infectious enthusiasm that can't be taught in a classroom. (I heard Vargas say, "It's exciting. I like to come to work every day. My wife thinks I'm nuts.") The plant's improvements keep freeing up resources. Half the production space had been emptied and six people freed up when I first visited. The six had joined Vargas to devote time to improvement projects, except when needed somewhere in a production capacity. Rather than detailing more of the wheres and hows, it is enough to say that R. W. Lyall, like FNOK, is the low-tech equivalent of the Northwest Technology Center. All three business units have the system, knowledge, and drive to adopt a version of the four-stage migration strategy.

RISK PROTECTION.
It should be understood that this kind of migration strategy is not at all like garden-variety takeovers and turnarounds that acquisition-minded companies have been doing for years. Those entail installing the buying companies' own management team and control system. In the four-stage strategy as applied at Freudenberg-NOK and R. W. Lyall, we are talking about sending a team of doers and teachers. Their expertise is not "tech and spec," nor is it even simply to install their proven lean management model. It is to build the same kind of human-improvement team that they are a part of in their home companies. FNOK might send mostly engineers and other college-educated masters of lean. Lyall could dispatch Mo, Gary, and their lean team, along with two or three college-degreed colleagues from the front offices.

Why should these manufacturers extend themselves in such a manner? Small companies like Lyall are usually content to stick to their knitting. They have, however, a rare set of skills and a unique opportunity to take their knitting sticks beyond their own walls. From the standpoint of owners and profit-sharing managers, there is personal wealth involved in such growth. Aside from that, small manufacturers dependent on one product line are at risk. It is too easy these days for a competitor to emerge somewhere on the planet and knock off the existing local or global market leader. The new rival might do so based on cost, technology, geography, size, or political pull. Best protection always has been—and the more so now—growth: new product lines, new sites, new alliances.

Competitive Advantage?

Can this really work—light a fire that refuels itself and burns brighter? There is a point of view that says no: continuous improvement is too easy to do. Industry has already implemented lean manufacturing. That negative view is belied by research data and by personal observation.

First, consider one of the companies that participated in the World Class *by* Principles Benchmarking project. That company has had thirty-nine of its manufacturing sites self-score on the sixteen principles. (Many of those sites' scores have been formally entered into the WCP database.) Here are the thirty-nine total scores out of eighty points maximum, five points per principle:

12.4	13.7	16.2	20.3	27	27	29.4	29.9	31.8	33.5	35.8	36	36.1
36.2	36.8	38	38	38.5	39.2	39.8	42.4	44.9	45	45	46	46.2
46.7	47	47	47	47.5	48.5	49.5	50	50.6	51.9	55.8	56.5	65.7

On average these are good scores—better by a few points than the average for all 480-plus manufacturers in the database. It is a high-performing company. Yet consider where the median score lies: at 39.8 points. After more than fifteen years' efforts in this company to adopt total quality, JIT, focused plants, design for manufacture, and the rest of the lean/extra-lean agenda, the majority of the company's plants muster only half of the eighty points in the scoring matrix. And the company's scores range all over the landscape.

The WCP benchmarking results offer another slant on the issue. Many of the manufacturers participating were handpicked for their existing excellence, and others asked to be included in the assessment. To even ask requires that the organization have above-average "world-class" credentials; otherwise, they would not even understand the language in the assessment criteria (terms such as "capability index" and concepts such as "quick changeover"). Despite this kind of screening a few participants could muster, by self-assessment, only ten points or less. If the WCP had been in operation in, say, 1975, it would have been rare for any Western manufacturer to score as many as ten points. That is an indicator of the enormous advances made in manufacturing company management in twenty-five years. We may draw another salient conclusion as well: In 1975 the gap between best, average, and poor manufacturers was modest; today it is a Grand Canyon. Part of the gap is explained by knowledge versus lack of it; the other part is an ability to execute successfully and the lack of it.

Another example comes from the automotive industry, the home and supposed paragon of lean. In 2001 I visited Ford's stamping and assembly plant in Hermosillo, Mexico, which produces several models of the Focus and Escort cars. This is the site identified in *The Machine That Changed the World* (1991) as the globe's "most efficient" auto assembly plant.[6] The factory has undergone its share of improvements since the MIT-sponsored team made its assessment. And it is an excellent plant, compared with its peers in the industry. (Peers, here, do not include new-era plants designed around module deliveries from suppliers). Among the positives in this plant: Changeover times on giant stamping presses are excellent; operators are well trained and in teams; and the assembly lines easily accommodate mixtures of models.

A glaring weakness at Ford-Hermosillo, as at the majority of auto assembly plants, shows up at the end of the line: Some sixty cars sit in a rework area.

This is the case even though every station on the assembly line is outfitted with easy-to-reach line-stop and help buttons. In this plant (and others in the industry), those buttons have become not much more than props—there because "the book" says lean production lines must have line-stop and help devices. The problem is in design of the lines. At Hermosillo, for example, the assembly line is composed of 145 conveyor-linked stations. If an assembler can't manage to affix a radiator correctly or misses tightening a bolt somewhere, will he push the red button to get it right (all "he's" among the operators in that plant), as is supposed to happen? Hardly ever, because that would stop all 145 stations. Instead, note the problem (if there's time and inclination) and let the end-of-line rework crew handle it.

In the early 1980s the question came up frequently in my own plant visits and seminars: How do you get the advantages of small teams and work cells on conveyored production lines? They got the standard answer from me: Break the lines into multiple small "chunks," each the purview of a small team; put small buffer inventories between the chunks. The additional buffer inventories, seemingly contrary to lean, will be a net gain, because they allow the teams to handle problems as they occur without stopping the entire flow. "Do it right first time" is a basic a tenet of lean, and it slashes the worst kind of inventory: rework after nearly all value has been added.

Another basic of lean that I and others hit hard in the early 1980s was underscheduling the line. The reason is so that even on a bad day, there's time at shift's end to meet the scheduled rate. Making that rate should be so dependable that all the stamping machines, all makers of engine and chassis components, and all suppliers of hundreds of items of trim can synchronize to it. (According to one report, Ford's redesign of its Haleswood, England, plant to produce Jaguars—formerly Ford Escorts—gets it right: The plant's design features assembly broken into chunks separated by a few cars of buffer stock, line-stop cords, *and* underscheduling.[7]) At Ford-Hermosillo, which has its own stamping, the lack of such synchronization is apparent: Racks and pallets are loaded high with hundreds of different stamped parts and dozens of different welded subassemblies.

Lean manufacturing is largely common sense; yet it is not easy to master. If all rivals were to gain parity in its mastery, it would offer no competitive advantage.[8] But, to return to the point of this discussion, the four-stage strategy, as described, is not merely lean and not a check-off sheet of defined methods. It is a whole-organization base of resources—one that reaches out into the value chain. It may also be one that amplifies itself in growth cycles of product development and migration.

Two UCLA economists have comparatively studied the resource base of U.S. and Japanese automakers. They did this in the context of what is being called, in management theory, a "resource-based view" (RBV) of the firm. One of their conclusions is as follows: "The RBV implies that differences in firms' performance are most likely to be determined by differences in organizational capabilities, which are hard for rivals to replicate."[9] As we see in the next section, a key organizational capability lies in setting strategy for the whole rather than the parts.

STRATEGIC INTEGRATION

It will take time for the four-stage strategy to catch on widely. One reason is that seeing its merits requires a multifunctional outlook. But conventionally, manufacturers divvied up the job of making strategy. Marketing had charge of strategic shifts in product lines and sales channels. Information technology plotted new systems. Human resources set strategic direction for hiring, paying, and training people. Operations was the authority for capacity. And so on.

That approach is a poor fit with today's realities. Two major forces are changing the face of strategic management. One is the multifaceted complexity of big, direction-changing pursuits under globally intense competition. To cope, companies need a whole-company way of setting strategic direction. The other is a new underlayer of stable, universal strategy that all companies should adopt—or else! Further discussion of these two topics concludes the chapter.

Multifaceted Complexity: How to Cope

The object of strategy is improved competitiveness. In the sleepy, soft, localized competitive environments of the past, strategies were simple. Under wide-open, globally turbulent commerce, a durable strategy must check all the angles. It must allow for multiple scenarios—including, as discussed earlier, external sources of products and production sites.

This requires shedding the fractionated approach. No more having each key function set forth its own component strategies, which then roll up to become the firm's overall business strategy. It was always possible, and now becomes necessary, for cross-functional teams to develop integrated business strategies directly. Each strategy is developed as a multidisciplinary team project. At the next higher level, there will be conflicts among the strategies, especially with regard to funding. That is the case regardless of how the strategies are developed. What is critical is that each initiative makes good business, not good functional, sense.

Exhibit 10.2 compares the two approaches: old-style business strategy was, more or less, the sum of functional parts. Often enough, the parts clashed and crashed, and a few iterations were needed before final approval. The iterations, however, were one box to another. For example, a marketing strategy for boosting sales 10 percent goes to operations, which simply says that requires 10 percent more resources. Finance says there's money enough for only 6 percent more capacity, and the whole sequence repeats. Why not a joint plan, weighing different sales strategies in new markets along with new technology and raw materials with new plant sites, all integrated with full cash-flow analy-

A. Functional strategy development:

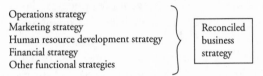

B. Integrated strategy development:

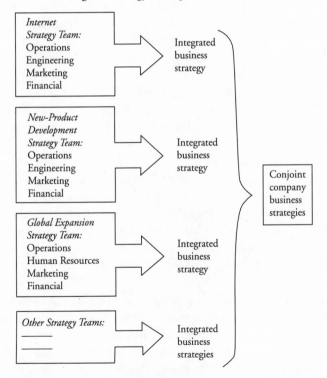

Exhibit 10.2. Functional and Integrated Strategy Development

sis? It was beyond the ability, or inclination, of the functions to work together. Moreover, the planners lacked today's access to simple spreadsheet planning tools and simulation models. But competitors were equally inept at planning. Weak planning was normal but survivable.

Examples: Information System Strategies

Say that a strategic opportunity—developing a new information system—is on the table. It would consist of hardware and software that will link supply chains, share technology, mine customer data, and transact factory receipts and shipments. No information technology department is capable of planning such a broad-scope endeavor. Yet in conventional practice, the IT department would have the job. A good IT department would invite other functions to participate. But participation is not the same as being on a team of responsible equals. The integrated approach starts with a multifunctional strategy development team. Their job is jointly to develop strategy for the project.

The typical ERP (enterprise requirements planning) project is large enough in scope to justify the multifunctional approach. An example is Lucent Technologies' Energy Systems business unit in Mesquite, Texas, which launched an ERP development project in 1998. (Energy Systems, in 1994 when still owned by AT&T, is the only Western manufacturer to be awarded Japan's Deming Prize; Florida Power & Light, a utility, has also received the prize. In 2000, Energy Systems was acquired by Tyco International.) The project was led by Mike Cassidy, who came out of operations management to be appointed director of business transformation. Cassidy headed up a full-time, co-located one-hundred-person team. Half were on-site vendor people, and the other half represented all of the affected Lucent functions. Strategic choices would have to be made regarding which of the many ERP subroutines should be activated and to what degree; thus the need for a closely interactive, multifunctional team effort. After development, most of the project's implementation is handed off to the more technical IT people.

Multifunctional strategy teams may operate at the level of a plant, a business unit or site (as at Energy Systems), or the parent corporation. Johnson and Thompson provide an example of the latter: a multifunctional ERP strategy team at Boeing. The team determined that full ERP was right for a small number of highly complex Boeing business units. Most units, being less complex, should, they felt, opt for one of three lesser versions: 1) simplified ERP—for variable-demand, stable processes employing visual controls and, usually, cellular layout; 2) simpler, process/product-family-focused ERP—for stable demand or options, with visual controls and, usually, cellular layout; 3) simplest, product-aligned ERP—for stable and predictable demand, few customers, few supplier-partners, visual controls, and, usually, cellular layout.[10]

Such holistic strategy development may even draw in key customers, suppliers, and other stakeholders. This approach has been called "great groups"—in contrast with "great leaders."[11] What emerges are strategies reasonably correct for the whole rather than biased for a single power center's narrow interests.

This discussion has centered on the variable, infrequent kind of strategy making. As noted at the start of the chapter, much of strategy is not of that type anymore. It is universal. The final chapter topic explains.

UNIVERSAL STRATEGY

Business strategy divides uneasily into two camps: trade-offs and no trade-offs. Trade-off thinking is conventional, though no one likes it: it means giving up something good in order to have something presumed better. Worse, the most strategic, customer-oriented trade-offs are among the golden goals: quality, speedy response, flexibility, value (QSFV).

The other camp sees ways to turn the trade-off arrows so they all run in the same, positive direction. In other words, have it all—for customers. Superior manufacturers, once Japanese but no longer nation-specific, have absorbed best practices that lead to improving Q, S, F, and V all at the same time. The book *The Hunters and the Hunted* echoes this point of view throughout, at one point saying, "Today, any competitor that wants to be the 'supplier of choice' must supply value with no trade-off in price, quality, and response."[12] As to the roots of this point of view, see the accompanying box.

Who Knew?

Among the first no-trade-off advocates were Ed Hay and William Wheeler, at the time senior consultants at Rath and Strong. In the early 1980s few Western consultants had a better understanding of Japanese manufacturing management than these two, who were in high demand giving presentations to clients. They often appeared on stage together, "finishing each other's sentences." They had special fun with the inevitable question from an audience member about trade-offs. In mock indignation, Hay or Wheeler would affect a look of derision and say something like "You've uttered the dreaded *T word*—say it again, and out you go!"

Characteristics of Contrary Strategies

Strategy itself has always been thought of as too important to entrust to any but senior management. As to trade-offs, the process is presumed to be one of sorting and sifting high-level either-or options and coming to a decision. For example, to gain strategic advantage in quality, the decision is to approve the hire of inspectors and acquisition of new equipment. The downside is that the rise in costs reduces value to the customer. Among the no-trade-off solutions are the following:

- Transfer quality to the operators (the total quality approach using process control charting and so forth).

- Get more quality out of present equipment by transferring basic machine care to the operators (the total preventive maintenance approach).

- Get still more through process capability upgrades, which pay for themselves quickly. TQ and TPM reduce staffs of inspectors along with preventive maintenance people from the plant maintenance department, which slashes costs.

The net effect is more quality and higher value.

The set of practices that lead to improving Q, S, F, and V all at once are not issues needing high-level analysis. They are just good business—dealing with ongoing matters. Executives need not hold a planning session to decide whether making money is a good strategy. Or generating products. Or serving customers. Nor should they be debating TQ, TPM, JIT, supplier partnerships, and cross-training. These and a whole set of related "best practice concepts" and tools are the arsenal of the no-trade-off camp. They are out of the realm of strategic contention. The arsenal belongs to all employees, not a select few, and it traverses the whole value chain. Putting it differently, the full tool set makes up the universal side of strategy. It is good medicine for any organization (but it allows for differing execution priorities within the mix). Executives, then, have that much more time to deliberate the other side of strategy, which is deciding on changes in the firm's architecture. Such decisions are infrequent but generally entail large expenditures. Examples include whether and when to do a joint venture in China, to buy back common stock shares, to stockpile land for future expansion, to mantle or dismantle an ERP system, and so forth.

Conventional strategy tends to be a project, with a start and an end—in other words, temporal. Universal (no-trade-off) strategies, on the other hand, tend toward stability and longevity. A break in the continuity may be considered a management failure.

	JUSTIFICATION	OWNERSHIP	LONGEVITY	APPLIED LIFE CYCLE	WHERE FOUND	EXAMPLE
Conventional (architecture)	Trade-off analysis	Senior management	Temporal	Projects	Most companies	High quality or low cost Growth or profit
Contemporary (ongoing business)	Universal	Whole organization	Unlimited	Continuous	Prestigious, globally competitive companies	Joint improvement in quality, throughput time, flexibility and value

Exhibit 10.3. Conventional and Contemporary Strategy Development

Note: In conventional strategy, the trade-off factors may be major or of little import, obvious or hidden. Boston Scientific's decision to close Redmond was based on expectation of large cost savings. The consulting firm that recommended the move probably saw a trade-off—loss of years of experience—but judged it minor. The hidden factor was collective expertise in process improvement, mutual dependence and trust, dedication to a lifesaving product, and pride in mastery of an exacting, demanding medical technology. All traded off without awareness of the loss.

Exhibit 10.3 summarizes differences between conventional and the contemporary contender. Six labeled columns contrast the two approaches: conventional strategy (architecture) is justified through trade-off analysis, is owned by senior management, has temporal longevity, and has the applied life of a project. It is still dominant in most companies, since most have not gone far with the lean/world-class agenda. Examples are quality-cost and growth-profit trade-offs. Contemporary (ongoing business) strategy is universal, enterprise-wide, unlimited in duration, continuously applied, found especially in prestigious, globally competitive companies, and exemplified by joint improvement in quality, throughput time, flexibility, and cost/value.

Strategic Transition

The transformation from conventional to contemporary has a short history. Exhibit 10.4 roughly tracks the shift. The shaded zone represents the degree

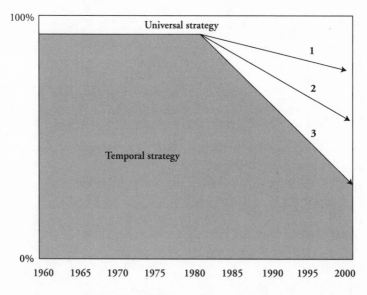

Exhibit 10.4. Influence of Temporal and Universal
Business Strategies over Time

Note: The initial date, 1960, in this graph is not significant, except that there seems to have been little awareness of strategy as an element of operations or business management much before that. Strategy had been strictly a military concept and is so defined in most early dictionaries.

of influence of trade-off-temporal thinking on strategy development. The clear zone represents stable universal's growing influence. The exhibit places the turning point at 1980, which is roughly when Western industry began to adopt such previously Japanese concepts as company-wide quality and just-in-time. How deeply the universalist zone has penetrated the totality of strategy development is a matter for conjecture. The arrow labeled 1 describes slight penetration, 2 moderate, and 3 deep.

The universal viewpoint will not supplant conventional strategy. Companies will always be faced, from time to time, with big, special issues. They are best handled, as noted earlier, by a multidisciplinary strategy team. Special issues require special studies sometimes involving trade-offs; for example, acquire another company, but go into debt doing so. There is no universal principle that tells whether and when to make an acquisition. Still, the strategic universals can at least help sharpen such decisions.

A typical acquisition candidate is an underachiever that, with better guidance, can become a star. If the acquisition-minded manufacturer is steeped in universals, it might look for candidates differently. Best prospect might be the underperformer that has invested heavily in training and application of continuous process improvement. But sometimes the results of those measures are a bit slow in coming. The problem may be the parent corporation. It may be imposing on its manufacturing units a cumbersome information system or heavy-handed financial controls. There are plentiful examples of that type of corporate oversight. It is still rare for a parent headquarters, or its consultants, to have the qualities of vision to be able to see and appreciate the less tangible strengths that NWTC had in Redmond. The final chapter topic considers that kind of vision with the Northwest Technology Center as an example.

How to Spot Intangible Excellence

Boston Scientific had acquired NWTC from its founder in 1995. A contract stipulation was that the site must continue to operate for a minimum of five years. Five years later its closure was announced. A consulting firm did the analysis and made the recommendation.

Our team of three—the two university professors and I—question the decision. But we have an advantage. In recent years we had visited and studied the site several times. Sometimes it was with students, once it was with a group of high-level executives on a study mission co-sponsored by the Hong Kong Productivity Council. We had access to our own and a variety of others' assessments, all highly favorable. We could see an impressive record of improvements. More than that, we became aware of a set of capabilities behind the improvements, capabilities that few other manufacturing sites are able to match.

The consulting firm, as well as Boston Scientific corporate, looked at NWTC with different eyes. They were concerned with BSC's erratic earnings and stock price, along with overcapacity in BSC as a whole. They saw, as well, high costs and valuable real estate in Redmond, as compared with those at BSC sites in Ireland and Florida. Though the NWTC operation was very profitable and had proven technical abilities, consolidation at the other two sites seemed to promise even better profitability. The downside—the breakup of a high-performing team with familylike cohesiveness and dedication—is an intangible that is rarely considered. It should be. This chapter and previous ones have shown, in various ways, why. Reasons include the following:

- The new environment of much elevated competitiveness, with new kinds of rivals popping up planet-wide.
- Growing awareness of the advantages of multifunctional teams for developing strategy.
- Higher levels of performance that come from organization-wide pursuit of a more universal, less trade-off approach to success.
- The virtuous-circle advantages of the four-stage strategy—generate, simplify, standardize, migrate: dynamic stability.

A *Harvard Business Review* article is entitled "Decoding the DNA of the Toyota Production System."[13] The authors had conducted a four-year study of forty plants to discover the system's inner workings. Their main finding is that there are things that do not stand out when merely looking at trend charts, performance numbers, and flow patterns. They speak of the existence of an *improvement system*. So does Fujimoto in his detailed history of development of Toyota's manufacturing system.[14] So does this chapter—for NWTC, FNOK, and R. W. Lyall. (For an insightful, on-target look at the wrongheaded, top-down way that most companies try to build an involved workforce, see the Roth and Potts article "Doing It Wrong: A Case Study," in *Quality Progress,* February 2001.)[15] In strategically managing a complex business—in this era of hypercompetition—awareness of the need to *look for* such systems may make the difference.

11

Continuous Improvement Up-to-Date

"Standardized Lean": That is the title of an article in *Automotive Manufacturing & Production* magazine.[1] The story reports on the documents issued by the Society of Automotive Engineers that define what lean is and how to do it. Nice idea. But I thought that had been done in the late 1970s and early 1980s with publication of thorough books on the subject. Four were from Japanese authors: Ohno and Shingo, fathers of the Toyota system; Monden, a professor with a deep understanding of the system and ability to write it up in English; and Suzaki, an American author-consultant who had emigrated from Japan.[2] Other authors included Hall, Harmon and Peterson, and myself,[3] followed later by numerous others with their own take on the system[4] or specialized parts of it.[5] Industry was following the formula nicely until the half-life syndrome hit. Womack and Jones to the rescue with a new name, "lean," and new evidence, which rejuvenated the movement.[6]

Still, there is plenty of dissatisfaction with the slow pace of adoption. Continuous improvement proves often discontinuous—or if continuous, snail paced. George Koenigsaeker is one of manufacturing's more astute experts in the whats and hows of lean execution. A former manufacturing executive of office equipment giant Hon Industries, he is now president of Lean Investments, which has answers to the problem of slow adoption. Part of the blame, Koenigsaeker believes, is that the usual Japanese approach requires too much time to bring everyone on board, team up, and learn by doing. His company will speed up the process: Find a fat prospect, acquire it, and staff it with a CEO and director of operations handpicked for their lean credentials.[7] The turnaround should not take long.

Quick, effective, lasting execution is the ultimate hope of any who have world-class aspirations. This chapter explores the possibilities. Topics include a "wedge" strategy, six sigma, *kaizen* and *kaizen* "blitz" events, "superblitz," total continuous improvement, and a few more remarks on the Lean Investments approach. We take up these topics in reverse order.

WAYS AND WHYS OF IMPLEMENTATION

Mr. Koenigsaeker has an excellent business plan. If I had switched from author to entrepreneur—and had the wits—I might have started up my own Lean Investments. But there is room for only one or two such businesses. For one thing, there is a scarcity of Koenigsaekers to lead this kind of venture. There is also a shortage of experienced, talented, committed executives to make the acquired weak manufacturers strong.

Does that mean that the majority of companies can cast off their wastes and delays only by a slow, learn-by-doing method? How about a fast, learn-by-doing approach—one having features of the two extremes that Mr. Koenigsaeker refers to? That in-between method is presented next.

The Third Way: Total Immersion

Chapter 6 presented an eight-point sequence referred to as "total continuous improvement." Its eight elements are repeated below:

1. All front-line employees receive application-linked training in process improvement and a "sense of the customer" view of competitiveness.

2. All employees gather process data.

3. Via data collection, employees become process managers.

4. Formatted data point to root causes.

5. Solutions become suggestions, often implemented by suggestors.

6. Trend charts in the workplace track direct-effect results.

7. Recognition closes the loop.

8. Derivative intrinsic rewards equal monetary awards in motivational impact.

Does this look like an effective approach to becoming a lean machine—but one that is turtle paced? It can be slow. On the other hand, consider the following, a real company, name disguised.

QUICK STUDY.

Engines, Inc., is a U.S.-based remanufacturer of internal combustion engines for automobiles. Its direct-labor workforce numbers about three hundred associates.

The co-owner and I had toured the facilities, noting large quantities of in-queue component parts throughout. Following the tour, we adjourned to a conference room where the management team self-scored on the sixteen elements of the WCP. (I was there as a listener and to help answer questions of interpretation.) The large work-in-process inventories—pistons and cylinders, crankshafts and camshafts, blocks and heads, push rods and rocker arms—translated into a low score on Principle 6: "Cut Total Flow Time, Flow Distance, and Start-up/Changeover Times." (See appendix 3 for the full set of criteria and fine points for Principle 6.)

After establishing a baseline score on each principle, next step is developing a plan for earning another point on the few principles that are most competitively vital. Principle 6 was the best candidate at Engines, Inc. I offered the following multistep plan. (The plan that day was sketchy. This more complete version emerged in the next day or so.)

1. The management team serves as an implementation task force.

2. The task force prepares a survey form, one for each of the three hundred hourly associates. The form asks each person to count the number of units in queue before his or her process and write it on the form. Next on the form is a blank calling on the operator's judgment. It says, "How many are really needed, in your experience, to avoid shutting down your process?"

3. The task force reviews all three hundred forms. In a few cases, the operator's estimate looks high. So a note goes back to the operator suggesting a lower number. Exhibit 11.1 shows an example of this exchange, for the engine block cleaning operation.

4. Final numbers become queue limits. These limits are printed on large signs (kanbans) in each work center. Another sign proclaims the monetary value of the inventory savings, plus the minutes and percentage reduction in throughput time. For block cleaning, those numbers are $1,000, and ninety minutes, or 75 percent. Part B of Exhibit 11.1 is an example.

A. Inventory survey and second estimate

Counting your idle inventory

Work Center: *Engine block cleaning*

Units waiting: <u>25</u>

Minimum needed to avoid serious work stoppage: <u>10</u>

To: Engine block cleaning

Question: *What would happen if units on hand were cut from present 25 to, say, 5?*

Your answer: <u>I guess we could get by.</u>

B. Queue limit and results

Work Center: **Engine block cleaning**

Maximum number of idle units: **5 engine blocks**

Estimated Savings

Before: 25 blocks at $50 each = $1,250
After: 5 blocks at $50 each = <u>   250</u>
Savings: **$1,000**

Reduced throughput time: **90 minutes, or 75%**

Exhibit 11.1. Inventory Forms and Displays: Engine Block Cleaning

5. Total savings in money, and in flow time and inventory, are posted in the cafeteria: $400,000 and 80 percent. The improved score on Principle 6, plus by-product improvements on other principles, go onto a visual display in the task force office. The score on Principle 6 rises from 1.5 to 2.5, and on Principles 3, 7, and 13, respectively, from 3.0 to 3.8, 2.3 to 3.0, and 1.0 to 1.7. Examples of the whole-plant results are shown in Exhibit 11.2.

Plantwide Inventory Reductions

Savings, to date: **$400,000**
Reduced throughput time and inventory: **80%**

Improved Scores on WCP

PRINCIPLE	POINTS BEFORE	POINTS AFTER
6*	1.5	2.5
7	3.0	3.8
3	2.3	3.0
13	1.0	1.7

*Main objective; other gains are by-products.

Exhibit 11.2. Whole-Plant Results

But wait. The improvement signs cannot go up until the result is realized. So here comes the fun part: draining the excess stocks throughout the plant to achieve the result. Bringing inventory levels down to the queue limits requires shutting down processes for a time. This occurs in a staggered manner: Last processes, final packing and shipping, do not shut down at all. First process, buying rusty, oil-belching, nonfunctioning engines stops almost completely—except buyers may still seek certain high-demand engines in scarce supply. Processes in between stop for progressively less amounts of time.

To put numbers on it, the whole stock-shedding sequence goes something like this: Engine buying ceases (with the noted exception) for, say, six weeks. Engine teardown halts for five weeks and cleaning for four and a half. Machining—biggest time consumer—stops for four weeks, subassembly for two weeks, final stock picking (kitting) for one week, and final assembly for three days. Final engine testing and shipping continue unabated, pulling in as much revenue as ever.

What happens to the people? With the plant on a cold-turkey diet, half the production stops—idling, in equivalent hours, half the workforce. So send them home? By no means—there is much to do!

DISCOVERY.

This purge period was preceded by zero training. That may seem to violate step 1 of total continuous improvement. What happens, though, is that the workforce begins its learning by the discovery method. Take the operator of engine block cleaning, who counted twenty-five blocks sitting idle on a long roller conveyor in front of a tank containing a cleaning solvent. Call him Emilio. In Emilio's initial judgment, he could get by with ten units but, after prompting, agreed to a maximum of five blocks. In thinking this through, Emilio had to consider the kinds of disruptions in supply of engine blocks from prior processes that he had experienced in the past. He may choose to confer with the preceding process folks about this. (Newer operators will have to confer with somebody.) That is exactly what is supposed to happen whenever kanban limits are being set. Prior to this time, the twenty-five idle pieces surely would not have concerned Emilio. If anything, they were "job security"—and thirty or forty idle blocks would have been more job security. Simply by being asked what minimum he could get by with (had he ever been asked for a job-related opinion before?), he begins to think like a business owner and to see idle stock for what it is: waste.

Those thoughts are reinforced when the sign goes up in his work center: Reduced-inventory savings: $1,000. Reduced flow time through his process: ninety minutes, or 75 percent. He will take some pride in contributing to this result.

For most of the workforce, the purge means weeks or days of nonproduction. An excellent time for more formal lessons. The main training topic is customer-focused competitiveness: why it requires becoming lean, the speedy-response factor, the inventory-as-waste concept. Operators may learn about work cells and quick setup, view videos, and visit other, already lean plants in the area to see for themselves. And has there never been time for training in the "seven basic tools"? There is now. There is time for learning, one tool at a time, and going right out onto the floor to apply the tool— the cell concept and quick setup being first in line, since they relate directly to Principle 6. The seven tools are next topics. Best training is just-in-time training: Learn one thing; go out and do it. Learn one more thing; go do it. And so on. (Step 2 of Principle 8, "Continually Train Everybody for Their New Roles," specifies that the training must be in the just-in-time mode. It is effective. All-at-once training sessions suffer from retention problems, more with lack of application. See appendix 3 for the full set of steps on Principle 8.)

Some of the work to be done is obvious. About twenty of the thirty feet of roller conveyor in Emilio's area is excess, in the way. Emilio may get busy removing it, then work with prior and next-process operators to move equipment closer together. This may happen before training on cells—the discovery method. Or perhaps formal training about compact cells will fit naturally into the mix.

SUPERBLITZ.

These six weeks will be the most profitable period Engines, Inc., has ever had or will have: Sales revenue comes in as usual. Almost no money goes out for fixable engines, and for much of the period little goes out for pistons, rings, gaskets, and dozens of other parts that are installed new instead of being remachined. (Payroll could be slashed as well by sending people home, but we've already nixed that idea.) And at the end of the eight-week "superblitz," large voids will have replaced all manner of containers and storage apparatus that had been chock-a-block with inventory. To make use of all the space, the company may wish to add another remanufacturing product line.

Fortunately, Engines, Inc., is privately owned and independent. There is no parent company and cost-accounting system to squelch the idea of halting production. (Cost-variance accounting cannot tolerate people being paid and not making things.)

What has been described is an aggressive, very quick implementation approach. It is in contrast with the agonizingly slow, "plan it to death" way that most companies handle most kinds of worthwhile change. A purported advantage of going slow, with extensive planning, is that it yields lasting gains. Using superblitz, however, Engines, Inc., got speedy results and at the same time laid the groundwork for long-lasting results. Exhibit 11.3 compares Engines, Inc.'s, superblitz with the eight-point total continuous improvement sequence.

As the exhibit indicates, the superblitz gives good coverage of the first three of the eight "total" items. Training takes place as a part of application. The applications are customer and competitively targeted. All the operators are contributing process data. And the slack period fills naturally with more training, swiftly applied.

In the fourth and fifth steps, seeds are sown. Training in the seven basic tools (flowcharts, check sheets, and so on) provides means of collecting and formatting process mishaps so as to point to root causes. Having the means to discover causes is key to a thriving suggestion system. Involvement in tearing out conveyors and racks gets operators involved in implementation of the waste-reduction plan.

Sixth, seventh, and eighth points refer to raising awareness, honoring in-

TOTAL CONTINUOUS IMPROVEMENT	SUPERBLITZ AT ENGINES, INC.
1. All front-line employees receive application-linked training in process improvement and a "sense of the customer" view of competitiveness.	Direct-labor force is highly involved in an application focused on quick engine turnaround, a key competitive factor in this remanufacturing business.
2. All employees gather process data.	From the start, front-liners generate process data. During the eight-week blitz, employees also receive formal training, via the just-in-time training method, including the seven basic tools of data collection and analysis.
3. Via data collection, employees become process managers.	Data collection involves all the direct-labor force from the beginning. Learning and applying the seven basic tools is key to making employees permanent process managers.
4. Formatted data point to root causes.	Sow seeds (e.g., the basic tools).
5. Solutions become suggestions, often implemented by suggesters.	Sow more seeds; asking employees for help starts the process—foundation for an effective suggestion program. Implementation includes removing stock handling and storage apparatus.
6. Trend charts in the workplace track direct-effect results.	Queue-limit signs are a starting point.
7. Recognition closes the loop.	Associates give their minimums; management recognizes and acts on them, with prominent displays of associates' queue limits and monetary and flow-time savings. Whole-plant results in the cafeteria help bind people together for competitive advantage. More seeds sown for more recognition of further improvements.
8. Derivative intrinsic rewards equal monetary awards in motivational impact.	The discovery method, using operators' experienced opinions, is high on the intrinsic-motivation scale.

Exhibit 11.3. How Superblitz Accommodates Total Continuous Improvement

volvement, and feeling pride thereby. Visual points on graphical displays—in the workplace (queue limits and results) and in well-trafficked places (whole-plant results in the cafeteria)—maximize the impacts. All told, the ground-work is well laid for the workforce at Engines, Inc., to end up with sustained high levels of motivation, especially the intrinsic kind.

Superblitz at a Major Manufacturer

Chapters 1 and 3 included warnings: Don't cut inventories arbitrarily. At Engines, Inc., it wasn't arbitrary. The reductions were based on judgments of those who know the processes best. On the other hand, a blitz that slashes stock irrespective of process conditions would be a bad idea. I was guilty of advancing such an idea in the mid-1980s.

The situation was this. I had been conducting management training at various business units of Emerson Electric Corp. On a Wednesday in the fall of 1986 I received a phone call. Could I attend a special meeting at Emerson's St. Louis headquarters that Friday? Charles Knight, the CEO, was angry. Emerson's "war on inventory" had been reducing stock to the tune of only $50 million a year, and that was not enough. The meeting was to do something about it.

By next day, I had a superblitz-like plan and was eager to deliver it on Friday. Over the phone (and maybe by fax) I explained the plan to St. Louis. The cover letter stated, "It may be applied full scale. . . . It could be applied to just some of the divisions or plants (but why do just part of a job?)." The four-page plan was in eight sections, briefly summarized as follows:

1. The reality: Corporate inventory was excessive—three to four months' supply. The "war" was mostly educational, igniting too few projects; it was scarcely touching bloated finished items, raw materials, slow-moving service parts, and nonmoving obsolete parts. The final point read, "Inventory won't go away as long as it continues to be produced."

2. Inventory clean-out strategy: Main features included a cycle of two-month partial plant shutdowns, beginning with plants whose business was slow. Meet all shipping commitments, running assembly, subassembly, and fabrication only for shippable products. Inform suppliers of reasons for curtailed buying. During the period, create work cells, convert to pull systems, adopt rate-based scheduling, cut setup times and lot sizes, and so on. Halt labor and variance reporting during the period while assigning everybody to full-scale training and implementation projects. Send nonessential

people home without pay (strong medicine, but for a large, one-time gain).

3. Timing: A time-phased plan over a ten-month period was laid out.

4. Training: Methods included videos, JIT simulation games, and bus trips to other, advanced plants to "see for yourself."

5. Permanent institutional changes: These included revamping the factory accountability system; considerably cutting lead times, finished goods, and distribution warehousing; transferring many people out of expediting, scheduling, material control, and so forth; halting many projects for automating material handling, tracking work flows, and generating work orders; and releasing and disposing of space and material apparatus.

6. Benefits: These would include, in 1987, $50 million to $100 million reductions in raw material and work in process and similar savings in finished goods, such savings continuing year after year; growth in market share; nearly all changes paid for out of scrap and rework savings alone; various cost avoidances; permanent "way of life" improvements; and exceptional bottom-line results during execution.

7. Risks: None. Main point: Customers are protected.

8. Obstacles: Four were mentioned, the last being "faintheartedness."

I don't recall all the details, but I believe I had my bags packed and air travel booked when a called came back from Emerson headquarters: Meeting canceled. It never was rescheduled.

This is the only blitz-like plan I have heard of aimed at a large corporation as a whole. That Emerson did not take the blitz challenge is no surprise. Manufacturing executives are conservative. They like to plan but not to do, and the blitz called for a whirlwind of doing. (As noted in chapter 4, Emerson has stayed the course since that time with its fairly successful Best Cost Producer program.) Would it have worked? Perhaps, but imperfectly. That is because most of the workforce would be involved only secondarily; they would be trained and participate only after the blitz was well under way.

While Emerson did not blitz, here is a company that did: Apple Computer. Apple had been "left for dead" in 1997 when founder Steve Jobs returned to work "the most unlikely comeback since the 1969 Amazin' Mets." Well-respected for his design and marketing acumen, Jobs has excellent manufacturing sense as well. He "slashed Apple's mind-boggling lineup of fifteen product lines to just a handful that share common components." Suppliers were cut from more than one hundred to just twenty-four and distributors from double digits to two. And half of Apple's manufacturing was outsourced to efficient contract electronic service companies. When Jobs took over, Apple's finished goods inventories were "the worst in the industry."[8] Apple's annual reports show total inventory turnover was a miserable 1.7 in 1997. By the next year, Jobs had raised the figure to 5.7. Still not satisfied, Jobs hired former Compaq procurement head Timothy Cook, who outsourced printed circuit boards and closed more than ten finished-goods warehouses. By the end of 1999, the inventory turnover number had soared to a phenomenal 22.2.

Jobs and Cook were not slashing and burning. They were aiming squarely at the kinds of wastes commonly attacked under the lean/world-class agenda. Nor should their efforts be seen as the kind of command-and-control, "make your numbers" *modus operandi* rebuked in chapter 7. Rather, they were a one-time shot, the kind of "get well" medicine needed when any company finds itself fat and unhappy about it.

Like the plan for Emerson, Jobs's actions did not engage the experience of the workforce—a flaw. Most plans, though, are imperfect, and Jobs's measures were vital; otherwise Apple may have been another DEC (Compaq "saved" Digital Equipment Corp. by acquiring it). Vital or not, the Apple example serves simply to demonstrate that superblitz can be applied even for a major corporation. Whether Apple can weather upcoming storms remains to be seen. (The same goes for Gateway Computer. When founder Ted Waitt reassumed Gateway's helm to stem losses in market share and earnings, a quick action was to cut and standardize components in order to reduce product variations from 23 million to 1,000.)[9] One issue that it and all companies face is how to make improvement continuous, not a one-time shot.

BLITZES AND BLACK BELTS

Continuous improvement goes as often by the internationalized Japanese word *kaizen*. Anand Sharma, president and CEO of a *kaizen*-specializing consulting group, notes that the term originally implied slow, step-by-step improvement. The Toyota model of *kaizen* applications has, Sharma says, swung the meaning of the term to something like "rapid evolutionary change."[10]

While *kaizen* continues to thrive in many companies, another driver of betterment, called "six sigma," has become equally prominent. Six sigma, too, has the ring of rapid evolutionary change. In following discussions of the two approaches, there is no need for a lot of details; sources of information on how they work are plentiful. Rather, the emphasis here is on how the two fit with the ideal of total continuous improvement.

Kaizen Events

Briefly, a *kaizen* is a quick-hit, two-to-five-day improvement event. It gets results and at the same time may get people excited about further application of the method. A *kaizen* may be a project with a single-minded focus: Re-layout the packaging area. More often the target is an area, such as packaging, but with just a general goal: Improve it. Outside experts or inside facilitators may lead the effort, with, typically, a mix of direct-labor and technical staff doing the data collection, task breakdown, analysis, and implementation. (But see the accompanying box regarding an alternative—a one-person, mini-*kaizen* approach.)

One-Person *Kaizen*

We've all heard of "management by wandering around." Less well-known is "management by standing in the circle." Teruyuki Minoura, president and CEO of Toyota Motor Manufacturing North America, describes the method as practiced by Taiichi Ohno, a mastermind of the Toyota production system: "Ohno, when teaching TPS, would take his students to a problem area and draw a circle on the production floor [from which to] observe, think, and analyze. He wanted us to watch and ask 'why' over and over again. If we did that, he knew the better ideas would come [and that] they come from true understanding of the process."[11]

My first awareness of this practice—call it a one-person *kaizen*—was in about 1984. I had continued visiting Kawasaki's Lincoln, Nebraska, plant. Kawasaki had the Toyota system down cold—including the stand-and-study method of process improvement. My hosts—American managers—delighted in pointing discreetly to the lone man standing still and watching a certain production area. It was the new Japanese plant manager. My thought at the time was that he probably had eyes for manufacturing like a safari tracker's eyes for big game. Yet something didn't seem quite right. Why should the top executive on-site be doing this?

Perhaps no company has ever tried assigning "stand, watch, and ask why" to a selected shop-floor associate. A knotty problem area would be the target. Then the assignment goes to another operative for another situation; and so on. Many shop employees, by turns, would be given the clipboard for the same kind of assignment. What they lack is wide experience and perspective. What they do not lack is common sense, detailed knowledge of the work itself, and a personal onus to make something work.

One-person *kaizen* makes sense—under the right pair of eyes.

Kaizen has been popularized through the efforts of Masaaki Imai and his 1986 book on the subject.[12] A close look at that and other books on the procedure (and at Imai's company Web site, kaizen-institute.com) shows that *kaizen,* in practice, takes in about any good idea for improvement. It's cells, visual management, and 5S; total quality, cross-training, and TPM; and more. But all that is beside the point: *kaizen* is an intensive attack on wastes in which a cross-functional team completes study and implementation in just a few days. So *kaizen* is anything but a plan-it-to-death process.

According to "Getting Dirty Together," a section of another book: "Kaizen is very much a *hands-on* process. Team participants not only plan, they clean equipment, sort tools, move machinery, . . . Rank is not recognized. . . . The team's job is to make change happen. To create and leave in place *a new way of doing things.*" The book's title is *The Kaizen Blitz.*[13] The label *blitz* was introduced by the Association for Manufacturing Excellence (AME) a few years ago. AME has sponsored many blitzes around North America in which *kaizen* veterans from other local companies volunteer their time to help a host manufacturer. Sometimes the host is a smaller supplier, and some of the volunteers are from customers of the supplier.

Earlier in the chapter, the Engines, Inc., case was referred to as "superblitz." Blitz—borrowing the AME term—for its quick results. Super for its company-wide scope. Some manufacturers gain wide-scope involvement by running *kaizens* continually: many per year, involving most of the workforce. Such intensive application of *kaizen* approximates the total continuous improvement model—presuming inclusion of all eight steps (trend charts, recognition, and so on).

For that matter, Engines, Inc., could have benefited from having an AME-sponsored *kaizen* blitz during the eight-week inventory-reduction time. Engines could today be using *kaizens* as a primary vehicle for maintaining high levels of work-force involvement. Turning the idea around, *kaizen*-event sponsors might add to their repertoire of techniques the use of the inventory form filled out by each operator—Exhibit 11.1. In these ways, the *kaizen* approach may fit well with this chapter's ideal: quick, effective, *lasting* continuous improvement.

Six Sigma: SPC-Plus

Speaking of lasting results, who could have thought, in the late 1980s, that total quality management would be subject to the half-life hex? What could be more elemental than total quality? Yet TQM (or TQ) half died. Its resurrection required a new name: six sigma. For a capsule review of it, see the accompanying box.

Six Sigma

Mathematically, six sigma means 3.4 defects per 1 million chances. That objective, however, is almost beside the point. As *Quality* magazine put it,[14] in practice the term *six sigma* "is used to denote much more than a simple counting of defects. It has come to imply a whole quality culture of strategies, statistics, and tools for improving a company's bottom line. 'Black belt' is the title used to describe people who are qualified experts in using those tools."

And what are six sigma's "pitfalls"? In the same article, Gerald Defoe, a six-sigma black belt for New York Air Brake Corp. of Watertown, New York, offers this: "We all have problems we solve on a daily basis as part of our normal jobs. Those don't—and shouldn't—become projects. The projects reserved for the black belt should be the ones where you've tried to fix it three or four times and it hasn't worked, or it's gone away and it's come back. That's when the black belt should come in to really understand what is the root cause. How do we get after it? And how do we keep it controlled in the best way possible?"

Actually, as in all these comebacks from reaching half-life, the offspring has a few different features. Six sigma has cachet: black belts, master black belts, green belts. These knights of process management are highly trained in statistics-based improvement. Done well, six sigma charters the "belts" to run improvement studies widely, crossing department lines wherever there is need.

TQ had (has) the same quality-science foundation. TQ is stronger in its customer focus and whole-workforce involvement. Six sigma may be stronger in its openness to any process problem (not centered on quality per se).

Although six sigma's birthplace was Motorola, its paragon of successful implementation is General Electric. And why not? In the 1980s, TQM and the hard sciences of quality were roaring at Motorola, also at Hewlett-Packard, Texas Instruments, Ford Motor Company, and many other major manufacturers. GE in the 1980s had other agendas. GE had publicly indicated that it would not be adopting TQM. Thus, in the mid-1990s, when CEO Jack Welsh elected to make six sigma an all-out GE strategic initiative, quality improvement opportunities of awesome proportions lay waiting. For a 1998 investment of $400 million, mostly for training, GE would derive an estimated $1.2 billion in benefits.[15] Unless there is a reversal of policy under new CEO Jeffrey Immelt, the training should yield dividends for many years. Such has generally been the case at TQM pioneers, including

Motorola; even so, Motorola elected to rejuvenate its quality crusade via its six sigma invention.

Still, no company executes like GE. According to an extensive report on six sigma at GE, "Welsh directed that every exempt employee . . . be trained in six sigma methodologies." In addition, "Across all GE businesses no one will be promoted without the full six sigma training and a completed project." And, "Likewise, across all GE businesses, it is corporate policy that 40 percent of each bonus given to all top managers is now tied to that manager's six sigma goals, progress, and successes. . . ."[16]

Can six sigma function in the superblitz mode? It is already intensive and widely applied. While whole-workforce involvement is missing, six sigma perhaps could accommodate it: a key role of green belts might be to devise data-collection devices and facilitate their wide use. There is precedent for this idea: In the 1940s, "work simplification" emerged out of the industrial engineering profession.[17] Industrial engineers (IEs) had acquired the "efficiency expert" label—an uncomplimentary term, to say the least. Under work simplification, IEs taught operators to do their own flowcharting, methods studies, workplace re-layouts, time studies, and so forth.

The improvement tools discussed so far range from old hat to mainstream new. A central theme of this book, however, is that hypercompetition requires a forward-reach mind-set. While we cannot know the future, it is not much of a reach to expect green belts to be engaging more and more in green projects. That is particularly likely in view of the groundswell of interest in becoming registered to the ISO 14000 series on management for the environment. (See discussion of ISO 14000 in chapter 4.)

Any improvement methodology—six sigma, TQ, *kaizen,* and others—is likely to face human barriers ranging from indifference to outright resistance. In such cases, starting with the right implementation step can make the difference.

WEDGE IMPLEMENTATIONS

One thing sometimes leads, helpfully, to another. Esco Corp. was host for an AME-sponsored *kaizen* blitz in Portland, Oregon. One of Esco's objectives had to do with the tendency to keep the work centers busy producing regardless of demand. An outcome of the blitz was conversion to producing only for customer orders and only in the customer's specific quantity. That practice cleared the floor between work centers. It was, according to the AME reporter on hand for the event, "a natural lead-in to . . . cell formation."[18]

At Boeing Company's Welded Duct facility in Auburn, Washington, safety was the lead-in. New management initiatives, including cells, kanban, and total preventive maintenance, were getting nowhere with the seven-hundred-plus employees. The safety features of TPM proved to be the wedge. In this welding environment, the danger of explosive welding gases was first on the minds of the unionized workforce and its leadership. TPM puts everything in proper, marked-off, color-coded places. By emphasizing how this enhances safety (marked-off safety lockout zones, safety checkpoints, and so forth), management won full support of the labor force. Next safety issue: fork trucks traversing the distances among tube bending, duct layup, tack welding, seam welding, X-ray, and other shops. Fork trucks are an accident waiting to happen. Moving processes close together into cells collapses fork-truck travel and cuts the risk, and emphasis on that point melted resistance to cells. Kanban was next. The work-order system put large quantities of in-process material throughout the plant. The more material, the more fork trucks and other handling, and the more chances for an accident. Since kanban greatly reduces those stocks, kanban became a reality, too.

The Welded Duct example is unique in using TPM as a wedge. More often, consulting firms with a TPM specialty (such as EFESO, headquartered in Milan, Italy, efeso.com; and Paris, France–based Proconseil, proconseil.fr) feature a broad repertoire to begin with. TPM blends naturally with a variety of related improvement tools: cells, kanban, and visual management; SPC and value engineering; *kaizen* and six sigma.

While, at this writing, six sigma enjoys favor in highest places and *kaizen* remains in wide use, the other improvement drivers have large followings as well. Probably a thousand manufacturers have a total preventive maintenance effort under way, and a thousand more (or many of the same ones) are embracing visual management along with 5S.

This brings us to a key summarizing point of the chapter: There are a wide variety of ways to jolt people, or companies, out of their complacency. Any of the tools of improvement can, like coffee, wake you up and get you going. You can switch tools—perhaps to the new one brought forth by the latest hot new program (like switching from coffee to a high-energy sports drink). As emphasized in this and earlier chapters, however, lasting results require not just tools, but a multifaceted system that involves everybody. A system involving eight such facets has been referred to as "total continuous improvement." It is a robust approach that can build effectively on a wide assortment of improvement tools.

12

Manufacturing's Burdens—and Responses

Chapter 11 proposed ways for manufacturers to raise their execution to the level of their planning and programming. Standing in the way, though, are the burdens of a complex world and the baggage of the inept past. Heavy among them are the way things grow beyond ability to manage them. These include too many suppliers, part numbers, end items, stockkeeping units, and customers and bewildering demand patterns. They strain the abilities of finite resources to cope, and inept coping practices worsen the problem. Burdensome as well are false signals: apparent good results from what really are flawed systems. This chapter considers each of these burdens.

TOO MUCH AND TOO MANY

A lesson from Japan, circa 1980: Don't have too many suppliers. So for twenty years manufacturers have been reducing suppliers "to a few good ones." The rationale is easy to understand. With multiple suppliers for each purchased item, efforts to pay each of them proper attention dissipate. Close partnerships work only with a modest number of suppliers.

A lesson from the United States, circa 1985: Don't have too many part numbers. This lesson is elemental in the works of Boothroyd and Dewhurst,[1] originators of DFMA (design for manufacture and assembly). Same rationale.

The good sense of the supplier-partnership *concept* is what convinces companies to trim their supplier lists. The impetus for cutting numbers and varieties of parts comes not so much from a concept as from the DFMA *methodology*, which reduces to a set of common-sense guidelines.

But where are the concept or guidelines that tell companies to reduce their product lines, customers, complexity, resource base, and size? All of these tend to grow to burdensome proportions. Often companies do not even seem to see these as problems. Notions of economies of scale cloud judgments. But problems they are. The size issue was addressed in chapter 9. Why the others are problems and a bit on what may be done about them is the following topic.

The "Too Many" Syndrome: Products

Having too many products or product lines should be, but often is not, seen as serious. One argument against proliferating products is the well-known 80–20 principle. It says that 20 percent of products garner 80 percent of earnings. Some of the other 80 percent probably are money losers. Oblivious to this, manufacturers tend to carry old products way past their profitable lives. And they add new models and model extensions that never do produce profits.

Earnings erode for several reasons. When product lines fatten, costly manufacturing capacity is eaten up by changeovers. Further, scheduling becomes tumultuous and invites costly, complex scheduling systems with large non-value-adding staffs to run them. High numbers of SKUs in the distribution and order-fulfillment systems require their own complex, costly systems. Purchasing and engineering have too much on their plates, as do sales and marketing. The "SKU'ered" organization loses its focus.

SALES TARGETS, VALUE ENGINEERING, AND TARGET COSTING.

Typically, the main culprit is company goals calling for tough-to-meet revenue targets. *Good* sales—of products that are profitable or have potential—are insufficient. So, to make the target, past-their-prime products are retained and new, unprofitable models are added.

The 80–20 concept is not powerful enough to overcome the ingrained practice (and illogic) of letting sales targets dominate. More ammunition is needed. Proof, in money, can help. An audit of real costs—using activity-based methods—can lay bare the likely truth: that many old products and some of the new ones are drags on earnings. Some money losers, of course, must be retained as a service to good old customers and potential new ones.

Losers that have been in the product line for many years sometimes can be resuscitated via an old and still excellent technique: value engineering (VE). Initially called "value analysis," value engineering originated in the purchasing department of General Electric in 1947. It is a structured way of analyzing any product's, or component's, function, cost, and worth. Teams of experts conduct the studies and usually are able to retain the function at much less cost. Often the improvement comes, simply, from using a better and cheaper kind of material, which may not have been an option originally. SAVE International is the umbrella organization for the value engineering discipline, value-eng.com.[2] In keeping with the elevation of value as a dominant, customer-driven business concern, SAVE has been promoting the term *value methodology* as a synonym for value engineering.

Preemptive action is better than delayed reaction. In other words, do not allow dubious products to make it out of development in the first place. Here we have the aid of an excellent tool: target costing. There are plentiful references on this methodology, which originated in Japan.[3] There is even a target-costing Web site, target-costing.com/target-costing.htm. The site is sponsored by CAM-I (Consortium for Advanced Manufacturing–International), which has been a leader since the 1980s in advancing cost systems that are better in tune with JIT and TQC ways of doing business.

If cost audits, target costing, and value engineering are not enough, best hope is to get at product proliferation through a multifunctional strategy team project, as presented in chapter 10. The charge in such high-level projects is to develop a holistic strategy—versus the one-dimensional kind that lets sales targets ride roughshod over what's good for good business.

SHAPING DEMAND.
If all else fails, try technology, à la Dell Computer. Here the purpose is not to reduce numbers of products, but to better manage capacity, inventory, prices, and profits for those already in sales catalogs. The example in chapter 8 showed how Dell order takers—and the supply chain—make good use of up-to-date electronic information. The following example presents a fuller picture of the system and its multiple benefits, including shaping the incoming orders.

Here's how it works. Dell salespeople take orders for any way you want your PC. If you specify an option that they lose money on, or that disrupts schedules and capacity plans, your salesperson may, over the phone or by e-mail, nudge you toward a different option. Say that, for a printer to go with your Dell desktop PC, you ask for the $149 HP DeskJet 932C on page 12 of the Dell catalog. While you are on the phone, the Dell saleswoman is keying in your preferences. Her screen says to instead suggest the HP 970Cse, which lists for $249 on the same catalog page. She tells you it's yours for $199 instead of the list price of $249. You take it. Why the good deal? Your sales woman doesn't know exactly why. But she knows that these advisories on her screen are for good business reasons. It could be that Dell negotiated a better deal with Hewlett-Packard on the $249 printer, so it is more profitable than the $149 model. More often the reason is scarcity of inventory or capacity: The $149 DeskJet, or some of its components in the supply chain, are on or near back-order status; it's the opposite for the $249 printer.

The system, as modified in 2000, also provides suppliers representing 90 percent of the company's purchasing with real-time visibility of Dell's usage of the items they supply.[4] With this information, suppliers take their own proactive steps to avoid the "bullwhip." Dell's ability to collaborate on capacity/inventory issues at the supplier end and shape demand at the customer end is unique; it has been called "two-knob control."[5]

Maybe Dell is also guilty of the "too many" syndrome. That is, it has too many printers in too many different suppliers' models in its catalog. But if so, keeping suppliers informed and shaping orders at order entry is, at least, a worthy, advanced way to cope.

Customers Beyond Reason

A related issue is that too many products invite too many customers. The reverse is true as well: marginal customers' demanding marginal products. As applied to customers, turnaround expert Don Bibeault proposes not 80–20, but 120–20. His "rule of profits" states that 120 percent of profits come from 20 percent of clients. The other 80 percent, he says, *lose* money.[6]

But wait a minute, you might say. How can a customer-focused company turn away customers or, from the previous topic, a customer's special product preferences? The simple answer is that true customer focus is doing well for a few, rather than doing poorly for too many.

Phone companies, banks, airlines, and mail-order houses seem to be way ahead of manufacturers in acting on that viewpoint. Many are busy installing software that tracks amount of customer activity. All sorts of demographic information is included. From that information come differentiated customer-management policies. Active clients get reduced prices, better seats, quicker service, and other kinds of special treatment. Other clients—maybe you and me? Too bad.

Those human services businesses, however, are much different from manufacturing. They deal with thousands or hundreds of thousands of small, random customer interactions per month or week. Manufacturers have large, ongoing business dealings, involving masses of inventory rather than masses of customer transactions. Their production comes from ultra-expensive capacity threading back through supply chains. Customer-preference software that automatically differentiates would mindlessly slash and burn. The 120–20 "rule of profits" may apply as well in manufacturing as in other sectors. Manufacturers, however, have more to think about in setting customer strategies.

One manufacturer that has given plenty of thought to customers is St. Louis–based Wainwright Industries, 1994 winner of a Baldrige national quality award. To receive the award, it is, above all, necessary to be customer-focused. Wainwright's dominant catch-phrase, "We want a few good customers," captures the essence. Their customer base, in the automotive and aerospace industries, is slim. Various ways that Wainwright dedicates itself to just those customers stand out at the company. For example, the customer service office resides in the midst of Wainwright's stamping plant. Its glass-windowed walls provide maximum connectivity from customers to where the metal gets stamped.

We also learned in chapter 5 about Nypro, perhaps the world's premier (and largest) injection molder. The odd thing it did some ten years ago was to cut its customer base from six hundred large, medium, and small-fry customers to just thirty-one big ones. What revenue was lost did not take long to recover. Nypro's stellar reputation for quality and service allows it to pick its customers rather than the other way around. Today Nypro has twenty-odd plants on several continents, each dedicated to a small number of large-volume customers (sometimes just one!).

Nypro is one of a tiny number of manufacturers that might meet the criterion for earning the fifth step on Principle 16 of the WCP, which reads as follows: "Reverse Marketing: Out of Strength, You Choose Whom to Sell To."

The LaGrange, Georgia, plant of Freudenberg-NOK, manufacturer of oil seals, is a year 2000 recipient of the Shingo Prize. One of the major steps on the plant's jerky road to the prize was cutting complexity. Bruce Warren and the leadership team did so by focusing on number of customers, along with numbers of part numbers, machines, and operators. In an article on the plant's transformation, Robert Hall observes: "The most dramatic simplification . . . was to drastically reduce the number of parts and the number of customers on which each person had to concentrate."[7]

Customer selectivity applies as well in the process industries. In the early 1990s, Polymers and Resins (P&R), the largest business unit of Rohm and Haas, was getting whipsawed on prices by new competitors. Its emulsions plants were all unfocused, handling mixtures of make-to-order and make-to-stock products for any customer. Customer service representatives had no formal way to obtain delivery promises, scheduling was chaotic, delivery performance was erratic, and costs were too high. So in 1995 P&R formed a redesign team. The team did the usual 80–20 analysis, which led to grouping its four thousand customers into four tiers: 1) partners and potential partners, 2 percent of the total but yielding 55 percent of gross profits; 2) strategically important customers, 6 percent of customers and 24 percent of profits; 3) important customers, 17 percent and 13 percent; and 4) other customers, 75 percent and 6 percent. Numerous decisions to realign products, plants, and customers followed, but with the involvement of good customers to ensure that their needs were not compromised. The changes "saved millions of dollars, increased productive capacity, and made P&R a leaner, more disciplined, and smoother operating unit."[8]

One more example: Illinois Tool Works (ITW) bought thirty-two manufacturers in 1999. Upon acquisition, an ITW team pays a visit to help find the profitable 20 percent of customers that make 80 percent of profits. It is then up to the purchased company to focus heavily on that 20 percent and to work down the numbers in the 80 percent—not with a meat ax, but with a rapier. ITW is twice as profitable as its peers.

How do these, and small numbers of other manufacturers, come to the realization that taking in any breathing customer is bad for best customers—and for good business? A multidisciplinary way of questioning past strategies and business plans is where to start. As with the "too many products" issue, a full, activity-based audit of costs can be the clincher.

New and Bulked-up Supplier Sectors

Sometimes the solution to the "too many, too much" problem is to call upon a new breed of supplier for help. If you are an end-item electronics manufacturer, you are in luck, because the new type of supplier exists. In industries other than electronics, the wait for this kind of help may not take long.

From nowhere a dozen years ago to a giant force today is the subindustry called EMS, for "electronic manufacturing service" (or CEM, "contract electronic manufacturing"). This newer kind of outsource sprouted in order to take over some of the burden of manufacturing from companies like IBM, Sony, H-P, Nokia, and Cisco. The latter relies almost totally on EMSs for its production.

Those customer companies have plants in many countries. To serve them locally, so do the EMS leaders—Solectron, SCI Systems, Celestica, Flextronics, Jabil Circuits, and others. These manufacturers mainly assemble but increasingly get involved in product design and other services. In many cases their plant was purchased intact from their customer. Why can the EMSs run those facilities better than their customers could? Volume economies, especially in purchasing. Quoting Robert Hall, "One rule of thumb is that, depending on the business, materials savings of 10–30 percent can be obtained just by letting an EMS with good supplier connections handle it all."[9]

Another, much smaller but growing, new subindustry is contract pharmaceutical services. Generally, the critical competencies of the major pharmas lie not in production, but in developing and marketing drugs. The manufacturing, and maybe the extensive clinical trials, are candidates for outsourcing to the new rank of contract services companies.

The automotive industry is also in the throes of transformation—from the majors to first-echelon suppliers. As with EMSs, the tier-one suppliers are taking on design as well as manufacturing for their customers. (When the supplier is given full design as well as production responsibility, Fujimoto calls it "black-box purchasing":[10] Instead of taking direction from the customer, the supplier becomes independent, a closed-off "black box.") A difference here is that the first-tiers do not make up a new subindustry. They've been around for most of the autmobile's history. Another wrinkle is that the first-tiers are expected to deliver complete, preassembled modules. Formerly, they did not. They delivered loose parts, and the auto assemblers had the enormous job of putting together ten thousand or more of them to make a car.

Right behind the auto industry is aerospace/defense (AD). Same idea. Offload responsibilities for large numbers of components to first-echelon suppliers and, where it makes sense, have them deliver in pretested modules. (The module as delivery unit is most likely where the end product is large in size and number of parts. Aerospace, defense armaments, and automotive products are prime examples. Machine tools and certain instruments and test equipment also qualify.) Why? Because AD companies have too much and too many resources—with excessive complexities and costs. They need relief. It seems likely that other industries—construction, furniture, and food and beverage, to name a few—will undergo similar devolution. (Food and beverage companies already rely heavily on suppliers, on everything from flavorings and additives to containers and labels. Next step is for food companies to contract out their manufacturing to a food manufacturing subsector.)

It never did make good sense for the major producers of complex products to, as Geoffrey Moore puts it, hoard the value chain. (See the accompanying box for Moore's take on how, in his favorite industry, the hoarding has been diffused.) Manufacturers did it because they lacked today's management expertise.

Links in the Chain

"In this new world, the companies that make the microprocessors (Intel, Motorola, MIPS), the people who make the memory (Toshiba, Micron, Samsung), the people who make the disk drives (Seagate, Quantum, EMC), the people who manufacture the subassemblies (Solectron, Flextronics, GE Harris), the people who sell to the end user (CompUSA, Fry's, and a host of value-added resellers), and the people who support the systems going forward (EDS, Unisys, Honeywell)—all are different.

"[These] value chains scale much faster and are more cost-competitive than vertically integrated ones. Frankly, they do not compete well on quality of integration or accountability—and in niche markets this still gives the advantage to a vertically integrated company...."[11]

They did not know how to develop suppliers, nor did they fully appreciate how futile it was to try to manage thousands or tens of thousands of parts.

This is not advocating wholesale offloading of parts to suppliers. There is a strong case to be made for retaining at least some understanding of how to design and make key items that are contracted out. Say, for example, that Honda makes the momentous decision to farm out stamping of its auto bodies. Honda would sell its stamping plants to stampers such as the Budd Company. (This is just as the major electronics majors have sold much of their assembly facilities to the EMSs). But not all of them. Prudence would dictate that Honda retain one or more of the plants. That may seem to defeat the purpose—taking advantage of savings and expertise of the stamping specialists. Nevertheless, Honda should do so in order to retain enough knowledge to effectively deal with the stampers.[12]

The measures suggested so far aim at simplification and gaining focus. In some businesses best efforts still seem for naught because of highly unpredictable demand.

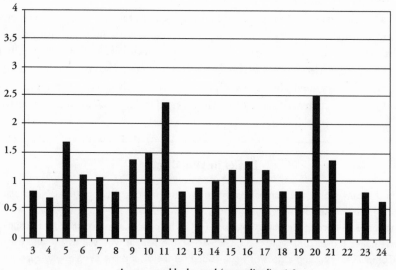

Average weekly demand (normalized) = 1.0
Coefficient of variation (standard deviation of demand ÷ average demand) = 0.55
From *A Stitch in Time: Lean Retailing and the Transformation of Manufacturing—Lessons from the Apparel and Textile Industries* by Frederick K. Abernathy et al.,
copyright © 1999 by Oxford University Press, Inc.
Used by permission of Oxford University Press, Inc.

Exhibit 12.1. Single-Breasted Men's Coat, Size 46 Regular

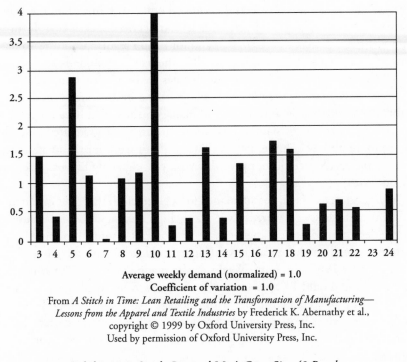

Average weekly demand (normalized) = 1.0
Coefficient of variation = 1.0

Exhibit 12.2. Single-Breasted Men's Coat, Size 43 Regular

Confounded Demand Patterns

There is nothing new in demand forecasting. As mentioned in chapter 2, that issue is one we might hope shall become the subject of the next breakthrough. The demand forecasting problem actually can be worse than it even seems. Abernathy, et al., provide an example from the apparel industry.[13] Included in their extensive research is a study of the manufacturer's demand for a certain type of men's coat. Exhibits 12.1 and 12.2 show actual weekly numbers for a popular and an unpopular size, respectively. We see considerable variation for the popular one, 46 regular: weekly demand peaks at nearly twice the coat's average demand. That is modest, however, compared with the less popular 43 regular: its peak-week demand soars to about four times that of the average week. Demand patterns for the two sizes do not coincide at all: the 43 regular peaks at week ten, which is just a normal week for the 46 regular.

Many manufactured items have demand patterns more variable than what we see for these coats. But here we have a product that is not seasonal and whose demand was not influenced by sales promotions. Moreover, it is sold in over a thousand retail outlets.

From the data, the researchers determined how much inventory the manufacturer must hold to provide the same level of service for each coat. It turns out to be twice as many weeks of demand for the 43 regular as for the 46 regular. And whereas all sizes of this coat sell in the tens of thousands per year, in the odd sizes, including 43 regular, yearly sales are only a few hundred.

It seems likely that 43 regular, and many other odd sizes, are money losers. If this were an industrial product, good management would have the manufacturer trying to work with the customer to arrive at graduated pricing: charge more for low-volume specials. That will not work for the men's coats, because the retailers could not get away with passing along higher prices for the odd sizes.

The good news here is that demands for a given cloth that goes into many different coat sizes can be forecast with fairly high accuracy. That is because of the well-established precept that you get low forecast error by grouping items with individually high forecast error. (Highs and lows within the group average out.) The 1967 Plossl and Wight classic made this clear.[14] So while the manufacturer should be able to get by with relatively small inventories of cloth, serving the retail customer with finished coats requires high inventories. At least it does in the absence of countermeasures. Manufacturers, however, should always be working on countermeasures. Four are worthy of comment here.

1. *Create focused units.* Put the low-volume, highly variable demand items into a special-order business unit or cell. Having its own resources and challenge to make money generally releases a flood of good ideas. (The all-important *focus* topic has taken up two full chapters in this book: chapters 8 and 9.) Treating low-volume items specially can be effective in many kinds of manufacturing, including apparel. I first saw an example at Russell Athletic in Alexander City, Alabama, in 1988. Russell had created a focused module (the industry's word for cell) just for athletic uniforms for professional teams. (This was probably one of the earliest Western applications of the modular or TSS sewing system.)

2. *Ensure flexibility for the low-volume units.* Higher-volume units do not require a high degree of flexibility. (Still, they should have multiskilled associates and, where possible, equipment on wheels.) A low-volume-specials unit must have much greater flexibility. The professional uniforms module at Russell did. If a new order came in from, say, the Boston Celtics, a product team would be assembled, patterns and materials pulled, and sewing machines pushed together just for that order. On finishing the order, the team would break up and move to other work.

Ruffa and Perozziello describe a similar application at Indianapolis-based Garrity Tool Company. Owner Don Garrity had joined the Ruffa/Perozziello research team studying lean manufacturing for aerospace-defense under an industry-sponsored grant. Garrity learned from the experience. In the three years following the AD industry study, his shop was 100 percent defect-free and 100 percent on-time to its aerospace customers. One ranked his company as its number one supplier, and in 1999 Garrity Tool received the Indiana Quality Improvement Award. According to Ruffa and Perozzielo, these honors stem in the main from creation of flexible units, which produce not only for aerospace, but also for material-handling and faucet-manufacturing customers. Garrity's multi-tasked machinists "can readily adjust to wide swings in demand for individual units, maintaining an overall level loading of [the] shop's activities."[15]

3. *Postponement.* This is making partially completed items to a forecast, then awaiting actual orders to finish the items. It is an old idea, whose old name is delayed differentiation. Zara, the Spanish clothing retailer and manufacturer, is a prime example. Zara has created a stir in its industry by its ability to get new fashions into stores in less than fifteen days.[16] Unlike most competitors, Zara produces 60 percent of its goods in-house. Fabric cutting and dyeing take place at its state-of-the-art factory. Then, using up-to-the-day information from stores, it sends the cut-and-colored fabric to local stitch-and-pack shops before shipping to stores around the world. Postponement is most effective with the kind of advanced information system that is a key to the Zara system.

4. *Modular design and production.* Modular plants, designs, and production were discussed in chapters 4 and 9.[17] Here the point is that modules may be produced to a forecast, then sit and wait for orders to arrive. The design allows mix-and-match assembly to actual incoming orders. Modular concepts fit well with focused facilities flexibly producing in a postponement mode.

These kinds of actions do not eliminate the forecasting problem. They just help manufacturers to reduce the severity of consequences. But even with perfect forecasts, things will go wrong, because demand-side problems are only one kind of constraint. The bottleneck/constraint issue is explored more deeply next.

BOTTLENECKS AND CONSTRAINTS

Nettlesome bottlenecks have plagued manufacturers "forever." Common sense has always meant giving bottlenecks intensive attention—usually a matter of marshaling resources. For example, throw extra operators, engineers, and technicians at the bottleneck. Run the constraining resources seven days a week to keep other, five-day-week resources well supplied. (This a less favored solution since it requires inventory buildups.) Or dust off otherwise unused equipment, or engage a subcontractor.

Despite its popularity, constraints management does not offer much that is new about managing the constraints. What it does well is give bottlenecks and constraints systematic, rather than haphazard, attention. A *system* has regular checks and balances. In the case of bottlenecks, a good system requires re-analyzing at frequent intervals or continuously; then, develop counteractions that dampen or cope with bottlenecks in preference to reacting to them.

With this brief introduction, we may take a closer look at constraints, their causes, and their effective solutions. As to causes, constraints may be grouped by those with roots external to the organization and those with internal sources. The external causes are few in number but very high in impact. Internal causes are the opposite: many in number but each usually low in impact. Following discussion includes examples.

External Constraints

The most serious constraints are largely self-inflicted. A typical manufacturer makes only halfhearted attempts to capture some of the most critical information. Namely, the deficiency centers on failing to find out true demand downstream and the state of capacity upstream in the supply chain.

On the customer side, here is the common situation: Orders arriving from the immediate customer are way out of phase with real usage farther downstream. Demand gets badly misshapen as each customer echelon engages in marketing promotions, panic ordering to meet sales quotas and budgets, scheduling to inaccurate forecasts, batching to gain production and transport economies, and warehouse space replenishment. Actual orders can end up as wrong as forecasts generally are.

With orders so badly mangled, the value chain is anything but lean. It is chock-full of inventory of wrong items: products that were selling well weeks ago but no longer are, and items that were forecast, budgeted, and promoted but for which customers really have little need. Excesses sell at a loss, after incurring high carrying costs. The whole system is unstable, with erratic ordering patterns commonplace. Sudden, large orders follow voids, as what customers are really buying ripples ponderously back through the supply chain. Constraints are everywhere as orders appear in large gulps without warning.

An extremely agile manufacturer in this system may proudly claim 98 percent on-time performance. But against what? Against orders that are wrong, especially deep in the value chain. That is because the manufacturer is passing the same sad pattern back to its suppliers and their suppliers. At each stage the constraints worsen, in what Hau Lee has labeled "the bullwhip effect."[18] Manufacturers have been so inward looking that they fail to see what is happening. They are like someone being pummeled in a fight but who won't fight back. Who just says, "Hit me again."

There is much that can be done to fight back—avoid the bullwhip. An aggressive outreach effort can make a world of difference. Collaboration with external players is what supply-chain management is, or should be, all about. *Industry Week* magazine's Census of Manufacturers for 2000 asked a question on the matter. A majority of responding executives said they are already using or plan soon to use the Internet for collaborative forecasting with their suppliers.[19] That will help.

The IT side of collaboration—the Internet and supply-chain management software—has its role but is incidental to where the real work is. It lies in persistent efforts to organize face-to-face events with counterparts up and down the chain. A main purpose is to hammer out ways of sharing demand and advance shipping information from farthest points downstream among all parties upstream. Other targets for agreements include advance notice of intent to change prices, to offer promotions, and to introduce new products in new channels. The *Industry Week* findings are a sign that a significant number of manufacturers have been at work doing groundwork.

The Dell Computer examples earlier in this chapter and in chapter 8 show how such agreements can lead to high sharing of capacity and true demand information among collaborators. An ultimate achievement is when the people taking orders are able, Dell-like, to shape demand away from pinched resources and toward gluts—and at the same time give customers equal or better value. Another Dell innovation is the way it pays sales bonuses. To avoid the end-of-period tendency of salespeople to sell madly and cause capacity constraints, each Dell salesperson's bonus period ends on a different day of the month. That way, "all sales personnel are not closing major orders at once."[20]

Somewhat opposite to collaboration is order refusal or deferment. Refuse orders? No, when capacity is plentiful. But yes, when capacity is lacking. Another book[21] describes how this works, a process called "*decomposing the order book.*" A multifunctional master planning team meets at least weekly. Its purpose is to do a thorough review of order backlogs or recent order history. In periods when orders exceed capacity week after week, the team flags orders that are money losers as well as those from pain-in-the-neck customers. Some of those kinds of orders are candidates for refusal. Not those already booked, but further orders of the same kind.

Alternatives to refusal are to go to the customer with options. One is deferment to a week when capacity looks to be more plentiful. The other is jacking up the price. If these options turn away a difficult customer ordering a money-losing item, so be it. Members of the review team must include operations, marketing, and finance: Operations knows capacities and capabilities. Marketing knows which customers to work with even though they might be difficult. And finance is there to do quick, activity-based cost analyses to show where the moneymakers and losers are at different volume levels.

Internal Constraints

Inside the business, there is no end to bottlenecks. Some are short-lived and roving, others sticky. Among the causes of the former are machine breakdowns, canceled orders, last-minute changes to orders, late parts, inaccurate stock records, absenteeism, tardiness, and more. Causes of the sticky include shortage of a critical skill or insufficient capacity on essential equipment.

Whether brief and roving or sticky and fixated, resolution may call upon a large array of solutions. Among these are the following kinds of tools:

- *Quality improvement.* With dependably high quality, bottlenecks due to rework's unwelcome appearance are avoided.

- *Total preventive maintenance.* With dependable machines, equipment-outage bottlenecks do not arise.

- *Just-in-time production.* The JIT tools convert the batch-and-queue system to rather smooth, continuous operations. Getting off batch-and-queue eliminates erratic demands whose peaks turn certain resources into bottlenecks.

Philip Quigley says, "You need only eyes, ears, shoe leather, and a grease board to resolve most bottlenecks—provided people are willing to work together." He is referring to tracking down bottlenecks via process flowcharting, then getting a group together to decide what to do about it.[22]

Eyes, ears, shoe leather—and kanban—offer another way to prospect for and fix bottlenecks. Felker Brothers is a Marshfield, Wisconsin, producer of stainless-steel piping for the process and building industries. Felker's flexible workforce keeps its eyes open and its shoe leather busy moving from where kanban squares are full to where they are empty. This is a simple, no-cost, roving bottleneck killer. The Felker plant had been organized into work cells governed by three work-cell "commandments": 1) "Never ever, ever stock out"; 2) "When the outbound squares are full, don't produce, help other [work cells]"; 3) "Never ever work out of sequence."[23] "Never" is a bit extreme. For any item on kanban, the receiving work center *should* run out of stock—but only infrequently and briefly. If there is never a stock-out, the queue limit is too generous; reduce it.

If stock-outs are frequent or long, one or both processes are bottlenecks. The providing process is the more likely offender, since it is failing to keep up. The using work center, however, may be part of the problem. If its performance is overly variable—in output rate, quality, or setup time, for example—the negative effects ripple back and forward through the processes. In either case, if not too severe, the bottleneck may be eliminated simply by upping the queue limit. For example, instead of three kanban containers, raise it to four. But don't rest. Attack the cause and reduce the kanbans anew.

More severe bottlenecks often cannot be resolved so easily. But there are plenty of exceptions that can make a big difference. Here is one: At R. W. Lyall the constraint was the coating line, which sprays epoxy protection on parts hung on an overhead conveyor. It could not keep up, except through costly overtime. An operator's simple idea, which engineering tested out as viable, relieved the problem. The solution was to decrease the distance between hangers from the former twelve inches to six inches. That doubled line capacity, which eliminated the bottleneck, along with the overtime. There may be nothing in work life so satisfying as coming up with that kind of solution—fixing a vexing root cause at scarcely any cost.

Paint and coating lines are among the commonest of manufacturing bottlenecks. More than a capacity problem, paint lines generally are not capable. (In quality management, the term *capable* means "able to meet specifications nearly every time." Its mathematical measure is called "the process capability index," Cpk.) Paint not right first time through? Send the part down the line again. This injects erratic demands on paint lines, which at their peaks overload the resource.

In automobile assembly, paint-line incapability is the norm. It means that the assembly plant cannot give suppliers of interiors and trim a definitive schedule until after paint. This has required suppliers to spend enormous sums for flexibility to ship interiors in the correct sequence with only hours' notice.

Regarding the automotive industry, Richard Morley observes that "many paint shops' typical state is 'line down.'" Or, he notes, the paint gun is clogged, truck to be painted is not ready, air pressure is wrong, painting modules are in repair or being reprogrammed. Also, "the trucks do not march down the line in order of their color; frequently no booth with the correct color will be available. Scheduling is a nightmare." He is referring to the configuration of multiple paint booths on a single assembly line. Patricia Moody and Morley describe, in their engaging book, *The Technology Machine*, a simple scheduling system devised by Morley. Done with "four lines of computer code," the scheduling system, owned by the booths, has the booths bidding on each job (truck) coming down the pike. The system will advise the booths that, say, an arriving truck needs black paint.

> A booth already loaded with black paint and near the end of its current job will bid very high for the black truck. A booth with another color, but almost empty, will bid slightly lower. A booth that is farther away, filled with red paint, broken down, or otherwise less suited for the job will bid lower still. Based on the outcome of this virtual biding war, the scheduling system will assign the truck to the highest-bidding paint booth. [It's an iterative sequence that] all happens in nanoseconds.[24]

Painting components instead of whole auto or truck bodies works differently. Commonly, the parts go on hangers pulled by overhead conveyor sequentially through painting and drying booths. Under that method, there are still troublesome problems of incapability. Steelcase, the giant office furniture manufacturer, largely avoids them in its Context plant in Grand Rapids. About ten years ago the company invested the necessary capital to install a state-of-the-art powder paint line that has uncommonly high capability.[25]

A usual cause of paint incapability is running the line faster than its rated capacity. Why? To avoid the considerable cost of putting in a second paint line. This is self-defeating. Speeding up the line to gain productivity generally ends up losing the gained productivity to rework—and creating bottlenecking peak demands besides. Rotary Lift in Madison, Indiana, producer of automotive lifts, has a better idea. Each of its two modest-size manufacturing buildings (sixty thousand and one hundred thousand square feet) has three paint lines, each dedicated to its own product-focused cells; a fourth air-dry paint line was recently removed from one of the buildings. The norm, even in half-million-square-foot factories, is to have just one paint line. That virtually guarantees bottlenecks, since different product lines will be competing unevenly for hooks on the line. Paint lines are expensive, but Rotary Lift finds that multiple lines avoid enough problems to pay for themselves.

These remarks about paint lines apply well to other expensive resources: heat treat, blast cleaners, sheet extruders and coaters, looms, environmental test chambers, and many others. It can be argued, or rationalized, however, that plenty of companies make money even without facing up to their bottlenecks and burdens. Some are living on borrowed time. Others muddle through with flawed systems.

FLAWED SYSTEMS

Even after twenty years of cogent reasons to get rid of them, or cut them back, companies hang on to discredited systems. Prime among them is overhead-absorption accounting. It seems to have scarcely any authoritative advocates anymore. Yet many, perhaps most, manufacturers still do it. Why? Because it "works." Material requirements planning also "works." So does activity-based management, which entails putting a cost slant on about any process; and finite-capacity scheduling—to name just a few of the more or less dubious systems.

How can they work if they shouldn't? Answers include these:

- A flawed system done well may equal a good system done poorly. Execution counts.

- A flawed system is much superior to no system. At least it is a system. As such, it can get people from high management down through staff departments and to first-line associates working together.

It may be that most of the major manufacturers have had success with getting lean and achieving low parts per million product defects. Irrationally, many of them still cling to standard costs, cost variances, and overhead-absorption accounting. Such cost management clashes with the lean/JIT pull system, in which production stops when the next process needs no more. Chapter 7 laid out a full set of related points against that conventional cost system. The combination of lean, high-quality practices with a heavy-handed cost system may yield acceptable numbers. But it will lose out to the growing number of companies that still have the cost system but are ignoring it. Finally, true lean will discard the system as non-value-adding waste.

The case against MRP is fairly well-known and is reviewed in the following chapter. Finite-capacity scheduling is also taken up in chapter 13. Activity-based management enjoys favor in most quarters and so requires a few comments here.

Activity-based costing, as a system, has been gradually giving way to ABC audits. Costs must be known for competitive decisions, but they are infrequent. They include pricing, make or buy, manual or automated, and hold 'em or fold 'em. Since costs must be known, do it accurately—by an ABC audit, as needed. Activity-based management (ABM) employs ABC. But it employs it for such purposes as prioritizing improvement projects.[26] A little bit of back-of-the-envelope cost analysis of candidates for improvement makes sense. Making a system out of it—cost analysts doing cost studies to justify each improvement project—is overkill. It's non-value-adding waste. So, by the way, is postmortem cost analysis: showing how much the improvement project saved. Reduction of wastes is sufficient; the savings go right to the bottom line. Costing the waste reductions just reduces the bottom-line savings by the cost of the cost studies.

Summary: Simplicity—Still the Key

Simplicity is still the key—as it was around the year 1300, when philosopher Sir William of Occam offered his famous test, called Occam's razor: The simpler of two otherwise equal explanations wins.

Simple systems win, too. Proactive, root-cause-fixing systems outdo reactive, control systems. Visual systems win out over IT systems. A system beats no system. We live and work, however, in a complex world. Every situational change introduces new complications. We have to fight back each time. The systems topic, peripheral in this chapter, is the main topic of the next.

13

Systems: Some Come with an "E"

It's everybody's favorite sport: pontificating about life and the Internet, that is. A hundred years ago, it was life and the horseless carriage. Reactions ranged from total adoration to sneers and ridicule. Your great-, or great-great-grandparent may have been in the second camp, yelling at the passing driver, "Get a horse!" Today's maximum ridicule, directed at the consummate Net surfer, goes, "Get a life!"

As it turns out, we all (or most of us, anyway) are getting a new life. Infotech has intervened. The early months of writing this book had me making repeated trips to the business library at the University of Washington and the King County regional library in Bellevue, Washington. Only a few months later, having signed on to DSL, the much faster link to the Internet, I was able to cut way back on the library trips.

As a user of the Net in my work, I was startled by how much I could get done. One topic in chapter 8 was Intel's copy exactly. Somewhere in my file cabinets would be my notes and clippings on the topic. But which one? Try the Intel file; surely I would have put copies of all materials on copy exactly there. No dice. After trying other files and finding only a few of my notes, I just keyed on to the Infoseek search engine and typed "copy exactly intel." There it was—better information than what I had been stuffing into file folders.

This final chapter, however, is not about the Internet or electronic business in general. Rather, the subject is systems, some of which are electronic. Our discussion looks at the essence of just a few IT applications that have been attractive to manufacturers.

THE E-MANAGEMENT AGE: A MIXED REVIEW

Quick! What do the following stand for—MRP, ERP, CIM, FCS, MES, APS, EDI, SCM, SOP, CRM, ATP, CTP, CM, MPS? Notable in this list (only a few of the prominent manufacturing IT acronyms) is this: The first seven require computers and software. The last seven do not, though software is plentiful for their application by computer—as explained next.

Tell any rationale layperson—say, your uncle Jack or your grandma—that your job is to develop supply-chain management (SCM) or sales and operations planning (SOP). They won't think it has anything to do with computers. Sounds like getting together. And it is; the IT side of SCM and SOP are optional and secondary.

Customer relationship management (CRM)? Probably it stands out at your uncle's or grandma's favorite store. And, if he's a traveler, perhaps your uncle experienced it at the hotel where the doorman signals to reception by a pull on his earlobe. The message is that the arriving guest has been here before (the doorman asked). At the front desk the receptionist greets the amazed guest by saying, "Welcome back!" CRM software—perhaps the application that records customers' buying habits—is good, too, but is no substitute for doing the basics of customer relationships simply, cheaply, and well.

Available to promise (ATP), capable to promise (CTP), capacity management (CM), and master production schedule (MPS) are all doable on spreadsheets. Paper spreadsheets will work, as will Microsoft Excel.

What is also notable about these seven is that they build value-chain bridges. Operations, sales and marketing, and the customer are jointly responsible for the master production schedule. They cannot develop an MPS properly without also engaging in capacity management: "What capacity options do we have, when, and at what cost?" are CM issues needing attention in order to do an MPS. Sales and operations planning enjoins this whole high-level bridge-building process.

SOP also applies at the level of making an order commitment to a customer. Useful commitment tools include available to promise and capable to promise: before booking an order, sales checks to see how much capacity is already committed and how much is still available to promise. Capable to promise is similar but more refined. That is, an available element of capacity might not be capable for certain special kinds of orders; sales would want to make sure one way or the other before promising.

ATP works well at Alstrom Pump, Mänttä, Finland, where people in every function like to use the term *rules of the game*. Operations has its rules—policies and practices, really—that add up to short, stable lead times. Sales and marketing love that and reciprocate by not overloading manufacturing's capacity. The main tool is a data sheet showing, week by future week, number of pumps already "sold" and numbers available to promise. The ATP sheet—joint property of operations, sales and marketing, purchasing, and engineering—visibly tracks adherence to the rules of the game.

Customer relationship management sharpens efforts of the company to get the right items and timing into the MPS and to commit to what customers really want and need. Supply-chain management (SCM) aims the bridge building in the other direction. And if those bridges are not built sturdily, what happens? A study on the value of supply-chain management by Singhal and Hendricks puts the answer in terms of plunging share prices. They followed up on stories of supply-chain failures reported in *The Wall Street Journal* and the Dow Jones News Service from 1989 to 1998. For the 861 companies involved, they found that after public announcement of the supply-chain malfunction, stock prices in the following three months fell an average of 8.62 percent and shareholder wealth by $120 million or more per company. What's more, stock prices fell by as much as 9 percent in the three months prior to the announcement. The explanation is that shock waves were reverberating through the system and reaching the ears of investors well before the company broke the bad news.[1]

And what of the first seven in our list of fourteen abbreviations? Four of them are well-known: MRP stands for material requirements planning, ERP for enterprise requirements planning, CIM for computer-integrated manufacturing, and EDI for electronic data interchange. Less familiar are FCS, finite-capacity scheduling; MES, manufacturing execution system; and APS, advanced planning and scheduling. None are bridge builders. Rather, they are tools that aim for accurate, efficient processing of data. Except for EDI, they operate on the provider's side of the bridge. See the box for further comment on the abbreviations.

Nouns and Names

The acronyms cited are all common nouns. English-language rules do not allow their capitalization except when reduced to acronyms. But many academic and professional journals (not *Harvard Business Review, Business Week,* and others that have professional copy editors) skip the rules and capitalize: Supply Chain Management, Finite Capacity Planning, and so on. Why should anybody care? Because it creates uncertainty as to whether the capitalized term is somebody's proprietary product or not. When Manufacturing Execution Systems, a common noun, is capitalized, it looks proprietary—as much so as SAP's Accelerated Enterprise Solution, which *is* proprietary.

This is not a legal thing—a matter of trademarks. Right use of capitalization here is better management of knowledge, yours and mine. We should know when a new idea is common domain and when it is a promoter's attempt to get us to accept its branded product as the world standard. Common ideas are free to all of us to adopt and adapt, bend and twist, for the sake of betterment. We should protect them from ideas bound to a hidden agenda.

Although data processing is still the strong suit for information technology, IT and e-management open new doors as well. Some doors are wide open, the Internet being the prime example. Others, such as bar-code scanning, are open to selected sectors. Still other IT tools are for use within the given firm. These levels of IT applications are the topics of the next three sections.

INTERNETWORKS

Manufacturers have an attractive new sales outlet: the Internet. If the manufacturer produces consumer goods, however, there is a problem. When a manufacturer of jeans, toasters, or jam tries to do an Internet end run around Costco, Carrefour, or Tesco, the latters' hackles elevate. They tell the manufacturer, Do it and we won't carry your product line anymore. That usually ends the end run.[2]

Too bad for us consumers. The stores are making it hard to bypass a physical visit (and incur the stores' extra costs). Still, the Internet is there, giving consumers new options. Before going to a retailer, we can drop in on various manufacturers' Web sites and study their array of offerings. (The same applies to a buying team evaluating, for purchase, the offerings of several machine-tool manufacturers.) As the Net is further enriched, we may be able to find out which jeans are double stitched. Those who care may check a watchdog site to see if the jeans were made in a sweatshop. All this and more may take place before deciding on a visit to a store. (Or maybe some of it can take place while in the store. Kenneth Kendall raises the specter of you the consumer going to the store with a personal device that can tap the Internet and also scan universal product codes. Before buying, you scan the store's price, which the device compares with what it finds on the Net. You are duly advised whether to buy or not.)[3] The enrichment angle—depth of information available electronically—bears further consideration, next.

Richness and Reach—and Speed

In *Blown to Bits,* authors Evans and Wurster maintain that the Internet eliminates the trade-off between information richness and reach.[4] Conventionally, enrichment happens when someone selling a luxury good takes the time to provide a prospect with details about the product. That kind of information, however, is costly to impart and therefore reaches out only to a select few. The Internet reaches with no end and with rich detail. After the one-time cost of richly loading a site, anyone anywhere can tap it with scarcely any additional cost. Furthermore (a point missed in *Blown to Bits*), the Internet provides speed—instantaneous transmission of rich, wide-reaching information.

That rich/reach/speed combination not only aids the customer, it also opens the door for the manufacturer finally to obtain a flood of valuable information about what customers really like and don't like, want and don't want. Heretofore, organizations have had only primitive methods of finding out customers' concerns. (Doing this well gains points on WCP Principle 2, presented in chapter 2 as a common "blind spot.") Most have not even tried.

FEEDBACK.

Say that you are in an automobile showroom. You get the salesperson's full attention. Then you clearly, pleasantly, and insistently say exactly what the main things are that you do not and do like about the car being shown. Even at the luxury car dealer, the salesperson will not record what you say, nor is there any form or procedure or requirement for doing so. After twenty years of customer-focused total quality under the business world's belts, this deficiency should be shocking. Yet it is the norm in businesses from autos to department stores to public transit.

In other words, the Net is not a substitute. The business world is not blown to bits. Customer-focused management—total quality, if you will—requires the front-line workforce to record every hiccup, glitch, suggestion, or complaint on the spot. Often corrections can take place on the spot. Many more are fixable soon thereafter as area improvement teams sift collected glitch data to find root causes. Most companies, however, fail to do these things well.

To continue with the auto case, Evans and Wurster note a perverse result of the lack of such feedback.[5] Customers in the showrooms rarely find just what they want. Maybe many are looking for a pale blue metallic color, which is scarce in dealers' lots. The salesperson's main job, therefore, is to steer the customer to an available car that is something like what customers want—pale *green* metallic. Not too happy about it, the customer buys. This happens at many dealers, which marketing at the automaker takes as a strong signal of demand for pale green metallic. So production schedules load up even more with that color. And salespeople must work even harder at selling colors customers really do not want. This phenomenon is not limited to consumer goods. Buyers of industrial goods—equipment, MRO (maintenance, repair, and operating supplies), and, to some extent, direct materials—also often buy what they don't really want.

The Internet to the rescue. Via the Net, customers can link directly to those who set master production schedules. An automaker could "require" that all auto buyers spend five minutes at the dealer checking off their strongest preferences on a touch-screen survey form. Preferences for pale blue metallic will be noted. The false feedback—people settling for pale green—will be overridden by what people say rather than what they reluctantly bought. The feed-forward survey data overrules the biased sales data.

HATE SITES.

Moreover, when a consumer is disgruntled about any product or service, there are fast-growing numbers of convenient outlets: hate sites. Or, less pejoratively, feedback sites. Some—for example, walmartsucks.com—are less for consumer feedback and more for someone to air a point of view.[6] Another, not quite of the same ilk, is dunkindonuts.org, created in 1997 by a customer mad that his Dunkin' Donuts store didn't carry skim milk. By August 1999, the site was receiving about six hundred comments monthly. So Dunkin' Donuts bought the site—as a useful source of customer feedback.[7]

Other sites, such as imdb.com (Internet Movie Database), are for polling. Consumers and critics rate and remark on their movie likes and dislikes. While the news media inundate us with movie reviews, this site enriches the data in that it boils down dozens or hundreds of moviegoer opinions. Still other sites are there just to collect consumers' raves and remonstrances about products and services of all kinds. Taking up a full wall of the Alaska Airlines concourse at Seatac airport in Seattle is an ad for one of them: planetfeedback.com. This site collects and demographically sorts wide-ranging complaints and sells the information to companies.[8] But will there be so much feedback that companies won't be able to handle it? The accompanying box

---

Coping with E-Message Overload

Feedback Processors.

Before many years, we all may carry around devices that we will use often for on-the-spot feedback. Will this overwhelm the bank or the taxi company—hundreds of messages per day? Yes, if those handling the feedback are managers. As this book has emphasized repeatedly, that would be poor practice. Instead, use technology to deliver whatever the message is directly to the teller or driver: root-cause improvement at the source. Such feedback could do more for shaping behavior and improving performance than supervisors could ever do using carrot and stick.

Quality Filters.

Speaking of being overwhelmed, how many e-mails do you get per day, and how many are worth even a read? How many magazines and books do you lack the time for—and wonder what you're missing? The info-overload mess requires quality filters.

Ackoff reports on an experiment he and colleagues did years ago. They started with over a hundred articles from five science journals. By a detailed procedure involving well-known experts, they boiled them down to four highly rated and four miserably rated articles. They had professional science writers rewrite and shrink the articles' lengths by two-thirds while retaining all content and then create a separate concise abstract. Next, the original authors were asked to develop test questions on the key messages of the articles. Graduate students read the articles—some the full versions, others the shrunk ones, still others only the abstracts—and took the test. For the four good articles, test scores on the full and reduced versions were the same, but on the abstracts they were much lower. Ackoff's conclusion: "Even scientific writing—which is generally considered to be very compact—could be reduced by at least two-thirds without loss of content." On the low-rated articles, scores for those reading only the abstracts were significantly higher than scores for those reading the article itself! As Ackoff puts it, "This suggested that the optimal length of bad writing is zero."[9]

The world needs more professional rewriters and post-publication critics. They are expensive but can save hundreds of executives and thousands of managers and professionals from wasting time on articles and books that turn out valueless. The other prominent option is computer filtering. For example, one digesting routine uses only first sentences of paragraphs plus bulleted lists. Many more of these crude but efficient routines will be developed. Information is the generator of knowledge, but bad information doesn't qualify.

addresses the question, plus the related one that faces the poor working stiff who receives one hundred–plus e-mails a day.

The planetfeedback.com kinds of feedback sites—those giving entrée to many companies—may not last. There may be no need for them. Instead, use a search engine to go to the provider's own Web site, many of which will take your complaint right there. Regardless of which kind of site, companies badly need the feedback information, for praise or "hate." And in providing both richness and reach, the Internet opens new doors. Most important for this purpose is reach. It is easy for customers to register their opinions, and it will become much more so in the future: easy-to-use devices for sending messages will be everywhere, including on our persons. Second in importance is richness: the Net makes it easy for customers to say a lot to the providing company. *Not* so important, here, is speed—at least in the case of products (for services speed *is* important). Complaint information from customers—preference information, too—needs to find its way to product and service designers and marketers, but it need not get there fast. That kind of feedback is for detecting broad patterns and dealing with more complex issues than can be handled by on-the-spot problem solving.

SCANNING THE SECTORS

On the other hand, for purposes of scheduling, purchasing, and delivery, speed may matter more than either richness or reach. The race starts with scanning a product's bar code to record a usage or a sale. The sprint continues with global positioning satellite (GPS) systems that unerringly dispatch and monitor deliveries. In some sectors, these applications are becoming necessities—keys to speedy response back through logistic, production, and supply stages. The ideal, in some sectors, is continuous replenishment—production and delivery synchronized to actual sales. According to the authors of the definitive work on the subject, bar codes "are one of the major innovations of the last quarter of the twentieth century."[10]

GPS and Bar Coding

Surprisingly, the low-tech cement industry harbors one of the more advanced users of GPS-guided logistics and Internet-based customer relationships. The company is Cemex, the giant Mexico-headquartered manufacturer. Adrian Slywotzky of Mercer Management Consulting, Inc., observes that Cemex has been able to "substitute the management of information for the deployment of costly assets such as trucks, ships, and employees." He considers Cemex to be in a league with Dell and Cisco as one of the world's leading digital reinventors.[11]

The ideal of continuous replenishment is not an issue in the cement industry. It is, however, in the apparel and textile industry, which was the first to employ bar coding for that purpose; other consumer goods sectors have followed. (Continuous replenishment had not been in the vocabulary, or dreams, of apparel people; it simply wasn't possible to replenish stores in the same season. Now it is routine.) While manufacturers in textiles and apparel led these developments, the chain retailers—Wal-Mart and Target, Zara and Benetton—soon took the baton. This is not surprising, since retailing possesses the immediacy of lined-up customers with goods and cash in hand.[12] The Wal-Marts of the world are now often providing manufacturers with much more than latest point-of-sale data. The challenge is to move goods from dock to store shelf in hours rather than the former five days. So manufacturers are increasingly expected to package goods complete with retail price labels, tags, and/or stickers—and sometimes, in the case of garments, on store hangers—provided by the retailer.[13]

Perhaps because the customer is not standing there, manufacturers of industrial products and items sold through distributors tend to lag in making use of bar-code speed. But in one industry, medical supplies, the customer sometimes is standing there, perhaps having a heart attack. Yet until recently, few medical supply manufacturers had been applying bar codes. Nor did hospitals and the rest of the using community press for it, even though the items—everything from gowns to beds to instruments to swabs—account for a considerable proportion of health care costs, not to mention the need for speedy responsiveness.

Pioneering Application in Health Care

An early exception is a three-hundred-bed nonprofit hospital in Bismarck, North Dakota: St. Alexius Medical Center. Frank Kilzer, longtime material resources director, recalls the inventory situation over two decades ago when his department could not account for 20 percent of its supply costs.[14] Fed up, and using retailing as a model, Kilzer got approval to spend $50,000 on a bar-code scanning system. It was a flop. Undeterred, Kilzer worked with the hospital's computer staff to cobble together a workable inventory-tracking system that employed a bar-code scanner, laptop computer, and homegrown software. The cost of the scanning software was only $150. Next issue. Most items received at St. A's lacked a bar code. So in 1985 Kilzer's material resources people began applying bar-code stickers themselves—to each item as it was received. With the system's elements in place and working well, material resources extended the system beyond the stockroom. Scanners went into all nursing stations, operating rooms, the pharmacy, the dialysis center, the print shop, and an off-site receiving warehouse. Inventory unaccounted for dropped to less than 1 percent of costs.

Next step was to apply the system to health care delivery itself. Kilzer's group equipped every patient room with a device that nurses use to record issuance of any kind of item, from a box of facial tissue to a medication from the pharmacy. In every patient room an Etch-A-Sketch-like device hangs in a cradle on a wall at the foot of the bed. The device is a CliniView RF scanner made by CliniCom, a subsidiary of HBOC Co. It has a screen with a wand on a cord and is linked by radio frequency (RF) communication to a central computer containing the patient record and item master file. Each time a procedure or medication is administered or a supply item is used, the nurse carries the CliniView RF unit bedside and records the event by wanding a bar code. This largely stamps out wrongful medications or procedures, chronic kinds of error in hospitals, according to a White House report.[15]

Greg Miller is chief financial officer at St. Alexius and a former materials manager himself. Miller conducted the cost analysis to show that the extra labor and equipment needed to apply their own bar codes easily paid for itself—even to the point of labeling a single, tiny bone screw. (The hospital has successfully tested a miniature bar-code tag the length of the top of a postage stamp and the depth of its border.)[16] The analyses employed activity-based costing methods, which capture nonobvious costs that spill over into multiple departments. Most of those costs, however, would have been avoided if the medical supplies industry had been doing the bar coding at the time of manufacture.

Much of the health care sector is still lagging in use of this technology. It is not too late to do something about it. Every nation frets over high health care costs, and there are few sure ways to make a large dent in those costs. Linking usage of medical supplies to providers and producers *is* a sure way. The Efficient Healthcare Consumer Response (EHCR) initiative, underwritten by a consortium of health care manufacturers, estimates that current distribution practices add up to $23 billion in the United States. The EHCR studies suggest that $11 billion of that, or 48 percent, could be eliminated.[17]

Given the industry's own inertia, it might take governmental action to get results. For example, governments and commissions charged with doing something about out-of-control costs might make the following a priority: 1) Institute measures that require all manufacturers of medical items to put bar-code labels on their products; 2) Provide seed money for hospitals and clinics to install and use bar-code scanners at points of use; 3) Follow through with whatever it takes to get the necessary software into the system to link usage back through the stages in the supply chains.

This book's early chapters presented research data and discussion about inventories as a symptom of much that goes wrong and right in the value chain. Technology was downplayed in those discussions. Here it has been up-played. The reason has to do with IT's power (bar coding's in this case) to connect far-flung elements of the value chain.

IT INSIDE

The 1980s witnessed plentiful debate at manufacturing conferences and in the journals about the role of material requirements planning. MRP had become *the* manufacturing information system. There was no other. The challenge to its domination had arisen out of the simplicity and visual features of just-in-time management. Through the first half of the 1990s, the dominant viewpoint went something like this: MRP was necessary for planning; JIT could take over for execution. Consultants and software vendors said it, and manufacturing people often echoed it.

Then along came enterprise requirements planning. ERP systems, built on MRP platforms, were furiously being installed to beat the year 2000 in-

formation system "crisis." Within months of the turning of the thousand-year calendar, manufacturing people were openly proclaiming their displeasure. ERP was for financial control; in manufacturing it created havoc by requiring inside-the-plant work-flow reporting. That reporting had been found to be redundant and wastefully costly among manufacturers that had simplified processes and slashed throughput times. As Patricia Moody put it, "ERP simply doesn't have the genetic makeup to solve simple factory flow problems—it's not in the genes."[18]

The lean movement had emboldened the manufacturing community. They would accept a little MRP and a little ERP, but no more. Guests touring Lockheed Martin Aeronautics Company in Marietta, Georgia, in connection with a manufacturing conference in that city heard tour guide Bill Rothery state the new, prevailing attitude: The company's lean team aims at reducing reliance on MRP systems, "to get rid of pure schedule-driven movement of parts."[19]

This resistance to new, complex manufacturing systems seems finally to be entrenched. The lean persuasion made it so. Complex systems will still arise and have their day, but manufacturers will no longer meekly accept glowing claims. The following addresses just one such system.

How to Schedule—If at All

IT power, it is claimed, will allow manufacturers to match orders to available capacity, right down to a stamping machine's stroke or a labor hour at a calibrating station. At that fine a level, the term of choice is finite scheduling. It comes as a software package offered by any number of vendors.

It is not hard to find testimonials as to the fine results some manufacturers get from their finite-scheduling package: big gains in on-time performance, higher throughput, and so on. In IT applications, however, the costs and system complexity often outweigh the gains. Also, often enough the fine payoffs might be much finer if the company instead pursued a simple, lean approach with minimal IT. To illustrate these points for the special example of finite scheduling, let us consider how customer orders lurch their way through the scheduling maze.

Infinite Capacity

Before computers and still today in most manufacturing companies, schedules build on the false presumption of infinite capacity. This occurs on three levels:

1. *Customer orders.* Sales beats the bushes to scare up every possible sales order and dumps the orders on manufacturing. The implicit assumption: infinite capacity. (It is not sales' fault that the company lacks a workable system of steering orders to where capacity to produce is or isn't.)

2. *Plant-level production orders.* Manufacturing puts the customer orders into a master production schedule (MPS) that is balanced against average capacity (in labor hours, machine hours, tons, or other units). The MPS aims to fit in all the orders without use of overtime, extra shifts, and other costly measures. Okay so far.

3. *Work center–level production orders.* The master schedule breaks down into detailed schedules of jobs scattered among the work centers. The detailed schedules presume infinite capacity. But, of course, the work does not load evenly. Some work centers will be overloaded, others underloaded. Manufacturing's response is a priority system: wherever jobs stack up, have the work center run the latest jobs first. Overtime, extra shifts, and so on are available in a pinch. It is an imperfect system: some orders will not make it on time, and the expediting to push latest jobs higher on the priority lists is costly and disruptive.

Finite Capacity

Finite scheduling is an alternative. What is required to run it? The U.K. Department of Trade and Industry says this: "FCS systems contain a model of the production process: This model holds details of throughput rates, capacities and other constraints which limit what the factory can do."[20] But will it work? Darrel Vande Hoef, explains the difficulty (using FFS, for "finite forward scheduling," rather than FCS):

> In order for an FFS to function well, information must be deadly accurate, from set-up time, to run time, to wait time, to move time, to queue time; from available capacity time to shift start and stop times to expected downtime; from vacation, holidays, overtime, operator illness or other absence to maintenance schedules. . . . [And] the shop cannot have the kind of variability found in most shops. Setups are expected to take the same amount of time every time.[21]

Accuracy of that data is for accurate planning. In addition, there are the data to be tracked, which Vande Hoef points out is enormous. While the tracking system can be automated, such systems "have their own forms of unanticipated downtime." Vande Hoef notes, further, that companies most in need of FCS (or FFS) are "large job shops with large numbers, divergent types of machines, and complex and diverse routings." That kind of manufacturing seems ripe for FCS, since it has the worst problems of capacity-workload mismatches. But that kind of manufacturer is least likely to be able to muster the data accuracy and invariability to make FCS work. Catch-22.

"In the case of 'simple' companies," opines Vande Hoef, "it is difficult to justify FFS." Yes, such companies are more likely to have good, invariable data. On the other hand, they are likely to have far fewer, more visible, and more manageable capacity problems. Lean flow management thrives when complexities have been removed. No need for FCS.

As to complex companies, what all this says is that they should, with all deliberate speed, devote their main energies to root causes of their complexity. Those were ticked off in chapters 8 and 9, whose main message is, "Get focused." That includes splitting large, complex entities into plants-in-a-plant and flexible cells. Chapter 12 offered specific guidelines, suggesting, by various means, shrinking part counts, suppliers, customers, space, number of people, and so on.

There is a more basic issue here: The preference under the lean way of thinking is to have a master production schedule—what to make and when to get it done—but *not* to do detailed scheduling. The way around scheduling is the pull system: let end-product orders (the MPS) be the trigger for pulling materials from kanban locations back through the production and supply layers. In the transition from large, complex manufacturing units to smaller, more manageable ones, IT-based scheduling is necessary. It starts out covering everything that moves—the MRP way. The first breath of JIT/lean simplicity drives out some of the scheduling. Continuous improvement keeps pushing out more of it as the company strives for zero scheduling. In custom manufacturing that ideal may never quite be reached. But, again quoting from Vande Hoef, "Even most engineer-to-order shops are predominantly repetitive," which means there is underlying simplicity there to exploit with simple, visual flow management systems.

IT'S SHIFTING ROLE: A SUMMARY

The intent of the preceding discussion has not been to dismiss FCS. It is to use FCS as an example, along with MRP and ERP, of how the "lean toward lean" has altered prevailing views of IT systems in manufacturing. In its early days, MRP was the only game in town. It really was. In the 1970s in Western industry, all of the following were deteriorating: care of equipment and of the workforce; closeness to suppliers and customers; product design and development; product costing; labor productivity; and in general, quality, responsiveness, flexibility, and value. As noted in chapter 3, early users of MRP, on the other hand, typically improved on-times and reduced inventories by around 25 percent each. Those were the glory years for production and inventory control and purchasing, since all the other functions were going the wrong way on the effectiveness scale.

Now the worm has turned. IT applications will still have their uses internal to the manufacturing company, though they will have to pass much stronger tests of value than in the past. Manufacturers seeking maximum bang for their IT investments should generally look beyond company walls. The main, untapped potential to get lean and serve the customer through information technology lies in facilitating collaborative activities along the value chains (*hard* value—as noted earlier in the chapter, namely, the study showing how sensitive stock prices are to glitches in the supply chains).

That point serves as a fitting summary message for the book. Manufacturers: Do continue to improve in all aspects of the business. Especially, do this in the outreach mode—bringing your customers and their chains, and suppliers and theirs, into a grand, whole-enterprise, rapidly improving, and continually shifting dynasty.

THE STRONG AND THE WEAK

What manufacturing sectors are most and least competitive, as judged by "leanness"? The half-century analysis of manufacturers' inventory turnovers casts light on the question. In a global sample of over 500 manufacturers, 437 have sufficient years of data to permit rank ordering into strong and weak sectors.

Exhibit A1.1 shows the rankings. To get them, inventory turnovers for each of the 437 companies were examined. Strongest companies were judged to be those showing a fifteen-to-fifty-year trend in improving inventory turnovers. Those manufacturers received two weighting points. A third weighting point went to the same companies *if their positive trends did not lapse in the most recent five to seven years.* All the companies had been placed in up to three industry sectors. The result is Exhibit A1.1.

INTERPRETATION

The fifteen manufacturers making up the semiconductor sector rank highest, and the forty-four companies in the total electronics sectors are next highest. Those sectors have the best records of getting lean as measured by improving inventory turns. Why? Best answer is that electronics is more globalized than other industries. The sector is so dynamic and the product so easily shippable, one's competitors may be anywhere in the world.

Furniture, next, has too few companies to be meaningful. Also, the sample is upwardly biased by inclusion of Hon Industries and Herman Miller, both of which were among the West's earliest manufacturers to embrace just-in-time.

Most of the other higher-ranked sectors—left side of the exhibit—have lean roots in Japan. That carries over to competitors elsewhere in the world. Most of the lower-ranked industries, those on the right, are opposite: most have lacked global and Japanese competition, which is the main trigger for improvement. One surprise is retail/distribution, ranked thirteen. The sector should have benefited greatly from point-of-sale scanning and electronic data interchange and now from Internet/Web technologies. Retailers such as Wal-Mart have pioneered innovations including cross-docking, supplier-managed inventory, and continuous replenishment. These drive out waste of various kinds and shrink inventories. Apparently, not enough retailers, wholesalers, and distribution centers have adopted these initiatives to put the sector on the left side of the exhibit.

	SECTORS	SAMPLE SIZE		SECTORS	SAMPLE SIZE
1	Semiconductors	15	13	Retail/Distribution	23
2	Electronics, including		14	Pump/Hydraulic/Pressure	21
	Semiconductors	44	15	Aerospace/Defense	23
3	Furniture	8	16	Food & Beverage	35
4	Heavy Industrial Vehicles	18	17	Basic Metal Processors	19
5	Autos/Light Trucks	16	18	Telecom	12
6	Machinery/Large Appliances	33	19	Pharmaceuticals	15
7	Sheet Metal	12	20	Chemicals	16
8	Automotive Parts	26	21	Liquids/Gases/Grains/	
9	Metalworking/Machining	33		Powders	56
11	Medical Devices	21	22	Paper Manufacturing	25
12	Plastic/Rubber/Glass/Leather		23	Paper-Converted Products	18
	(Incl. Floor Tile and Insulation)	32	24	Printing	11

*Positive trend of 15 to 50 years weighted 2 points; lack of recent lapse 1 point

*Exhibit A1.1. Lean Manufacturing Trends
Evidenced by Positive Inventory Turnover Patterns
Without Recent Lapses—Best to Worst, by Sector**

SUBGROUPS

Exhibits A1.2 and A1.3 provide backup data. A1.2 shows sector rank ordering based on companies that have fifteen-to-fifty-year improvement trends. All fifteen companies in the semiconductor sector have fifteen or more years of inventory improvement. Exhibit A1.2 shows, however, that two of the fifteen (13 percent) lapsed in the last five to seven years. To explain the weighting system, thirteen of the semiconductor group received three weighting points; the other two in the group received two weighting points.

INDUSTRIAL SECTOR	SAMPLE SIZE	PERCENT OF SAMPLE EXHIBITING IMPROVEMENT PATTERN (BEST TO WORST)
Semiconductors	15	100%
Heavy Industrial Vehicles	18	94
Electronics, incl. Semiconductors	44	89
Furniture	8	88
Sheet Metal	12	83
Automotive Parts	26	81
Autos/Light Trucks	16	80
Machinery/Large Appliances	33	79
Metalworking/Machining	33	79
Medical Devices	21	76
Plastic/Rubber/Glass/Leather (including Floor Tile/Insulation)	32	72
Average, All 23 Sectors	**437**	**72**
Aerospace/Defense	23	70
Telecom	12	67
Pharmaceuticals	15	67
Pump/Hydraulic/Pressure	21	66
Basic Metal Processors	19	63
Retail/Distribution	23	61
Food & Beverage	35	60
Liquids/Gases/Grain/Powders	56	57
Chemicals	16	50
Paper-Converted Products	18	44
Paper Manufacturing	25	36
Printing	11	36

Exhibit A1.2. Lean Manufacturing Trends—Evidenced by 15-to-50-Year Rising Inventory Turnover, by Sector

INDUSTRIAL SECTOR	SAMPLE SIZE	PERCENT OF SAMPLE EXHIBITING RECENT LAPSES (BEST TO WORST)
Semiconductors	15	13%
Furniture	8	14
Retail/Distribution	23	21
Electronics, including Semiconductors	44	23
Machinery/Large Appliances	33	23
Autos/Light Trucks	16	33
Food & Beverage	35	33
Metalworking/Machining	33	35
Plastic/Rubber/Glass/Leather (including Floor Tile/Insulation)	32	35
Pump/Hydraulic/Pressure	21	36
Average, All 23 Sectors	**437**	**40**
Sheet Metal	12	40
Basic Metal Processors	19	42
Automotive Parts	26	43
Medical Devices	21	44
Liquids/Gases/Grain/Powders	56	44
Paper Manufacturing	25	44
Heavy Industrial Vehicles	18	47
Aerospace/Defense	23	50
Printing	11	50
Pharmaceuticals	15	60
Telecom	12	62
Paper-Converted Products	18	62

Exhibit A1.3. Lapsed Positive Trends in Lean Manufacturing—Improved Inventory Turnover Patterns Halted in Recent 5 to 7 Years, by Sector

Notable among lowest-ranking sectors are paper-converted products, printing, and paper manufacturing. Only 44 percent, or eight, of the eighteen paper-converted products companies have get-lean trends of fifteen years or more. And of that eight, 62 percent, or five, lapsed in recent years. Printing and paper manufacturing are similar. Interviews with executives at two of the manufacturers, Weyerhaeuser and Boise Cascade, yielded no insights as to why.

WCP INTERNATIONAL BENCHMARKING STUDY PARTICIPANTS AND GLOBAL BENCHMARKING PARTNERS

PARTICIPANTS

United States

AAI Corp., Hunt Valley, MD (defense products: unmanned aerial vehicles; test and simulation devices)

A-C Compressor Corp., Appleton, WI (compressors)

Accurate Partitions, Lyons, IL (toilet partitions)

ADAC Laboratories, San Jose, CA (diagnostic medical imaging)

Aeroquip Corp, New Haven, IN (marine products and Teflon bulk hose)

Aeroquip Corp., Middlesex, NC (air-conditioning products)

Aerospace company (anonymous), Los Angeles, CA

Ahlstrom Pumps LLC, Easley, SC (centrifugal process pumps)

Ajax Boiler, Inc., Santa Ana, CA (heat transfer boilers, water heaters)

Alaris Medical Systems, Creedmoor, NC (infusion pumps, patient monitoring devices, and disposable medical components)

Albany International, Albany, NY (paper machine press felts)

Alcatel Network Systems, Inc., Raleigh, NC (telecommunications equipment)

Alcatel Network Systems, Richardson, TX (telecommunication equipment)

Alcatel Submarine Networks, Inc., Portland, OR (underwater fiber optic cable systems)

Allergan Inc., Hormigueros, Puerto Rico (pharmaceuticals)

Allied-Signal, Inc., Kansas City, MO (non-nuclear components for nuclear weapons)

Allied-Signal fluid systems, Tempe, AZ (starters, valves, actuators)

Amadas Industries, Suffolk, VA (agricultural machinery)

American Steel Service Center, Kent, WA (steel distribution)

Analog Devices Inc., Wilmington, MA (electronics, semiconductors)

Andrew Corp., Orland Park, IL (heliax cable and accessories)

Anonymous, U.S. (paper towel and napkin products)

Arkansas Eastman Div., Eastman Chemical Co., Batesville, AR (specialty chemicals)

Armour-Swift-Eckrich, Downers Grove, IL (packaged and frozen meat products)

Arrow Group Industries, Breese, IL (metal storage bins)

Arrow Group—Whole company, Haskell, NJ (metal storage bins)

A. T. Cross Co., Lincoln, RI (quality writing instruments)

Atlantic Envelope Co., Shelbyville, KY (envelopes)

ATL, Bothell, WA (medical ultrasound equipment)

Automated Assemblies Corp., a Nypro Co., Clinton, MA (robots and automated work cells)

Avery Dennison, Specialty Tape Division, Painesville, OH (pressure-sensitive adhesive tape)

AVX, Kyocera Group, Vancouver, WA (electronic components, ceramic capacitors)

A. W. Chesterton Company, Groveland, MA (fluid sealing systems, chemical maintenance products)

Baldor Electric, Fort Smith, AR (industrial electric motors)

Bama Pie, Ltd., Tulsa, OK (fresh and frozen bakery products, trucking)

Barry Controls Aerospace, Burbank, CA (engine vibration isolation/cabin noise reduction)

Baxter Healthcare Corp, Cleveland, MS (pharmaceuticals)

Baxter Healthcare Corp., Mountain Home, AR (plastic disposable medical products)

Baxter Healthcare, Marion, NC (intravenous solutions)

Bayside Motion Group, Port Washington, NY (precision gearheads, linear motion products)

Bearse Manufacturing Co., New Windsor, NY (soft luggage, office machine covers, other sewn products)

Becton Dickinson, Sandy, UT (intravenous catheters)

Becton Dickinson, Sandy, UT (medical scrub brushes)

Becton Dickinson, Holdrege, NE (hypodermic needles)

Bio Clinic, Ontario, CA (health care pressure reduction products)

Blackmer, Compressor Div., Oklahoma City, OK (gas compressors)

Blount, Inc., Oregon Cutting Tools Div., Portland, OR (cutting chain for chain saws, accessory products)

Boeing Defense & Space Group, Oak Ridge, TN (sheet metal, machining, assembly)

Boeing Door Center, Renton, WA (aircraft doors and hatches)

Boeing Welded Duct plant, Auburn, WA (aircraft ducting)

Borden Chemical, Kent, WA (resins and chemicals)

Boston Scientific Corp., Redmond, WA (medical devices for coronary artery disease via less invasive surgery)

BPI, Kent, WA (office furniture)

Brady ISST North America, Milwaukee, WI (portable printers, software, labels, ribbons, applicators)

C. Lee Cook, Louisville, KY (sealing devices)

Cadillac Gage/HR Textron, Greenville, OH (turret control systems)

Capsugel—Greenwood, SC, Plant, Greenwood, SC (hard gelatin capsules)

Carpenter Technologies, Reading, PA (specialty steels)

Carrier Access Corp., Boulder, CO (telecommunications equipment)

Case Corporation—Racine Transmission Plant, Racine, WI (heavy-duty transmissions and axles, hydraulic control valves)

Charles Machine, Perry, OK (underground construction equipment)

Chicago Metal Rolled Products Co., Chicago, IL (custom metal bending, curving, rolling)

Chief Automotive Systems Inc., Grand Island, NE (collision repair equipment)

The Clarkson Co., Sparks, NE (industrial valves)

Coach Leatherwear, Lars, PR (leatherwear)

Coach Leatherwear, Medley, FL (leatherwear)

Coherent, Inc., Auburn, CA (laser manufacturing)

Columbia Forest Products, Greensboro, NC (hardwood plywood)

Continental-General Tire, Mt. Vernon, IL (passenger and truck tires)

Cook Airtomic, Louisville, KY (piston rings)

Cooper Automotive-Wagner Lighting Products, Hampton, VA (automotive exterior lighting)

Copeland, Sidney, OH (air-conditioning and refrigeration compressors)

Dana Corp., Minneapolis (hydraulic control valves)

Dana Corp., Parish Frame Div., Stockton, CA (truck frames)

Dana Corp., Spicier Heavy Systems Assembly Div., Lancaster, PA (heavy truck chassis assembly)

Dana Spicier Axle Div., Columbia, MO (automotive axle assembly)

Darling Store Fixtures, Paragould, AR (store fixtures)

Deere and Co., John Deere Horicon, Horicon, WI (lawn and garden ride-on products)

Dell Computer, Round Rock, TX (assemble-to-order personal computers)

Digital Systems International, Redmond, WA (call management systems/services)

DJ/Nypro, El Paso, TX (injection molding)

Double G Coatings, Jackson, MS (galvanized and galvalume sheet steel)

DovaTech, Ltd., Beecher, IL (welding guns, torches, plasma cutting products)

Dover Elevator Systems, Middleton, TN (cabs, entrances, signals)

Dover Elevator Systems, Walnut, MS (elevator controllers)

Dover Elevator, Horn Lake, MS (hydraulic power units, jacks, car slings, platforms)

Dow Corning, Hemlock, MI (silicone elastomer, tubing, misc. fluids)

Dow Corning, Midland, MI (silicon intermediates and finished products)

Dow-Key Microwave, Unit of K&L Microwave, Ventura, CA (switch products)

Du Pont Furnishings, Camden, SC (nylon carpet yarn)

Dynametal Technologies, Brownsville, TN (powder metal bearings and structurals)

Eastman Kodak Co., C.I. Worldwide Single-Use Camera Business, Rochester, NY (single-use camers)

Eaton Corp., Everett, WA (optical control devices)

Eaton Corp., Forge Division, South Bend, IN (custom gear blanks)

Eaton/Cutler Hammer, Automation Products Div., Watertown, WI (printed circuit boards)

Ennis Automotive, Ennis, TX (remanufacture of armatures, copper motor windings, stators)

Exxon Baytown, Baytown, TX (chemicals)

Federal Signal Corp., University Park, IL (industrial signals)

Fender Musical Instruments, Corona, CA (guitars and amplifiers)

Fireking International, Inc., New Albany, IN (fireproof files, safes, gun safes)

Fluke Corp., Everett (electronic test instruments)

Folger Coffee Co., Kansas City, MO (roast and ground coffee)

Ford North Penn Electronics, Lansdale, PA (automotive electronics)

Four Seasons, Coppell, TX (remanufacture of auto A/C compressors, etc.)

The Foxboro Co., Foxboro, MA (process instrumentation)

Framatome Technologies, Lynchburg, VA (nuclear fuel)

Freudenberg-NOK General Partnership, Cleveland, GA (oil seals and valve stem seals)

Furon Co., Cape Coral, FL (heat-traced lines)

Gabilan Mfg., Inc., Salinas, CA (custom manufacturing—OE products)

Gates Rubber, Denver, CO (industrial belts and hoses)

GE, ED&C Div., Auburn, ME (components for electrical devices)

Gelman Sciences, Inc., Ann Arbor, MI (cartridges and capsule microfiltration devices)

Genie Industries, Redmond, WA (industrial lifts)

Gentex Corp., Zeeland, MI (automatic dimming rearview mirrors, commercial bldg. fire-protection devices)

Geon Co., Terre Haute, IN (vinyl compounds)

Gilbarco, Inc., Greensboro, NC (service station gasoline pumps and control equipment)

Gillette, Andover Manufacturing Center, Andover, MA (toiletries, blade shaver assembly)

Gleason Works, Rochester, NY (machine tools)

GM Corp., Delphi Energy & Engine Mgmt. Systems Div., Grand Rapids, MI (valve lifters)

Graco, Minneapolis, MN (industrial and paint pumping equipment)

Grafalloy Div., True Temper Sports, El Cajon, CA (composite golf shafts)

Graphics Microsystems, Inc., Sunnyvale, CA (industrial controls)

Guidant Corp., Temecula, CA (disposable and implantable medical devices)

Hach Company, Loveland, CO (water analysis instrumentation)

Hallmark Cards, Kansas City, MO (greeting cards, boxed cards, envelopes)

Harland Co., SE Regional Printing Facility, Greensboro, NC (check printing)

Harris Corp.—Farinon Div., San Antonio, TX (full-featured, high-capacity, custom microwave radios)

Haworth, Inc., Holland, MI (office furniture)

H. E. Microwave, Tucson, AZ (microwave/millimeter wave—T/R modules)

Hewlett-Packard, San Jose, CA (optocouplers, fiber optics, etc.)

Hill-Rom, Batesville, IN (medical headwall systems)

Hitachi Automotive Products, Torrance, CA (remanufacturing and distributing generators and alternators)

Homexx International, Corona, CA (ceramic faucet handles and decorative cabinet knobs and pulls)

Honeywell Home & Building Control, Golden Valley, MN (HVAC controls)

Honeywell Industrial Automation Systems, Phoenix (process, field, and production control systems)

Honeywell Sensor and Guidance Products, Clearwater, FL (navigation systems)

IBM Corp., Rochester, MN (AS/400 midrange commercial computers)

Instromedix, Hillsboro, OR (cardiac monitoring products)

Intel Puerto Rico, Las Piedras, PR (desktop mother boards, server boards, network adapter cards)

Intel, Fab 6, Chandler, AZ (semiconductors)

Interface, Inc., Scottsdale, AZ (load cells)

Intermec, Everett, WA (barcode printers, readers, scanners)

International Rectifier, Temecula, CA (semiconductors—hexfets)

ITT McDonnell & Miller, Chicago, IL (boiler controls)

ITW-Signode Engineered Products, Glenview, IL (strapping tools, machines and strapping heads)

JE Pistons, Huntington Beach, CA (high-performance race-car pistons)

JLG Industries, McConnellsburg, PA (mobile aerial work platforms)

Joerns Healthcare, Stevens Point, WI (nursing home beds, furniture)

John Crane Belfab, Daytona Beach, FL (edge-welded metal bellows)

Johnson & Johnson Medical, Inc., Southington, CT (peripheral intravenous catheters)

Johnson Controls, Inc. Battery Plant, Middletown, DE (automotive batteries)

Johnson Controls, Milwaukee, WI (valves, screw machine parts)

Jostens, Denton, TX (class rings)

Jostens Cap and Gown, Laurens, SC (graduation apparel)

Jostens Diplomas, Red Wing, MN (diplomas)

K&L Microwave, Coles Circle Plant, Salisbury, MD (tunable/wireless microwave products)

K&L Microwave, Northwood Facility, Salisbury, MD (microwave components and subsystems)

Kawasaki, Maryville, MO (small gasoline engines)

Kennametal Inc., Metalworking Manufacturing Div., Johnson City, TN (metalworking products)

Kennametal, Inc., Latrobe, PA (carbide cutting tools)

Kennametal, Inc., Solon, OH (tool holders and work holding products)

Kerr-McGee Chemical Corp., Hamilton Electrolytic Plant, Hamilton, MS (electro-chemicals)

Kinetic Concepts, Inc., San Antonio, TX (medical devices)

KMC Systems, Merrimack, NH (medical devices)

Kondik Advertising & Printing, Inc., Bedford Heights, OH (offset and screen printing, distribution of promotional products)

K-Products, Inc., Orange City, IA (promotional headwear and wearables)

K2 Corp., Vashon Island, WA (skis, inline skates)

Landa, Inc., Portland, OR (pressure washers and water cleaning systems)

Lebanon Seaboard Corp., Lebanon, PA (fertilizers and seeds)

Lemco Miller Corp., Danvers, MA (contract machined parts)

Lifeline Systems, Inc., Cambridge, MA (emergency/personal-response services)

Lincoln Industrial, St. Louis, MO (lubrication equipment and pumps)

Linfinity Microelectronics, Garden Grove, CA (integrated circuits)

Lockheed Martin, Gov't. Electronic Systems, Moorestown, NJ (phased-array radars and sophisticated electronics)

Logistix, Fremont, CA (integrated supply-chain management, turnkey supplier)

Lucas Aerospace Cargo Systems, Jamestown, NY (aircraft cargo handling systems, aerostructures)

Lucent Technologies, Columbus, OH (telecommunications systems)

Lucent Technologies, Oklahoma City, OK (wireless, switching, networking comm. infrastructure products)

M&M/Mars Confectionery Co., Hackettstown, NJ (confectionery products)

Mark Andy Inc., St. Louis, MO (flexographic web presses)

Marlow Industries, Dallas, TX (thermoelectric heat pumps and cooling systems)

McDonnell Douglas Helicopter, Mesa, AZ (helicopters)

Medtronic Promeon, Brooklyn Center, MN (medical device components)

Melroe Company, Bismarck, ND (compact mobile construction equipment)

MEMC Electronic Materials, Inc., St. Peters, MO (polished and epitaxial silicon wafers)

Merix, Portland, OR (printed circuit boards)

Metrex Valve Corp., Glendora, CA (self-contained water-regulating valves for HVAC industry)

Mid-America Packaging Div., Gaylord Container, Pine Bluff, AR (multiwall bags)

Midland Communications Packaging Inc., Louisville, KY (custom looseleaf binders, etc.)

Milgard Manufacturing Co., Tacoma, WA (doors)

Miller Brewing Co., Trenton, OH (beer)

Milliken, Business A (textiles)

Milliken, Business B (textiles)

Milliken, Business C (textiles)

Milliken, Business D (chemicals)

Milton-Bradley Co., East Longmeadow, MA (games, puzzles, toys)

Mine Safety Appliance Co., Instrument Div., Pittsburgh, PA (instruments)

Mine Safety Appliance Co., Safety Products Div., Murrysville, PA (safety equipment)

Mine Safety Appliances, Murraysville plant, Murrysville, PA (safety equipment)

Mine Safety Appliances, Jacksonville, NC (personal safety products)

MKS Instruments, UTi Div.—East, Walpole, MA (process monitor equipment, gas analyzers)

Monarch Marking Systems, Miamisburg, OH (marking equipment)

Murrary, Inc., Brentwood, TN (lawn and garden equipment, bicycles, snow removal equipment, toys, gokarts)

Nashua Corp., Nashua, NH (dry toners and developers for copiers and printers)

Nicolet Instrument Corp., Madison, WI (infrared spectrometers)

Northwest Manufacturing, Inc., Redmond, WA (precision sheet metal fabrication)

Novacap, Valencia, CA (multilayer chip and specialty capacitors)

Novartis Consumer Health, Inc., Lincoln, NE (pharmaceuticals)

Nypro Alabama Inc., Dothan, AL (injection molding)

Nypro Asheville Inc., Asheville, NC (injection molding)

Nypro Atlanta, Marietta, GA (injection molding for automotive, consumer, industrial, telecommunications)

Nypro Chicago, Gurnee, IL (plastics injection molding)

Nypro, Clinton, Clinton, MA (custom-molded plastic components)

Nypro Colorado, Inc., Loveland, CO (custom injection molding and related manufacturing solutions)

Nypro Iowa, Mt. Pleasant, IA (custom injection molding)

Nypro Medical, Inc., Clinton, MA (medical disposable valves)

Nypro Oregon, Corvallis, OR (custom-molded injection plastic parts)

Nypro Puerto Rico, Inc., Cayey, PR (plastics)

OPW Fueling Components, Cincinnati, OH (dispensing products)

Oral-B Laboratories, Iowa City, IA (manual and interdental toothbrushes)

Parker Hannifin Corp., Brookville, OH (tube fittings)

Peerless Chain, Winona, MN (chain and wireform products)

Pella Corp., Pella, IA (windows and doors)

Physio Control, Redmond, WA (defibrillators)

Pilot Chemical Corp., Red Bank, NJ (detergents)

Piper Impact, New Albany, MS (cold-forming; impact-extrusion of metals)

Pitney Bowes, Inc., Stamford, CT (postage meters, mailing machines, inserters)

Planters-Lifesavers, Fort Smith, AR (peanuts and tree nuts)

PowerBar, Boise, ID (athletic energy goods: Performance/Harvest bars)

Powerware Small Systems Group, San Diego, CA (uninterruptible power supplies)

PRC Laser, Landing, NJ (high-power CO_2 lasers)

Precor, Bothell, WA (aerobic exercise equipment)

Printronix, Irving, CA (computer printers)

Quickie Designs, Inc., Fresno, CA (manual and power wheelchairs)

R. A. Jones, Covington, KY (packaging machines)

Raychem Corp., Palo Alto, CA (cross-linked polymer products)

Raytheon-TI Systems, Lewisville TX (missiles, radars, forward-looking infrared components)

Reliance Electric, Flowery Branch, GA (electric motors)

Richards/OPW, Rockwood, TN (remanufacture gasoline nozzles, valves, and fittings)

Riverwood International, Perry, GA (folding cartons)

Rockwell Automation, Drives & Motions Control Group, Mequon, WI (industrial automation)

Rockwell International, Collins Avionics & Communications Div., Cedar Rapids, IA (avionics and communications products)

Rosemount Measurement, Chanhassen, MN (pressure products)

Rotary Lift, Madison, IN (automotive lifts, alignment racks)

R. W. Beckett, Elyria, OH (residential and commercial oil burners)

R. W. Lyall, Corona, CA (gas-distribution products)

Safetran Systems Corp., Rancho Cucamonga, CA (railroad communications and signal devices)

Sanmina Cable Systems, Carrollton, TX (cable and electronic manufacturing services)

Sargent Controls & Aerospace, Tucson, AZ (hydraulic valves and bearings)

Schindler Elevator Corp., Clinton, NC (escalators)

Schrock Cabinet. Co., Hilliard, OH (kitchen cabinets and bathroom vanities)

Senco Products, Inc., Cincinnati, OH (precision, collated nails and staples)

Servend International, Sellersburg, IN (ice machines, drink/ice dispensers)

Shade Foods, Inc., New Century, KS (food ingredients)

Siecor Corp., Hickory, NC (telecommunications fiber-optic cable)

Siecor Corp., Keller, TX (telecommunications fiber-optic connection equipment)

Signicast Corp., Milwaukee, WI (investment castings)

SLC Technologies, Inc., Hickory, NC (security equipment)

Smith & Wesson, Springfield, MA (firearms)

Solectron Washington, Marysville, WA (electronic manufacturing services)

Sonic Industries, Inc., Torrance, CA (aerospace fasteners)

Spartan Engine Supply, Phoenix, AZ (remanufactured automobile and truck engines)

Square D Co., Middletown, OH (electrical switchgear and heavy-duty safety switches)

Square D Company, Asheville, NC (electrical distribution equipment)

Square D Company, Groupe Schneider NA, Columbia, SC (motor-control equipment)

Stanadyne Automotive Corp., Diesel Systems Div., Windsor, CT (diesel fuel injection equipment)

Stryker Instruments, Kalamazoo, MI (surgical powered instruments)

Stryker-Osteonics Corp., Allendale, NJ (orthopedic implants)

Super Sack Manufacturing Corp., Savoy, TX (flexible intermediate bulk containers)

SWF Companies, Sanger Plant, Sanger, CA (packaging equipment)

System Sensor, St. Charles, IL (commercial smoke detectors)

Tarby Progressing Cavity Pumps, Claremore, OK (pumps)

Taylor Building Products, West Branch, MI (insulated garage doors and entry doors)

Tektronix Cable Analysis Networks Div., Redmond, OR (cable testers)

Teledyne Analytical Instruments, City of Industry, CA (analytical instruments)

Teledyne Controls, Los Angeles, CA (airborne/ground-based electronics)

Teledyne Electronic Technology, Advanced Manufacturing, Lewisburg, TN (contract manufacturing—aerospace, medical, and communications)

Teledyne Electronic Technology, Electronic Devices, Kinetics, San Diego, CA (SMT connectors, aerospace switches, and wire strippers)

Teledyne Electronic Technology, HQ, Los Angeles, CA (electronics)

Teledyne Electronic Technology, Medical Devices, Los Angeles, CA (pacemakers, EEG amplifiers and recorders)

Teledyne Electronic Technology, Halco, Londonderry, NH (hot-air solder leveling, spray application systems)

Teledyne Electronic Technology, Vacuum Technology, Rancho Cordova, CA (traveling wave tubes)

Teledyne Micro Electronics, Los Angeles, CA (solid-state, fiber optics, and RJ modules)

Teledyne Printed Circuit Technology, Hudson, NH (flexible and rigid-flex printed circuits)

Teledyne Relays, Hawthorne, CA (electromechanical devices)

Teledyne T.E.T. Microwave Components SBU, Mountain View, CA (microwave components)

Teledyne T.E.T. Hastings Instruments, Hampton, VA (vacuum and flow measurements instruments)

Tellabs, Inc., Bolingbrook, IL (telecommunications transmission and access products)

Tennalum—Kaiser Aluminum, Jackson, TN (hard-alloy aluminum machining stock)

Tennant Co., Minneapolis, MN (industrial floor sweepers and scrubbers)

Texace Corp., San Antonio, TX (headwear: caps, visors, hats, straw hats)

Texas Instruments, Lubbock, TX (semiconductor chips)

Textron Marine and Land Systems, New Orleans, LA (marine craft and combat vehicles)

Textron Systems Corp., SFW Manufacturing/Engineering, Wilmington, MA (sensor-fused weapons)

Thomas Steel Strip Corp., Warren, MI (cold-rolled steel strip, plain and plated)

3M Printing & Publishing, Weatherford, OK (proofing film)

3M Valley Plant, Valley, NE (industrial respirators and medical devices)

Timken Co., Altavista, VA (tapered roller bearings)

Titeflex, Inc., Springfield, MA (custom industrial hoses)

Trident Precision Manufacturing, Inc., Webster, NY (sheet metal fabrication, electromechanical assemblies)

Tri-Tronics, Inc., Tucson, AZ (electronic dog-training equipment)

TRW—Sterling Plant, Sterling Heights, MI (automotive steering and suspension components)

TRW Inc., Vehicle Safety Systems Inc., Cookeville, TN (automotive safety components)

Tulsa Winch, Jenks, OK (industrial winches and speed reducers)

United Electric Controls, Watertown, MA (temperature and pressure controls, sensors, recorders)

United Electric Supply Co., Inc., Wilmington, DE (electrical supplies)

United States Pipe & Foundry, Birmingham, AL (ductile iron water pipe)

U.S. Steel, Irvin Plant, Dravosburg, PA (low-carbon sheet steel, galvanized sheet steel)

Varian Associates, Oncology Systems, Palo Alto, CA (linear accelerators)

Varian Associates, Palo Alto, CA (nuclear magnetic resonance instruments)

Varian Vacuum Products Lexington, Lexington, MA (vacuum products)

Vectron Labs, Hudson, NH (oscillators, saw filters, timing recovery units)

Vectron Labs, Norwalk, CT (crystal oscillators)

Vermeer Manufacturing Co., Pella, IA (balers, other heavy agricultural equipment)

VIOX Corp., Seattle, WA (electronic glass products)

Vitronics Soltec, Stratham, NH (reflow soldering ovens, curing/cleaning equipment for semiconductor industry)

Vitt Kogyo S.A. de C.V., San Ysidro, CA (machine-shop and wholesale industrial supplies)

Wainwright Industries, St. Peters, MO (aerospace and automotive components)

Warner Electric Motors & Controls, Bristol, CT (AC-DC motors and electronic controls)

Waukesha Bearings Co., Antigo, WI (fluid film bearings, torque tools)

West Bend Company, West Bend, WI (small electrical appliances and cookware)

Wheelabrator, LaGrange, GA (shot-blasting machines)

Whirlpool Corp., Clyde, Ohio (clothes washers)

Whirlpool Corp., Fort Smith, AR (major home appliances)

White Cap, Downers Grove, IL (metal and plastic closures for glass and plastic jars and bottles)

Wilson Greatbatch Ltd., Clarence, NY (batteries, components, devices)

Wilson Sporting Goods Co., Humboldt, TN (golf balls)

Woodford Manufacturing Co., Colorado Springs, CO (valves, plastics)

Wood Tech, Inc., Cottage Grove, OR (massage furniture)

Wright Line Div., Applied Power, Inc., Worcester, MA (technical environments and enclosures)

XEL Communications, Aurora, CO (telecommunications)

York International Corp., San Antonio, TX (commercial air-conditioning equipment)

Zebco Corp., Tulsa, OK (fishing tackle, trolling motors, and associated equipment)

Zebra Technologies, Vernon Hills, IL (printers)

Americas (Other than United States)

A. G. Professional Haircare Products Ltd., Burnaby, BC, Canada (shampoos, conditioners, styling products)

Albany International, Perth Forming, Perth, ON, Canada (forming fabrics)

Axa Yazaki, Monterrey, Mexico (automobile wire harnesses)

Baxter Corp., Alliston, ON, Canada (IV solutions, nutritional and irrigation solutions)

Becton Dickinson Vascular Access, S.A. de C.V., Nogales, Sonora, Mexico (medical disposable devices)

Bird Packaging, Guelph, ON, Canada (corrugated packaging solutions)

Câble Alcan—Lapointe, Div. of d'Alcan Aluminium Limitée, Jonquiére, Québec, Canada (wire and cable)

Dover Elevator, Mississauga, ON, Canada (elevators)

Ford Electronics, Markham, ON, Canada (automotive electronics)

G. E. Multilin, Markham, ON, Canada (microprocessor-based power system protection relays)

Grote Industries de Mexico, S.A. de C.V., Monterrey, Mexico (lights for trucks and trailers, harnesses for trailers)

Harris Farinon Div., Québec, Canada (digital microwave radios)

Inglis Ltd., Cambridge, ON, Canada (clothes dryers, trash compactors)

Johnson Controls, Inc., Juárez, Chih, Mexico (pressure/temperature electromechanical devices)

KI Pembroke, Pembroke, ON, Canada (filing, storage, and desk manufacturing)

Krupp Fabco, Windsor, ON, Canada (metal stamping for automotive industry)

Levical division of Leviton, Tecate, BC, Mexico (electrical products)

Mercedes-Benz do Brasil—Axles, São Bernado do Campo, SP, Brazil

Metalsa S.A., Apodaca, N.L., Mexico (fuel tanks and pickup frames)

Multibras, Rio Claro Plant, Brazil (clothes washers)

Nhumo, Altamira, Tamaulipas, Mexico (chemicals)

Northern Telecom, Calgary, Alberta, Canada (telephones)

Nypro Precision Assemblies, Tijuana, BC, Mexico (contract assembly)

Philips Component Group, Juárez, Chih, Mexico (transformers)

Philips Consumer Electronics, El Paso/Juárez, Chih, Mexico (TVs, etc.)

Philips Modular Systems Plant #4, Juárez, Mexico (remote control, PC boards)

Philips Plant #5, TV plant, Juárez, Chih, Mexico (TVs)

Plamex, Tijuana, BC, Mexico (headsets)

Polywheels Manufacturing Ltd., Oakville, ON, Canada (aftermarket and OEM wheeled products)

Powerware Small Systems Group, Tijuana, BC, Mexico (uninterruptible power supplies)

Raychem Interconnect, Tijuana, BC, Mexico (electronics)

Rockwell Automation, Allen-Bradley, Cambridge, ON, Canada (adjustable frequency drives and system products)

Transmissiones de Patencia Emerson SA de CV, El Salto, Jalisco, Mexico (ball bearings, sprockets, gears)

TRW Canada Ltd., Tillsonburg, ON, Canada (automotive linkages and suspension products)

United Technologies Automotive, Juárez, Chih, Mexico (wiring harnesses)

Whirlpool Puntana S.A., San Luis, Argentina (refrigerators, washing machines)

Yazaki—Autocircuitos de Obregon, YNA-CBU, Cd. Obregon, Sonora, Mexico (automotive wiring harnesses—Chrysler)

Yazaki—Autoelectonica de Juárez, Cd. Juárez, Chih., Mexico (auto wiring harnesses)

Yazaki—Circuitos Mexicanos de Nogales, Nogales, Sonora, Mexico (automotive wiring harnesses)

Yazaki-EWD Group, Pedsa Operations, Cd. Juárez, Chih, Mexico (auto wiring harnesses)

Yazaki—Productos Electricos Diversificados, Cd. Juárez, Chih. Mexico (auto wiring harnesses)

Europe/United Kingdom

Ahlstrom Pumps Corp., Mänttä, Finland (specialty pumps)

Aritech Europe, Dusermond, Holland (security equipment)

BICC Components Ltd., Prescott, Merseyside, U.K. (cable components)

Caradon Trend, Horsham, West Sussex, U.K. (advanced electronics for building control)

Dell Computer, Limerick, Ireland (desktop and notebook PCs)

Dow Corning, Barry, Wales, U.K. (silicone liquids and rubber)

Enermet GmbH, Dulsburg, Germany (electronic control devices)

FMC Corp., Cork, Ireland (pharmaceutical and food ingredients)

Hamberger Industriewerke GmbH, Stephenskircken, Germany (hardwood flooring, laminates, toilet seats)

Herdmans Ltd., County Tyrone, N. Ireland (linen yarn)

Hewlett Packard FCO, Ipswich, Suffolk, England (opto-electronic components)

Honeywell Scottish Operations, Motherwell, Lamarkshire, U.K. (heating/cooling/microswitches)

ICI Chlor-Chemicals, Runcorn, Cheshire, U.K. (chemical plant and spares for chlor-alkali industry)

Interlux Louvre Manufacturing, Milton Keynes, U.K. (louvre controls for lighting)

K&L Microwave Ltd., Bridlington, East Yorkshire, U.K. (microwave filters)

Killeen Corr Products, Dublin, Ireland (paper)

Knürr AG, München, Germany (sheet-metal enclosures)

Lilly (Eli), Fegersheim, France (pharmaceuticals)

Microsoft, Dublin, Ireland (software manufacturing)

Munster Simms Eng. Ltd., Bangor, N. Ireland (water systems for rec. vehicles)

Norelem, Cedex, Paris, France (work holding products)

Power-Packer Europa B.V., Unit of Applied Power, Inc., Oldenzaal, Holland (customized hydraulic/electromechanical motion-control actuation systems and components)

Saman, Vitrolles, France (food products)

Schroff SAS, Betschdorf, France (electrical products)

Sew Usocome, plant no. 1, Haguenau, France (motors and engines)

Sew Usocome, plant no. 2, Haguenau, France (motors and engines)

Sew Usocome, plant no. 3, Haguenau, France (motors and engines)

Sew Usocome, plant no. 4, Haguenau, France (motors and engines)

SWEP/Tranter Group, Compact Brazed Business Unit, Landskrona, Sweden

Telemecanique-Ireland, Cophridge, Ireland (contactors)

Timken, Colmar, France (tapered roller bearings)

TRW Airbag Systems GmbH & Co., Aschau, Germany (inflators for car passenger safety systems)

Unipart Industries—Ketlon, Kent, U.K. (gears, shafts)

Vitronics Soltec, Oosterhaut, Netherlands (reflow soldering ovens, curing/cleaning equipment for semiconductor industry)

Waterford Crystal, Kilbarry, Ireland (crystal glasses)

Whirlpool Europe, Amiens, France (clothes washers, dryers)

South Africa

Adcock Ingram Critical Care (critical health care products)

Adcock Ingram Pharmaceuticals (pharmaceuticals)

Amalgamated Beverage Canneries (carbonated soft drinks)

Autoflug (safety restraints for motor vehicles)

Beier Albany & Co. (high-tech textiles, e.g., for filtration, etc.)

Cullinan Refractories (refractory products)

Eddels (footwear manufacture)

Illovo Sugar Ltd. (sugar)

Lever Brothers (detergents)

Mercedes-Benz of So. Africa (passenger cars and commercial vehicles)

MG Glass, Durban (beverage containers)

Power Engineers (distribution transformers)

Rhomberg Electronics Manufacturing (industrial electronics)

SAD Saf Medication (EL) (self-medication and personal care products)

South African Nylon Spinners (synthetic fibers and polyester polymers)

Toyota Auto. Comp. (exhausts, fuel tanks, seats, chassis, box bodies, fabrication)

Australia and Asia

Adaptec Manufacturing (s) Pte Ltd., Singapore (raid server products, SCSI host adapters, ASIC, and software)

All Head Services, Braeside, Australia (vehicle cylinder head reconditioning)

Bonlac Foods, Melbourne, Australia (cheese, milk powder, dairy products)

Davey Products, Huntingdale, Vic., Australia (pumps)

Dulmison Australia, Wyong, NSW, Australia (transmission and distribution goods for power industry)

Dulmison (Thailand) Co., Bangkok, Thailand (transmission and distribution goods for power industry)

Dulux Australia, Vic., Australia (surface coatings and paint)

Knight Wah Technology Ltd., Hong Kong (contract electronic manufacturing)

Morgan Zibo Insulators, Shandong, China (ceramic insulators)

Morlynn Insulators, Yarraville, Vic, Australia (ceramic insulators)

National Dairies, Muray Bridge, Australia (dairy dessert/cheeses)

National Dairies, Tiaree, Australia (yogurt, yogo, desserts, powder)

Nypro Shenzhen, Shenzhen, China (injection molding)

Olex Cables, Tottenham, Vic., Australia (cables)

Tetra Pak Jurong Pte Ltd., Singapore (packaging for beverages)

TWO ELEMENTS OF THE WORLD CLASS BY PRINCIPLES (WCP) INTERNATIONAL BENCHMARKING PROJECT

1. The Sixteen Principles and Self-Scoring Criteria
2. Survey Questions and Responses for Each Principle

This appendix weaves together two elements of the WCP International Benchmarking project:

- Each of the sixteen principles and self-scoring criteria, in stair-step format. Below the criteria for each principle are "fine points" that shed more light on the principle and scoring criteria.

- Sample of survey questions and responses. The survey was conducted in 1997 through 2000. The participants were companies attending Richard Schonberger's Manufacturing Institute seminars in various cities and on-site at several manufacturing companies. Each attending company was asked, on a voluntary basis, to submit just one completed survey form. The number of companies choosing to respond averaged thirty and ranged from seven to sixty-seven. Results were generally compiled and reviewed with the audience during the seminar. The total number of survey questions was 105. Included here are 32 of them, 2 per principle. (Results of the full survey will be reported elsewhere.)

The survey questions are interwoven with the sixteen principles so that the questions line up with the principles they relate to.

Regarding the participating companies, it seems probable that they are well above average. Otherwise they would not be attending seminars to learn something. On the other hand, on average they may not be the highest-performing manufacturers, many of which have internalized much of their training. In most cases, the audience comprises a spectrum of functions, usually including sales and marketing, finance and accounting, and so on, and ranks from most senior to factory operatives. Via the seminar, they will have been exposed to topics underpinning each question.

I. GENERAL

1. Team Up with Customers; Organize by Customer/Product Family

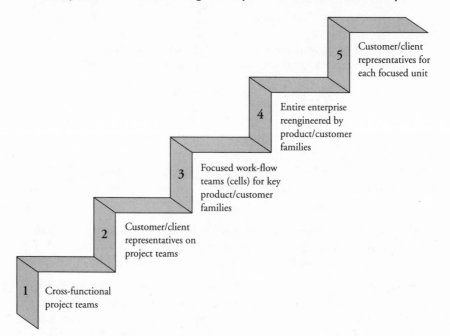

5 Customer/client representatives for each focused unit

4 Entire enterprise reengineered by product/customer families

3 Focused work-flow teams (cells) for key product/customer families

2 Customer/client representatives on project teams

1 Cross-functional project teams

Fine Points

■ Best is to be organized by (focused on) customer families (conventionally, marketing usually is; accounting and finance may be; production, staff support, and the supply chain rarely are)

■ Next best is focus by product families—what customers buy

■ Sometimes it's possible to be focused on both customer and product families—for instance, a power-tool maker with one set of resources making and selling to professional tradespeople and another set making and selling to home users

■ Lowest level of points (step 1) is for getting in league with one's internal customers, which happens when cross-functional teams are formed

- Many manufacturers earn points on step 3 (cells) without having done much on the steps 1 and 2 (which are easier and cheaper to do than massively moving equipment to form cells)
- Companies should be forming cells not just in production, but in staff support, too (order-entry cell, buy-receive-pay cell, and so on)

WCP Survey Questions

Brief summary on the general format of the surveys. Usually a seminar audience received one page of questions on just one of the sixteen principles. Most questions call for answers on a one-to-seven-point scale. The scale is shown below for this first principle but will be omitted for the fifteen remaining principles. Participants were asked to circle a number from 1 (low) to 7 (high). Mean score for the participating companies is given below, along with brief, sometimes rather opinionated comments.

PRINCIPLE I: CUSTOMER FOCUS

Topic of questions for this principle. "Extent of 'strategic collaboration' in your organization."

To what extent has your organization developed "horizontal, co-located product-flow teams (cells)" . . .

A. in manufacturing?

Hardly at all						A great deal
1	2	3	4	5	6	7

B. in "office support" areas?

Hardly at all						A great deal
1	2	3	4	5	6	7

Responses

Mean response to question A: 4.32

Mean response to question B: 2.95

BRIEF DISCUSSION

Responding companies appear to have gone about halfway in implementing work cells and cell teams in manufacturing. Some progress has also been made in breaking up departments in office environments to create cells (examples: order-entry cells, buy-receive-accounts payable cells).

I. GENERAL

2. Capture/Use Customer, Competitive, and Best-Practice Information

5 Broad implemen-
tation of better-
than-best practices
for customer service

4 All associates involved
in customer/competitive/
best-practice assessment

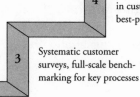

3 Systematic customer
surveys, full-scale benchmarking for key processes

2 Gather customer needs
and best-practice data,
and noncompetitive metrics

1 Gather customer
satisfaction data,
and competitive
samples and metrics

Fine Points

■ This principle taps outside information/knowledge; it's your main antenna

■ Information/knowledge (especially external) is the spark of innovation

■ Aim: Drive your improvement efforts with external data—from customers (customer satisfaction/needs surveys), competitive products (competitive analysis), and noncompetitive best practices (bench-marking studies)

- Though customer surveys and competitive analysis are old tech-niques, few companies have done them well or systematically; it's been haphazard
- Benchmarking is a newer approach, developed by Xerox, that seeks out best-in-the-world practices (best at stock picking, paying in-voices, and so on)
- Lowest point level (step 1) is getting data from customers and com-petitive analysis; higher points require benchmarking as well—each done systematically; at step 3, "noncompetitive metrics" refers to data on best practices, most of which will not be found in one's own industry; highest points require all-employee involvement and supe-rior uses of the data

WCP Survey Questions

PRINCIPLE 2: EXTERNAL INFORMATION

Topic of questions for this principle. "Extent to which your organization employs external information to drive continuous improvement."

Competitive Analysis

A. How extensively does your organization conduct competitive analysis?

B. To what extent does your organization make competitive analysis in-formation widely known to your workforce?

Responses

Mean response to question A: 3.05

Mean response to question B: 1.80

BRIEF DISCUSSION

Responding companies feel their conduct of competitive analysis is weak (a point below the midpoint on the scale). Their reported commitment to pre-sent competitive analysis information to the workforce is weaker still. Lack of full awareness of rivals' strengths invites complacency.

I. GENERAL

3. Continual, Rapid Improvement in Universal Customer Wants

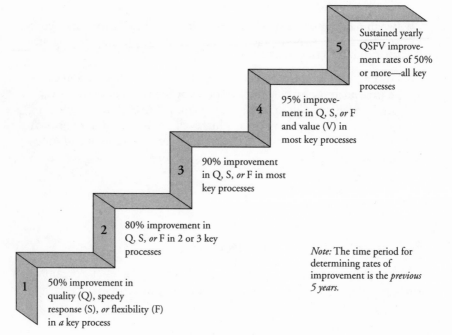

5 — Sustained yearly QSFV improvement rates of 50% or more—all key processes

4 — 95% improvement in Q, S, *or* F and value (V) in most key processes

3 — 90% improvement in Q, S, *or* F in most key processes

2 — 80% improvement in Q, S, *or* F in 2 or 3 key processes

1 — 50% improvement in quality (Q), speedy response (S), *or* flexibility (F) in *a* key process

Note: The time period for determining rates of improvement is the *previous 5 years.*

Fine Points

- This is the achievement principle, measuring improvement in the eyes of customers
- All customers, internal and external, want quality (Q), speedy response (S), flexibility (F), and value (V); these are universals of continuous improvement in the customer-focused organization
- Customers also want certain specifics, in the form of detailed *specifications*—not the topic of this principle
- S includes multiple flow-time elements: production, purchase to production, stockroom to production, order fulfillment, design to market, cash to cash, and so forth
- Q, S, and F are well-developed concepts; we know how to measure them; V, coming into play at step 4, is less well defined—but emergent as a vital customer concern
- An obvious element of V is price/cost; related to this is inaccurate

costing, which activity-based costing (ABC) attempts to address; other measures of value are warranty costs, late shipments, and so on

■ QSFV are also subjects of Principle 13—where the issue is use (not achievement) of QSFV internally in performance management

WCP Survey Questions

PRINCIPLE 3: CONTINUAL, RAPID IMPROVEMENT IN UNIVERSAL CUSTOMER WANTS

Topic of questions for this principle. This is the attainment principle—attainment of quality, speedy response, flexibility, and value. Survey questions aim at factors directly supporting these attainments. The second question deviates from the 1-to-7-point scale format.

    A. **Process vs. delayed-result metrics.** To what extent has your organization shifted emphasis from second- and third-order metrics to "the basics" and key direct-effect metrics?

Response

Mean response to question A: 3.42

    B. **Nonobvious wastes.** Which of the following eight nonobvious wastes does your organization try to *reduce or eliminate,* or does not do at all (check all that *generally* apply)?

*12*___ a. Promotional waste (negative selling).

*20*___ b. Tracking the orders through every process.

*20*___ c. Physical automation (conveyors and storage systems).

*16*___ d. Handling container to container.

*17*___ e. Staff or consultants needed to determine wastes to be eliminated.

*13*___ f. Tracking the savings arising from waste elimination.

*14*___ g. Determining costs of bad quality.

*14*___ h. Reporting utilization and labor efficiency/productivity.

RESPONSES
The italicized numbers to the left of each of the eight questions is the number of companies in the sample that checked that "nonobvious" waste—as one being reduced.

BRIEF DISCUSSION

Re question A, responding companies rate their movement away from aggregated performance metrics and toward root measures fairly low (just below the midpoint on the scale).

Re question B, on waste elimination, thirty-two companies contributed survey forms. On items b, c, d, and e, half or more of the companies indicated they are trying to reduce the waste. Top scores are for eliminating order tracking and physical automation. Only twelve, thirteen, fourteen, and fourteen of the thirty-two companies checked off reduction of promotional waste, costing the waste eliminations, costing the bad quality, and reporting utilization and labor productivity. This finding suggests that the overhead organization, responsible for "knowledge" wastes, is slow to change as compared with those involved in physical wastes.

I. GENERAL

4. Whole Workforce Involvement in Change and Strategic Planning

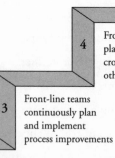

5   Front-line teams help develop strategies and set numeric goals, self-monitored

4   Front-line teams plan and implement cross-functionally with other teams

3   Front-line teams continuously plan and implement process improvements

2   Front-line teams assist in planning and implementing changes in own processes

1   Front-line associates assist in planning changes in own jobs

Fine Points

- This principle provides a framework for empowered, self-managed teams; "front-line" includes professionals/technicians as well as operations/clerical people
- Example: Zytec (Baldrige award, 1991) five-year strategic planning in four steps:
  1. External data—from customers, market research, benchmarking
  2. Six cross-functional teams, from all areas, develop five-year plan, critiqued by 20 percent of the workforce, plus key customers and suppliers; executives finalize and state as general one-year objectives
  3. Every employee, team, and department develops its own quality and action plans with measurable monthly goals (rationale: locally set numeric goals are often tougher, surely more relevant, than goals down from "on high")
  4. Translated into financial plans
- Contrast: Policy deployment (PD), a top-down approach with Japanese roots, fits with typical Western executive processes; but, while PD can provide strong guidance in early stages of "world class" implementation, it conflicts with empowerment ideals—especially step 5 (Gary Hamel: At next meeting on "strategy" or "innovation" in your company, make sure that 50 percent of attendees have never been to such a meeting before)

Observation: Steps 1 through 4 of this principle match up fairly well with what Ackoff labels as "the new functions of management" (except as applied to *operatives-as-managers*), which are as follows:

1. To enable and motivate subordinates to do as well as they know how.
2. To develop them so they can do better in the future than the best they can do now.
3. To manage their interactions, not their actions.
4. To manage the interactions of the unit they manage with other internal and external organizational units and organizations.[1]

WCP Survey Questions

PRINCIPLE 4: WORKFORCE INVOLVEMENT IN CHANGE AND STRATEGIC PLANNING

Topic of questions for this principle. Empowerment, teaming, and dispersal of professional/technical people to locations close to the action.

A. **Strategic transition.** To what extent has your organization shifted from management by procedures and/or policies to management by customer-focused, data-based principles *driven by the whole workforce?*

B. **Dispersed expertise.** To what extent have the professional and technical staffs been dispersed to proximities of those they support?

Responses

Mean response to question A: 3.17

Mean response to question B: 4.06

BRIEF DISCUSSION

Responding companies feel their transition to whole-workforce-driven competitive principles is weak (a point below the midpoint on the scale). The companies apparently are doing better at moving professional and technical people to locations near those they support (midpoint of the scale).

II. DESIGN

5. Cut to the Few Best Components, Operations, and Suppliers

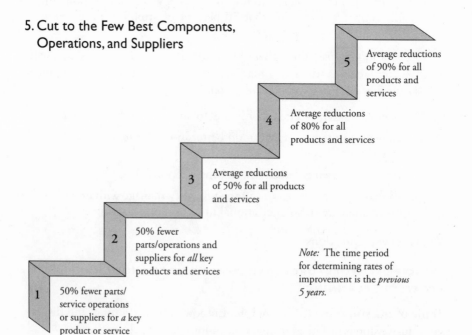

5 — Average reductions of 90% for all products and services

4 — Average reductions of 80% for all products and services

3 — Average reductions of 50% for all products and services

2 — 50% fewer parts/operations and suppliers for *all* key products and services

1 — 50% fewer parts/service operations or suppliers for *a* key product or service

Note: The time period for determining rates of improvement is the *previous 5 years.*

Fine Points

- This single design principle includes both product design and design of the supply chain, which are related as follows:
    - Both call for simplification and numerical reductions
    - Reducing number of suppliers is unlikely to reach a lower limit, because new/revised products, part numbers, operations, and outsourcing usually add new suppliers—requiring renewed efforts to simplify and reduce supply-chain breadth
    - Diligence in holding down growth of part numbers/operations at the same time holds down additions of suppliers
- Internet/Web: Provides wide exposure to potential new suppliers and customers; each business unit must evaluate them, do trial business with some of them, but contain and reduce their numbers
- Reducing parts/operations and suppliers involves wide-ranging product-development and supplier-partnership improvement measures
- Design for simplicity/modularity/etc. is key to achieving *customized mass production* (more accurate term than "mass customization")— and key to making *agility* affordable
- Job shop (no product line): Get involved in 1) partnering with customers on all fronts, including 2) improving customers' designs

WCP Survey Questions

PRINCIPLE 5: CUT TO THE FEW BEST COMPONENTS, OPERATIONS, SUPPLIERS

Topic of questions for this principle. Simplifications.

A. How extensively does your organization employ design for manufacture and assembly (DFMA)?

B. To what extent is your organization 1) serving as a value-added supplier of modules instead of piece parts; *or* 2) developing its piece-parts suppliers into value-added suppliers of modules?

Responses

Mean response to question A: 2.73

Mean response to question B: 2.93

BRIEF DISCUSSION

Responding companies rate themselves low on both questions (over a point below the midpoint on the scale). Both concern simplified product design, which has effects that ripple beneficially through most of what manufacturers do. Thus it seems manufacturers are neglecting one of their surest routes to improved competitiveness.

III. OPERATIONS

6. Cut Total Flow Time, Flow Distance, and Start-up/Changeover Times

5   Cross-functional teams achieve 90% average reductions

4   Experts help associates achieve 80% average reductions

3   Associates achieve 50% average reductions across *all* processes

2   In key processes, associates cut get-ready/ changeover time, flow time, and distance 50%

1   Train associates in readiness, changeover/ setup time and lot-size reduction, and queue limitation

Note: The time period for determining rates of improvement is the *previous 5 years.*

Fine Points

- Principles 6 and 7, under "Operations," are closely associated with just-in-time, quick response, and time-based competition
- Principle 6 focuses on measuring flow-time speed, queue-limitation (kanban) methods, preplanning of flow time via queue limitation, buffer-stock issues, and quick setup/changeover; next principle (7)

concerns scheduling and synchronization to the drumbeat of demand, *takt* time, monitoring schedule performance, seasonality, distribution centers/distributors, and *kaizen* events; flow time is total elapsed time through multiple work stations (production cycle, design-to-market cycle, and so on) (in some industries it is called "cycle time," though for much of Europe, cycle time retains its original engineering meaning: completion of a work cycle at a single work station)

- Synonyms for JIT: *continuous-flow manufacturing* (CFM is an early IBM term that has migrated to other companies), *short-cycle manufacturing* (often used by Motorola, probably originating with Ed Heard, an early Motorola consultant), *demand flow* (term coined by J-I-T Institute of Technology consulting firm), *full pull* or *pull system,* and *continuous replenishment;* closely associated with JIT are *kanban* and the Toyota system

WCP Survey Questions

PRINCIPLE 6: CUT FLOW TIME AND DISTANCE, AND START-UP/CHANGEOVER TIMES

Topic of questions for this principle. First of two just-in-time principles—this one on reducing flow time and related factors.

A. **Measurement of flow time.** To what extent does your organization measure and endeavor to improve setup time (or changeover time, start-up time, make-ready time, and so on)?

B. **Setup/changeover/make-ready time.** To what extent are your organization's setup/changeover reduction efforts driven by operators (as opposed to technical/professional people)?

Responses

Mean response to question A: 4.05

Mean response to question B: 3.75

BRIEF DISCUSSION

Responding companies rate themselves moderate on attention to setup time (midpoint on the scale). They rate themselves only slight lower on operator involvement in setup-time reduction, which is a good sign.

III. OPERATIONS

7. Operate Close to Customers' Rate of Use or Demand

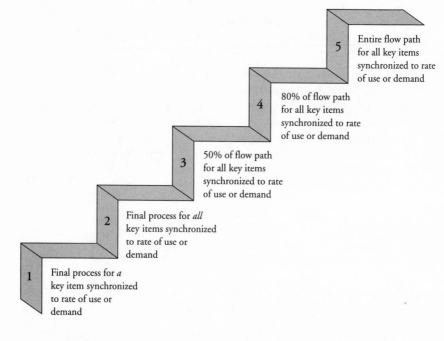

5 Entire flow path for all key items synchronized to rate of use or demand

4 80% of flow path for all key items synchronized to rate of use or demand

3 50% of flow path for all key items synchronized to rate of use or demand

2 Final process for *all* key items synchronized to rate of use or demand

1 Final process for *a* key item synchronized to rate of use or demand

Fine Points

- Highest level of points is for getting synchronized to the "drumbeat" of final-customer demand
- For maximum points, if you are several echelons in advance of final use, you must work actively with your customer chain to get schedules in synch with actual demand (or a smoothed representation of it); working similarly with your supply chain increases your ability to synchronize downstream
- Any racks, stockrooms, or tanks holding large inventories are evidence of *lack* of good synchronization
- Usually, it's easiest to synchronize final processes (such as final assembly, packing) with customer demand; hence, this qualifies for lowest level of points
- Rate-based scheduling can even apply to purchased items, such as sawblades in a sawmill

■ Job shop: Rate-based scheduling may be suitable only for parts you make for a higher-volume customer; lower-volume, erratic-demand items may require work orders or simple first-come, first-served sequencing

WCP Survey Questions

PRINCIPLE 7: OPERATE CLOSE TO CUSTOMERS' RATE OF USE OF DEMAND

Topic of questions for this principle. Second of two just-in-time principles—this one on synchronizing to the "drumbeat of demand."

A. **Mixed-model production.** If your business is engineer-/make-/configure-to-order, please check here and go on to next question [eighteen of thirty-two did check here and go on]. Otherwise, to what extent are your organization's products scheduled at repeating minimum-ratio, mixed-model rates equal to the mixed rate of sales?

B. **Seasonal scheduling.** If your organization lacks seasonal product lines, please check here and go on to question 5 [twenty-two of thirty-two did check here and go on]. Otherwise, to what extent are your seasonal product lines scheduled differently by season: 1) make-to-plan during the finished inventory buildup season; and 2) make-to-order during the finished inventory shortage season?

Responses

Mean response to question A: 4.28

Mean response to question B: 3.49

BRIEF DISCUSSION

Responding companies ratings are fairly high on the mixed-model scheduling question, which is worded quite restrictively. Ratings on two-season scheduling, which has scarcely been discussed in books and articles, are respectable. Both scores are higher than might be expected, and they come from companies attending seminars in Boston, St. Louis, and Anaheim—a cross section of the United States.

IV. HUMAN RESOURCES

8. Continually Train Everybody for Their New Roles

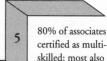

5 — 80% of associates certified as multi-skilled; most also certified trainers

4 — 50% of associates certified as multi-skilled; most also certified trainers

3 — 25% of associates certified as multiskilled

2 — 40 hours yearly "train-do, train-do" skills/process-improvement training for all associates

1 — Key managers and teams receive overview training on process improvement

Fine Points

- Lowest points are for *some* degree of training in process improvement (though on-the-job training in job skills is commonplace, training in process improvement was virtually nonexistent before the current period of industrial renewal)

- Step 2 calls for systematic training (job/process improvement):

  - At least forty hours yearly (*Industry Week* study: Some 11 percent of 2,789 plants said they provide over forty hours of training *every year*)

  - Follow the train-do mode, sometimes called "just-in-time" training—train just in time for use (train, go do it; next class evaluate results; repeat for each training topic)—which is far more effective than all-at-once training overload

  - At Johnson Controls, it's "training-with-a-purpose" (ten topics—for instance, 5S and visual management, fail-safing, standard work, quick changeover, kanban), typically a two-hour classroom session plus eight to twelve hours of on-the-job application

■ Steps 3, 4, and 5 call for certifiable training (systematic, account-able)—which requires periodic recertification

WCP Survey Questions

PRINCIPLE 8: CONTINUALLY TRAIN EVERYBODY FOR THEIR NEW ROLES

Topic of questions for this principle. Career breadth for staff people; oper-ators taking over roles conventionally owned by support people.

A. **Cross-careering.** To what extent does your organization employ cross-careering for professionals, technicians, clerical/administra-tive people, and other nondirect labor—other than "fast trackers" and senior managers?

B. **Functional training.** To what extent does your organization pro-vide the front-line workforce with training in functional expertise such as budgeting, hiring, scheduling, purchasing, maintenance, and so on?

Responses

Mean response to question A: 2.08

Mean response to question B: 2.07

BRIEF DISCUSSION

Ratings on both questions are very low. This indicates that human resources management in this sample of manufacturers—sixty companies—is stuck in the past.

IV. HUMAN RESOURCES

9. Expand Variety of Recognition, Rewards, and Pay

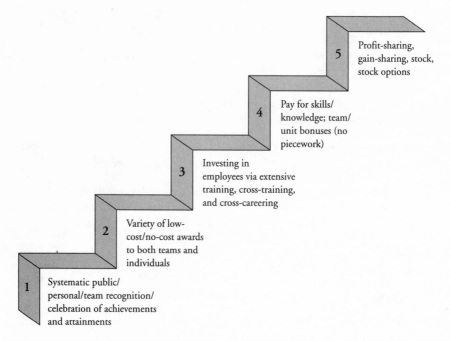

5 — Profit-sharing, gain-sharing, stock, stock options

4 — Pay for skills/ knowledge; team/ unit bonuses (no piecework)

3 — Investing in employees via extensive training, cross-training, and cross-careering

2 — Variety of low-cost/no-cost awards to both teams and individuals

1 — Systematic public/ personal/team recognition/ celebration of achievements and attainments

Fine Points

- Principle 9 "closes the loop," returning value to the workforce for value created (a modern take on J. Stacy Adams's equity theory— 1960s) through continuous improvements—necessary to keep process improvement "evergreen"
- Follows the "basket of values" concept: Multiple sources of value wash out unfairness of any narrowly based scheme
- This is stepwise reward and recognition that won't "break the bank"
    - Lowest point level: Based on systematic (not random) public recognition events (but irregular recognition—consistent with random-reinforcement theory—to any one team/ individual); includes pride and self-motivation derived from public displays of projects, successes, attainments
    - Next point levels: no-cost/low-cost, easy-to-do awards; then, training (half of *Fortune*'s fifty best-to-work-for plants average forty or more hours of yearly training per employee)

■ Finally, monetary rewards: Companies offering stock options to nearly all employees include Amgen, Cisco, General Mills, W. L. Gore, McCormick, Merck, Procter & Gamble, Intel, Microsoft

WCP Survey Questions

PRINCIPLE 9: EXPAND VARIETY OF RECOGNITION, REWARD, AND PAY

Topic of questions for this principle. Closing the loop with recognition for process improvements. Since question B deviates from the low-high 7-point scale of most other questions, its alternate scale is included below.

A. To what extent does your organization make use of *public recognition* and *low-cost/no-cost awards* for team/individual contributions?

B. Does your organization place more emphasis on *monetary reward or recognition*?

Monetary reward						Recognition
1	2	3	4	5	6	7

Responses

Mean response to question A: 3.26

Mean response to question B: 3.88

BRIEF DISCUSSION

Responses on both questions indicate that companies are paying for what they could get for free. It's not good business to pay so little heed to public recognition, which probably has motivational value as high as money.

Application of Stepwise Recognition to Supplier Partnerships

This reward and recognition scheme—five upward steps—has potential application beyond human resources. With small modifications it works fairly well for bestowing recognition upon suppliers. The lowest degree of recognition might be supplier certification. Formal recognition ceremonies are next up the ladder. Then comes collaboration with the supplier, for example, on product design, pricing, and sales targeting. Long-term contracts with the supplier make up step 4. Finally, at the fifth step, ways of sharing saving with the supplier are worked out.

These five steps are shown in the accompanying schematic. The following examples for each step—but not the five-step schema—come from a benchmarking study:[2]

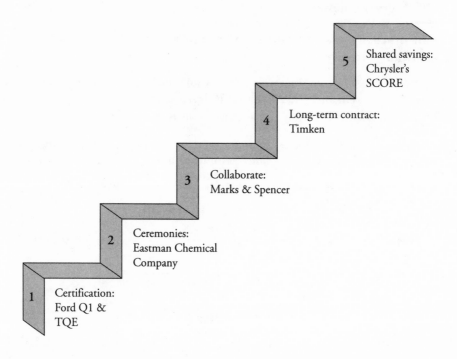

- Step 1. Ford Motor Company has a well-developed system of supplier certification. Its Q1 level of certification is based on product quality, and its higher level of certification, total quality excellence (TQE), goes beyond that to include excellence in delivery, engineering, the business relationship, and commitment to continuous improvement.

- Step 2. Eastman Chemical, Kingsport, Tennessee, holds an annual supplier recognition banquet at its world headquarters. Senior executives give a keynote talk emphasizing key roles of invited suppliers in meeting customer needs and sustaining competitiveness. A half-day in-depth tour of the Eastman facility follows.

- Step 3. Marks & Spencer, the U.K.-based department store chain, has a reputation for working with troubled suppliers to restore their financial health, rather than cutting them off.

- Step 4. Timken's Faircrest Steel plant in Canton, Ohio, seeks long-term relationships locally, where it considers Canton as its "supplier city." Its twenty-year purchasing agreements—not detailed contracts—seek 10 percent value improvements each year but encourage suppliers to limit their sales volume with Timken to 25 percent.
- Step 5. Chrysler's supplier cost reduction effort (SCORE) aims at continuous improvement and backs it up with money—savings shared between the supplier and Chrysler. At least before Chrysler's year 2000 profit problems, an intent of SCORE was to help maintain suppliers' profit margins.

This way of sizing up a company's supplier recognition is not basic enough to be considered as a separate principle. Rather, it may be useful as a technique supportive of a principle. In this case that principle is number 5, which concerns design of effective supplier partnerships. It is presented here rather than under Principle 5 in order to relate it to recognition and reward for human resources.

V. QUALITY AND PROCESS IMPROVEMENT

10. Continually Reduce Variation and Mishaps

5 — 2.0 Cpk; defects below 10 PPM; 99% reductions

4 — 1.33 Cpk; defects below 100 parts per million (PPM); rework, defects, lateness, unsafe incidents cut 95%

3 — 1.0 process capability (Cpk) for key processes; rework, defects, lateness, and unsafe incidents cut 85%

2 — In-control capability analysis for key processes; rework, defects, and lateness cut 50%

Note: The time period for determining rates of improvement is *the previous 5 years.*

1 — Training in and use of the "seven basic tools" of process control and improvement

Fine Points

- Seven basic tools: Everybody should know and use these mostly statistical (but simple) tools of capturing variation, mishaps, and unsafe or environmentally hazardous incidents, and isolating their causes
- Process control and capability analysis: At step 2, achieve process control first, then conduct capability (Cpk) analysis; step 3 adds reducing unsafe incidents
- Cpk: Means "process capability index," a numerical measure of ability to meet product and process (including safety and environmental) specifications without excessive variation; for equipment Cpk is calculated from variables measurement data; for office support, sales, and the like, Cpk may be calculated using attribute (yes-no) defect data
- PPM: Means parts per million defective or nonconforming
- First-pass yield is often a worthy measure of attainment on this principle
- Job shop: For short production runs, consider short-run process control-chart methods

WCP Survey Questions

PRINCIPLE 10: CONTINUALLY REDUCE VARIATION AND MISHAPS

Topic of questions for this principle. The quality sciences, including safety.

A. To what extent has your organization trained its employees in the *seven basic tools* (flowchart, check sheet, Pareto, fishbone, histogram, scattergram, SPC charts)?

B. To what extent does your organization employ behavior-based (no blame) safety?

Responses

Mean response to question A: 1.90

Mean response to question B: 2.90

BRIEF DISCUSSION

Deming, Juran, and Feigenbaum had industry's attention for a whole decade. Yet the companies rate themselves below 2 on training the workforce in the seven basic tools. Behavior-based safety is still not well known, yet companies rated their level of use of it a full point higher—good news for the state of safety, which had been bogged down for years in tracking accidents rather than potentials for accidents. (But the sample size on this question is, because of oversight, only seven companies.)

V. QUALITY AND PROCESS IMPROVEMENT

11. Front-Line Teams Record and Own Process Data at the Workplace

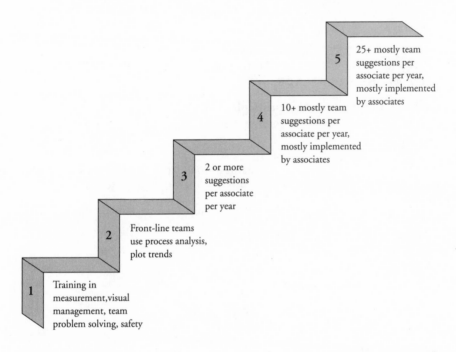

5 — 25+ mostly team suggestions per associate per year, mostly implemented by associates

4 — 10+ mostly team suggestions per associate per year, mostly implemented by associates

3 — 2 or more suggestions per associate per year

2 — Front-line teams use process analysis, plot trends

1 — Training in measurement, visual management, team problem solving, safety

Fine Points

■ Who's in charge? Effective management of quality and process improvement requires that front-line employees, not just managers and technical experts, be in charge

■ Ownership: To be in charge, front-liners must be collectors and owner-users of the process data

■ Visual management: Hidden data get less use than visual data; thus, visual management is a training topic in step 1, visual plotting of process data is a requirement in step 2

- Suggestions: Best evidence of front-line process ownership is high levels of employee/team suggestions
- Counting/recording suggestions:
  - If suggestions are not recorded and celebrated, high involvement in continuous improvement is less likely to be sustained (because "you get what you measure")
  - You don't count suggestions but do get the equivalent—for instance, two implemented suggestions per employee? At step 3, score half a point; gain the other half point by counting/recording

WCP Survey Questions

PRINCIPLE 11: FRONT-LINE TEAMS RECORD AND OWN PROCESS DATA AT THE WORKPLACE

Topic of questions for this principle. This is the companion to the previous questions on the quality sciences; this one concerns ownership of those sciences.

A. To what extent do your organization's first-line (direct/indirect labor, clerical, and so forth) employees have process ownership?

B. To what extent are your organization's processes visually managed?

Responses

Mean response to question A: 3.00

Mean response to question B: 2.10

BRIEF DISCUSSION

Respondents rate themselves low on question A (a point below the midpoint of the scale), despite all the attention that has been given to the idea that front-line associates are proper owners of quality. Ratings are a point lower on visual management of processes, which is a key facilitator of empowerment. (But the sample size on this question is, because of oversight, only seven companies.)

VI. INFORMATION FOR OPERATIONS
AND IMPROVEMENT (CONTROL)

12. Control Root Causes and Cut Internal Transactions and Reporting

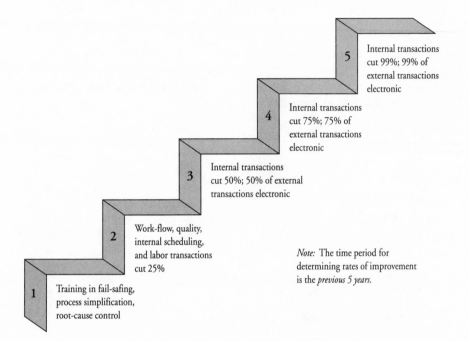

5 — Internal transactions cut 99%; 99% of external transactions electronic

4 — Internal transactions cut 75%; 75% of external transactions electronic

3 — Internal transactions cut 50%; 50% of external transactions electronic

2 — Work-flow, quality, internal scheduling, and labor transactions cut 25%

1 — Training in fail-safing, process simplification, root-cause control

Note: The time period for determining rates of improvement is the *previous 5 years*.

Fine Points

- Principle: Follows the notion of *economy of control*
  - Controls are needed most when processes are complex, incapable, failure-prone, variable; processes that are simple, capable, and rarely nonconforming thus need few formal controls
  - Best control is no *controls*; instead fix the processes
- Measurement:
  - Most internal transactions—and subsequent control reports—have to do with process failures and variation (defects, scrap, warranty claims, breakdowns, lateness, just-in-case inventories and related transactions) and complexity (work orders, move tickets, order tracking); thus points are earned on Principle 12 for eliminating internal transactions

- Exceptions: Direct controls (for example, real-time com-
  puter-executed corrective action) and fail-safing transactions
  (alerting an operator to a problem while the process is active)
- External transactions—with customers and suppliers—are
  necessary but should be done efficiently for instance, electronically via the Internet/Web, EDI, or fax

WCP Survey Questions

PRINCIPLE 12: CONTROL ROOT CAUSES TO CUT INTERNAL TRANS-ACTIONS AND REPORTING

Topic of questions for this principle. The concept underlying these questions is best control requires the fewest controls.

To what extent has your organization reduced . . .

A. labor transactions and reports?

B. scheduling transactions?

Responses

Mean response to question A: 2.50

Mean response to question B: 3.08

BRIEF DISCUSSION

Respondents rate themselves low on reducing dependence on transactions
and reports. Low ratings on labor reporting suggests that companies are still
generally labor-productivity focused, despite the low percentage of cost that
labor usually represents. Reducing scheduling transactions is closely related to
JIT/lean manufacturing and thus is rated somewhat higher.

VI. INFORMATION FOR OPERATIONS AND IMPROVEMENT (CONTROL)

13. Align Performance Measures with Universal Customer Wants

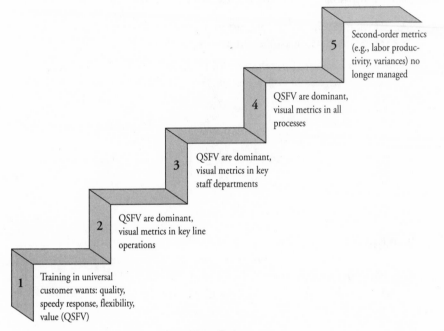

5 — Second-order metrics (e.g., labor productivity, variances) no longer managed

4 — QSFV are dominant, visual metrics in all processes

3 — QSFV are dominant, visual metrics in key staff departments

2 — QSFV are dominant, visual metrics in key line operations

1 — Training in universal customer wants: quality, speedy response, flexibility, value (QSFV)

Fine Points

- This principle concerns extent of use of QSFV (universal customer wants) as internal performance metrics (measures); Principle 3 is different, since it is devoted to measuring extent of *attainments* on QSFV

- One test: Ask a random employee, "What do they measure you on?"; if the answer isn't even close to Q, S, F, or V, no points are deserved

- Best practice: Large visual signboards in every work area showing QSFV-related trends and related improvement projects

WCP Survey Questions

PRINCIPLE 13: ALIGN PERFORMANCE MEASURES WITH UNIVERSAL CUSTOMER WANTS

Topic of questions for this principle. What are people measured on?

A. To what extent is your organization focused on external (customer) versus internal measures of performance?

B. To what extent does the workforce (teams/individuals) track its own improvements on visual charts?

Responses

Mean response to question A: 3.85

Mean response to question B: 2.40

BRIEF DISCUSSION

Respondents rate themselves reasonably well on customer-focused measures (quality, speedy response, flexibility, value). Ratings are nearly a point and a half lower on the workforce visually tracking its own performance. That suggests that managers are not giving enough responsibility to operators.

VII. CAPACITY

14. Improve Present Capacity Before New Equipment and Automation

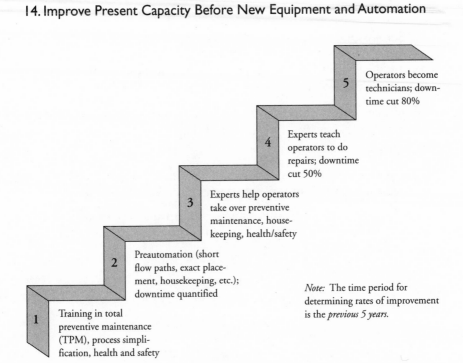

5 — Operators become technicians; downtime cut 80%

4 — Experts teach operators to do repairs; downtime cut 50%

3 — Experts help operators take over preventive maintenance, housekeeping, health/safety

2 — Preautomation (short flow paths, exact placement, housekeeping, etc.); downtime quantified

1 — Training in total preventive maintenance (TPM), process simplification, health and safety

Note: The time period for determining rates of improvement is the *previous 5 years.*

Fine Points

- Training topics: Improvement of present physical capacity (plant and equipment) via 1) TPM (also called "total *productive* maintenance"); 2) simplifying operation, maintenance, setup, and process control; and 3) upgrading safety and health

- Ownership: Operators must acquire ownership of maintenance and safety (including safety from environmental hazards and degradation), just as they have with quality, and participate in equipment selection/improvement; maintenance/safety people must be teachers/ facilitators, just as quality people had to become under total quality management

- Pre-automation: Usually makes operations more effective and efficient, while at the same time preparing for economical (lean, low-complexity) automation

- Automation: While increased automation is likely over time, there is no customer-focused principle recommending it (automation is just a tool, like a hammer or wrench); best (first) targets of automation: dirty, difficult, dangerous work

WCP Survey Questions

PRINCIPLE 14: IMPROVE PRESENT CAPACITY BEFORE NEW EQUIP-MENT AND AUTOMATION

Topic of questions for this principle. These questions pertain to the first of two principles on capacity—this one aimed at upgrading and maintaining existing capacity.

   A. To what extent are your organization's front-line associates responsible for selection of new equipment?

   B. To what extent is your organization able to avoid the costs of facility automation through pre-automation (exact, nearby positioning)?

Responses

Mean response to question A: 3.10

Mean response to question B: 3.20

BRIEF DISCUSSION

Respondent ratings are nearly the same on both questions (one point below the midpoint of the scale). Question A refers to what was almost unheard before the 1980s but now is catching on: operators helping to select their own equipment. Pre-automation, the subject of question B, is not written about much but received a respectable rating.

VII. CAPACITY

15. Seek Simple, Movable, Scalable, Low-Cost, Focused Equipment

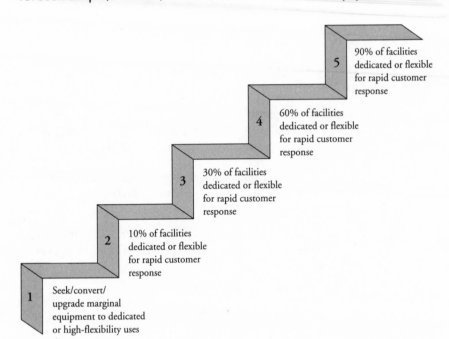

5 — 90% of facilities dedicated or flexible for rapid customer response

4 — 60% of facilities dedicated or flexible for rapid customer response

3 — 30% of facilities dedicated or flexible for rapid customer response

2 — 10% of facilities dedicated or flexible for rapid customer response

1 — Seek/convert/ upgrade marginal equipment to dedicated or high-flexibility uses

Fine Points

- Conventional capacity: High- and low-volume, and high- and low-mix products share the same capacity units (space and equipment)—no focus or ownership by product type, so poor QSFV response to customer demands
- Ideal capacity
  - For a family of high-volume standard products, the ideal is a dedicated team with dedicated, minimal-setup capacity, operated like a largely self-contained business unit
  - For low-volume, high-variety products, the ideal is a dedicated team with flexible skills and flexible, quick-change capacity; example: a March snowstorm kept most Ford Romeo, MI, Engine Plant associates home, but the Niche Line ran because it takes just a single, small team to build engines on that line
  - In either case, facilities should be as movable as possible— buildings equipped with solid floors, few impediments, all utilities available everywhere, rectangular shape; standardized

equipment, often on wheels; modular tanks and piping; and so forth.

WCP Survey Questions

PRINCIPLE 15: SEEK SIMPLE, MOVABLE, SCALABLE, LOW-COST, FO-CUSED EQUIPMENT

Topic of questions for this principle. These questions pertain to the second of two principles on capacity—aimed more at new capacity and re-layout of capacity.

A. To what extent has your organization preferred multiple, smaller-scale (instead of single, larger-scale) machines, mixing tanks, production lines, and so forth?

B. To what extent is your production performance constrained or hampered by policies on maintaining very high utilization of capital equipment?

Responses

Mean response to question A: 4.00

Mean response to question B: 3.70

BRIEF DISCUSSION

Company ratings reach the scale's midpoint on question A, the "economy of multiples" question. Ratings are close to the midpoint on question B, which does not call for abandoning the machine utilization metric, only ceasing to pay heed to it. Both ratings reflect fairly good practices with regard to facilities.

VIII. PROMOTION AND CUSTOMER PRESENTATION

16. Promote, Market, and Sell Every Improvement

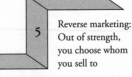

5 — Reverse marketing: Out of strength, you choose whom you sell to

4 — Global/national awards (e.g., Baldrige); over 90% customer retention

3 — Registrations, certifications, local awards (ISO 14000, Ford Q1, state award, etc.)

2 — Positive QSFV trends featured in selling, bids, proposals, ads

1 — General advertising slogans ("Absolutely, positively overnight," "Team Xerox," etc.)

Note: The time period for determining rates of improvement is the *previous 5 years.*

Fine Points

- Steps 1–2: Promoting QSFV works only if backed by true achievements; QSFV supplements the "4 Ps of marketing" (product, price, place, promotion)
- Steps 3–4: *Going for* awards juices your improvement rate; *winning* awards lets customers know about it
- Ultimate result: The organization delivers QSFV so impressively that its customers come to it; examples:
  - "[Solectron's] markets are so diversified, and its capabilities so advanced, that when one customer sneezes, another is waiting in line to take its place" (Alex Blanton, Wall Street analyst, March 12, 1997, "Notes")
  - Injection molder Nypro delivered some 2 billion defect-free contact lenses to Vistakon—an example of why Nypro grows and grows even after cutting its customer base from six hundred small and large to thirty-one big ones

■ Marketing/sales issues are also addressed under other principles, especially 1 (seller-buyer collaborations), 3 (voice of the customer), 5 (customer-supplier partnerships), and 7 (shrinking/changing roles of distributors)

WCP Survey Questions

PRINCIPLE 16: PROMOTE, MARKET, AND SELL EVERY IMPROVEMENT

Topic of questions for this principle. These questions concern the culminating principle, which is to convey important information, especially to customers.

A. To what extent are your organization's local successes in quality, response time, flexibility, and value communicated to other parts of your organization for learning/sharing purposes?

B. To what extent do your organization's marketing and sales activities emphasize improvement in quality, response time, flexibility, and value?

Responses

Mean response to question A: 4.00

Mean response to question B: 4.40

BRIEF DISCUSSION

Company ratings on these two questions are the highest of the thirty-two questions in this appendix. The surveyed companies are at the scale's midpoint in conveying success information to other parts of the organization. For a company to rate much above the midpoint requires establishing a system for this kind of knowledge sharing. Question B's good rating shows understanding of the new, customer-oriented instead of an internally focused way of thinking about competitiveness.

Note on Web citations: The initial Web address characters, usually http://www, have been omitted, except where the form is nonstandard, in which case the full address is written out.

Preface

1. John A. Byrne, "Visionary vs. Visionary," in cover story entitled "The 21st Century Corporation," *Business Week,* August 28, 2000, pp. 210–214.
2. Richard J. Schonberger, *Japanese Manufacturing Techniques: Nine Hidden Lessons in Simplicity* (New York: Free Press, 1982).

Chapter I

1. See Marvin B. Lieberman and Lieven Demeester, "Inventory Reduction and Productivity Growth: Linkages in the Japanese Automotive Industry," *Management Science* 45, no. 4 (April 1999): 466–485; and Lieberman and Rajeev Dhawan, "Assessing the Resource Base of U.S. and Japanese Auto Producers: A Stochastic Frontier Production Function Approach," unpublished paper, UCLA, August 4, 1999.
2. An interview with Federal-Mogul's interim chairman and chief executive, a turnaround artist, deals with the bankruptcy rumors: Joann S. Lubin, "Tips from a Turnaround Specialist," *Wall Street Journal,* December 27, 2000, pp. B1, B3.
3. Jamie Paton, "CEO Departures at Federal-Mogul and ICG Follow Profit Warnings," TheStreet.com/NYTimes.com, September 19, 2000.
4. Gregory L. White and Karen Lundegaard, "Ford Says Last Year's Quality Snafus Took Big Toll—Over $1 Billion in Profit," *Wall Street Journal,* January 12, 2001, pp. A3, A6.
5. Jeffrey E. Garten, "The War for Better Quality Is Far from Won," *Business Week,* December 18, 2000, p. 32.
6. L. Weiss and G. Pascoe, "The Extent and Permanence of Market Dominance," paper presented at annual meeting of European Association for Research in Industrial Economics, August 1983; D. Dueller, *Profits in the Long Run* (Cambridge: Cambridge University Press, 1986).
7. Jeffrey Garten, op. cit.

8. Kathy Chen, "Weak Economy Puts the Brakes on Job-Hopping," *Wall Street Journal,* March 27, 2001, pp. B1, B18.
9. Robert W. Hall, *Attaining Manufacturing Excellence* (Homewood, Ill.: Dow Jones-Irwin, 1987), p. 173.
10. Of companies responding in *Industry Week*'s year 2000 Census of Manufacturing, 9.1 percent say they are delivering at least forty hours of training per year for their employees: Jill Jusko, "Manufacturers Measure Up," *Industry Week,* December 11, 2000, pp. 23–43.

Chapter 2

1. Richard J. Schonberger, *World Class Manufacturing: The Lessons of Simplicity Applied* (New York: Free Press, 1986), pp. 217–18. The following year, Robert W. Hall included a table of sixteen "principles" of manufacturing excellence in his book *Attaining Manufacturing Excellence* (Homewood, Ill.: Dow Jones-Irwin, 1987), p. 264.
2. Richard J. Schonberger, *World Class Manufacturing: The Next Decade: Building Power, Strength, and Value* (New York: Free Press, 1996).
3. Geoffrey Boothroyd and Peter Dewhurst, *Product Design for Assembly* (Wakefield, R.I.: Boothroyd-Dewhurst, Inc., 1987).
4. For example, the Durango and Jeep have different windshield wipers and the five platform teams came up with three different types of corrosion protection for a rolled steel reinforcer used in plastic bumpers: Alex Taylor III, "Can the Germans Rescue Chrysler?" *Fortune,* April 30, 2001, pp. 106–112.
5. These quoted passages are from Chester Dawson, "Machete Time," *Business Week,* April 9, 2001, pp. 42–43. The story notes, further, that Nissan is facing up to its high costs by teaming up with Renault (its parent) to buy standardized parts at big savings from fewer suppliers.
6. This according to John Helyar, "Sittin' Pretty," *Fortune,* June 11, 2001, pp. 133–140.
7. Tom Archer, "How Productive Are You?," *Manufacturing Engineering* (April 2000): 120.

Chapter 3

1. Eamonn Fingleton, *In Praise of Hard Industries* (New York: Houghton Mifflin, 1999).
2. Richard Wise and Peter Baumgartner, "Go Downstream: The New Profit Imperative in Manufacturing," *Harvard Business Review* (September–October 1999): 133–141.
3. See, for example, the handbook, Geoffrey Boothroyd and Peter Dewhurst, *Product Design for Assembly* (Wakefield, R.I.: Boothroyd-Dewhurst, 1987).
4. Moon Ihlwan, Pete Engardio, Irene Kunii, and Roger Crockett, "Samsung: The Making of a Superstar," *Business Week,* December 20, 1999, pp. 136–140.

5. Cited in Alex Taylor, "The Man Who Vows to Change Japan Inc.," *Fortune,* December 20, 1999, pp. 189–98.
6. Kermit Whitfield, "Building Better Powertrains," *Automotive Manufacturing and Production* (May 2001), pp. 70–73.
7. Roger G. Schroeder, John C. Anderson, Sharon E. Tupy, and Edna M. White, "A Study of MRP Benefits and Costs," working paper: Graduate School of Business Administration, University of Minnesota, May 1980.
8. Brian Cargille, Steve Kakouros, and Robert Hall, "Part Tool, Part Process: Inventory Optimization at Hewlett-Packard Co.," *OR/MS Today* (October 1999): 18–24.
9. Hank Zoeller, "Going Outside," *APICS—The Performance Advantage,* January 2001, pp. 34–38.
10. Ibid.
11. Udo Nabitz, Giovanni Quaglia, and Paul Wangen, "EFQM's New Excellence Model," *Quality Progress,* October 1999, pp. 118–120.
12. David Drickhamer, "Standards Shake-Up," *Quality Progress,* March 5, 2001, pp. 37–40. The other two principles under ISO 9000:2000 are leadership (no surprise) and system approach to management.
13. While of the opinion that the ISO series is too broad in scope, Tito A. Conti notes that "the ISO 9000:2001 series finally incorporates many of the features of the so-called total quality management or excellence models," in "How to Find the Correct Balance Between Standardization and Differentiation," *Quality Progress,* April 2001, pp. 119–121. Conti, an Italian, is (in my opinion) perhaps the quality community's best thinker and writer—in English; see, for example, his remarkable book on quality theory (hailed by Joseph Juran), *Building Total Quality: A Guide for Management* (London: Chapman & Hall, 1993).
14. Australia's prerevision model is described in Robert J. Vokurka, Gary L. Stading, and Jason Brazeal, "A Comparative Analysis of National and Regional Quality Awards," *Quality Progress,* August 2000, pp. 41–49. The revised model, giving less emphasis to process-based quality, may be found in aqc.org.au/abef/index.html.
15. Another stock index, the Quality Progress Q-100, may be a truer test of the proposition that quality yields shareholder value. Created by Robinson Capital Management in 1998, the index tracks stock market performance of companies they consider as high users of quality tools and systems. In its first 3½ years, the index out-performed the S&P 500: Q-100 up 41.95 percent, S&P up 33.45 percent. "Q-100 Drops 9.3% in Volatile Market," in "Keeping Current," *Quality Progress,* April 2001, p. 28.

Chapter 4

1. The half-life concept, in a business context, was introduced by Arthur M. Schneiderman in "Setting Quality Goals," *Quality Progress,* April 1988, p. 51.
2. Jill Jusko, "Turning Ideas into Action," *Industry Week,* October 16, 2000, pp. 105–106.

3. The origins of "process mapping"—the term—are unclear, but a Web search produces several hits; for example, Canada's National Institute of Quality offers a one-day workshop on it (nqi.ca/English/lle-pmap.htm). "Value-stream mapping"—the term—may have been coined by James P. Womack or Daniel T. Jones in their book, *Lean Thinking: Banish Waste and Create Wealth in Your Corporation* (New York: Simon & Schuster, 1996).

4. Gene Bylinsky, "For Sale: Japanese Plants in the U.S.," *Fortune,* February 21, 2000, pp. 240[B]–240[D].

5. J. A. Byrne, "Management Theory—Or Fad of the Month?" *Business Week,* June 23, 1997, p. 47.

6. Robert C. Camp, *Benchmarking: The Search for Industry Best Practices That Lead to Superior Performance* (Milwaukee: ASQ Press, 1989).

7. Jeff Sabatini, "Old News," *Automotive Manufacturing & Production,* September 2000, p. 96. Also suggesting the reaching of lean's half-life is a book by Michael Cusumano and Kentaro Nobeoka, *Thinking Beyond Lean: How Multi-Project Management Is Transforming Toyota and Other Companies* (New York: Simon & Schuster, 1998). Moreover, in February 2001 North Carolina State University sponsored the "second international conference on Beyond Lean Manufacturing."

8. Lee Clifford, "Why You Can Ignore Six Sigma," *Fortune,* January 22, 2001, p. 140.

9. Paula Phillips Carson, Patricia A. Lanier, Kerry David Garson, and Brandi N. Guidry, "Clearing a Path through the Management Fashion Jungle: Some Preliminary Trailblazing," *Academy of Management Journal* 43, no. 6 (2000): 1143–1158.

10. R. J. Ricardo, "Strategic Quality Management: Turning the Spotlight on Strategic as well as Tactical Issues," *National Productivity Review,* 13, no. 2 (1994): 185–196.

11. Paula Phillips Carson et al., op cit.

12. Hitoshi Kume, "Quality Control in Japan's Industries," *The Wheel Extended* IX, no. 4 (spring 1980): 20–27.

13. Russell L. Ackoff, *Re-creating the Corporation: A Design of Organizations for the 21st Century* (New York: Oxford University Press, 1999), p. 260.

14. Charles F. Knight, "Emerson Electric: Consistent Profits, Consistently," *Harvard Business Review* (January–February 1992): 57–70.

15. H. Thomas Johnson and Anders Bröms, *Profit Beyond Measure: Extraordinary Results Through Attention to Work and People* (New York: Free Press, 2000).

16. Stephen A. Ruffa and Michael J. Perozziello, *Breaking the Cost Barrier: A Proven Approach to Managing and Implementing Lean Manufacturing* (New York: Wiley, 2000).

17. Charles Standard and Dale Davis, *Running Today's Factory: A Proven Strategy for Lean Manufacturing* (Cincinnati: Hanser Gardner Publications); the book's index references *variability* more than any other term.

18. Directly quoted from Richard J. Schonberger, *World Class Manufacturing: The Lessons of Simplicity Applied* (New York: Free Press, 1986), pp. 14–15.

19. Robert Green, "Reshaping Six Sigma at Honeywell," *Quality Digest,* December 2000, pp. 24–28.
20. For a partial listing, see Mark R. Hagen, "Quality Awards Listing," *Quality Progress,* August 2000, pp. 64–74.
21. Richard J. Schonberger, *World Class Manufacturing: The Next Decade: Building Power, Strength, and Value* (New York: Free Press, 1996), pp. 227–228.
22. Communication with NIST, January 2, 2000.
23. Stanley Fielding, "ISO 14001 Brings Change and Delivers Profits," *Quality Digest,* November 2000, pp. 32–35.

Chapter 5

1. Jerry Useem, "Boeing vs. Boeing," *Fortune,* October 2, 2000, pp. 147–160.
2. Dean Foust and Davie Rocks, "Nucor: Meltdown in the Corner Office," *Business Week,* June 21, 1999, p. 37.
3. Personal observation based on a visit to the company in the mid-1990s.
4. Zachary Schiller, "A Model Incentive Plan Gets Caught in a Vise," *Business Week,* January 22, 1996, pp. 89–92.
5. L. Gabriele, R. McInturff, and M. Perview, "Nypro's Team Efforts Put the Customer First," *Target,* November–December 1993, pp. 45–48.
6. Presentation by Michael A. Simms in connection with a plant visit and public seminar, St. Peters, Missouri, May 21, 1999.
7. *The New Encyclopaedia Britannica,* 15th ed., vol. 6 (Chicago: Encyclopaedia Britannica, Inc., 1989), pp. 825–826.
8. Robert W. Hall, "The Eighth Waste and Distributed Excellence," *Target,* third quarter 2000, pp. 8–15.
9. Richard J. Schonberger, *World Class Manufacturing: The Lessons of Simplicity Applied* (New York: Free Press, 1986), pp. 229–236.
10. The author's own observations of the two companies while he lived in IH/Deere country (the Quad Cities in Iowa and Illinois) in the late 1960s.
11. Takahiro Fujimoto, *The Evolution of a Manufacturing System at Toyota* (Oxford: Oxford University Press, 1999), p. 61.
12. Peter Landers, "Japan Takes a Second Look at Outsourcing Electronics," *Wall Street Journal,* January 18, 2001, p. A21.
13. Norihiko Shirouzu, "Honda Bucks Industry Wisdom, Aiming to Be Small and Efficient," *Wall Street Journal,* July 9, 1999, p. A12.
14. Brett C. Smith, "System Skills," *Automotive Manufacturing & Production,* November 2000, p. 32.
15. This discussion excerpts from a book review: Richard J. Schonberger, "Another Look: Not Built to Last," *Target,* fourth quarter 1999, p. 53 (of the book by James C. Collins and Jerry I. Porras, *Built to Last: Successful Habits of Visionary Companies* [New York: HarperCollins, 1994]).
16. Matthew Boyle, "How the Workplace Was Won," *Fortune,* January 8, 2001, pp. 139–146.

Chapter 6

1. Charles Handy, *Beyond Uncertainty: The Changing Worlds of Organizations* (Boston: Harvard Business School Press, 1996), p. 42.
2. Jeffrey Pfeffer and John F. Veiga, "Putting People First for Organizational Success," *Academy of Management Executive* 13, no. 2 (1999): 37–48.
3. Russell L. Ackoff, *Re-creating the Corporation: A Design of Organizations for the 21st Century* (New York: Oxford University Press, 1999), p. 9.
4. H. Thomas Johnson and Anders Bröms, *Profit Beyond Measure: Extraordinary Results Through Attention to Work and People* (New York: Free Press, 2000.)
5. Steve Broermann, "Competency-Based Initiatives at Abbott Diagnostic Division, Dallas, TX," *Target,* second quarter 2000, pp. 18–31.
6. "The Open-Book Revolution," cover story, *Inc.,* June 1995.
7. David Drinkhamer, "America's Best: The 1999 Winners," *Industry Week,* October 16, 1999, p. 82.
8. Personal site visit, October 21, 1993.
9. Dexter Roberts, "The Great Migration: Chinese Peasants Are Fleeing Their Villages to Chase Big-City Dreams," *Business Week,* December 18, 2000, pp. 176–188.
10. Myers, M. Scott. *Every Employee a Manager* (New York: McGraw-Hill, 1981).

Chapter 7

1. Portions of this chapter are excerpted from two articles: Richard J. Schonberger, "Economy of Control," *Journal of Quality Management* 6, no. 1 (1999): 10–18; and Richard J. Schonberger, "Time-Relevant Metrics—Avoiding the *Un*balanced Scorecard," electronic proceedings, Association for Manufacturing Excellence annual conference, October 11–15, 1999.
2. Henri Fayol, *General and Industrial Management* (London: Pitman Publishing Company, 1949), p. 97.
3. Robert N. Anthony, *Planning and Control Systems: A Framework for Analysis* (Boston: Harvard Business School, Division of Research, 1965).
4. H. Thomas Johnson, *Relevance Regained: From Top-Down Control to Bottom-Up Empowerment* (New York: Free Press, 1992).
5. H. Thomas Johnson and Robert S. Kaplan, *Relevance Lost: The Rise and Fall of Management Accounting* (Boston, Mass.: Harvard Business School Press, 1987).
6. Ibid., pp. vii and viii.
7. For more on how these four fit with the self-adjustment notion, see Richard J. Schonberger, "Economy of Control," *Journal of Quality Management* 6, no. 1 (1999): 10–18.
8. Ludwig von Bertalanffy, *General System Theory: Foundations, Development, Applications* (New York: George Braziller, 1968).
9. Gwendolyn Galsworth, *Visual Systems: Harnessing the Power of a Visual Workplace* (New York: AMACOM, 1997), p. 14. See, also, Michel Greif, *The Visual*

Factory: Building Participation Through Shared Information (Portland, Ore.: Productivity Press, Inc., 1991); originally published as *L'Usine S'Affiche* (Paris: Les Editions d'Organisation, 1989).

10. Marion Harmon, "Solectron Continues to Win with the Baldrige," *Quality Digest,* November 1996, pp. 46–48.

11. Information provided by World Class International, Denmead, Hampshire, U.K., about 1995.

12. David Rocks, "Reinventing Herman Miller," *Business Week E.Biz,* April 3, 2000, pp. EB 88–EB 96.

13. Personal visit, May 1998.

14. Robert S. Kaplan and David P. Norton, "The Balanced Scorecard—Measures That Drive Performance," *Harvard Business Review* (January–February 1992).

15. Russell L. Ackoff, *Re-creating the Corporation: A Design of Organizations for the 21st Century* (New York: Oxford University Press, 1999), p. 10.

16. The newsletter, called *TPM,* is published four times yearly by the Japan Institute of Plant Maintenance, Shuwa Shiba-koen 3-Chome Bldg. 5F, 3–1–38, Shiba-koen, Minato-ku, Tokyo 105–0011, Japan.

17. Gary S. Vasilash, "Continental Teves Morgantown: Where Rhetoric Is Meeting Reality," *Automotive Manufacturing & Production,* July 2000, pp. 69–71.

18. John E. Ettlie, "Surfacing Quality at GE," *Automotive Manufacturing & Production,"* August 2000, p. 44.

19. Anaheim, Calif., May 11–12, 2000.

Chapter 8

1. Nancy L. Hyer and Karen A. Brown, "The Life Cycle Dynamics of Manufacturing Cells: Continuation, Drift and Dissolution," *Proceedings of Decision Sciences Institute Annual Meeting,* Orlando, November 2000.

2. Robert Townsend, *Up the Organization* (New York: Alfred A. Knopf, 1970).

3. Personal visit to H-P, Singapore, 1994. Townsend, op. cit., abolished not only the PR department, but also HR, turning over personnel responsibilities to line managers.

4. Robert Sobel, *The Rise and Fall of the Conglomerate Kings* (Briarcliff Manor, N.Y.: Stein and Day, 1984); see also Edward R. Bagley, *Beyond the Conglomerates* (New York: AMACOM, 1975), chapter 3, "The Swinging Conglomerates of the 1960s."

5. When stock markets get bent badly out of kilter, so that valuable companies are under-appreciated, corporate raiders (Carl Icahn, KKR, and others) lick their lips. This is when, to avoid being acquired/merged, leveraged buyouts occur. Commonly, a group of current executives borrows heavily to take the company private. If the firm really is in good shape, earnings will allow the debt to be paid down in a few years. Then it's the time to go public again, making those executives super rich so they can sail off to the South Pacific in newly acquired yachts.

6. Dover Corp., once recognized largely for its Dover Elevators business, no longer can be. Elevators was sold off to Thyssen Elevator in 1999.

7. Byeong-Ho Gong and Chung-Ho Kim, "The Chaebols: Myth and Reality," found in cfe.org/book/book08/09/, August 1, 2000.

8. Yuji Akaba, Florian Budde, and Jungkiu Choi, "A Cure for Sick Chaebol," *Asian Wall Street Journal,* November 19, 1998; found in mckinsey.com/articles/sick_chaebol.html, August 1, 2000.

9. Joshua Karliner, *The Corporate Planet: Ecology and Politics in the Age of Globalization* (San Francisco: Sierra Club Books, 1999); found in corpwatch.org/trac/feature/planet/japan_k.html.

10. Risaburo Nezu, "Carlos Ghosn: Cost Controller or Keiretsu Killer?" *OECD Observer,* April 28, 2000.

11. Michael Williams and Peter Landers, "When Keiretsu Lose Their Way, It's Time for a Name Change," *Wall Street Journal,* April 27, 2000, pp. A1, A12.

12. "Ratan Tata" in "Steel Intelligence Profiles," Steel Information Agency (steelprofiles.com, 1997).

13. Manjeet Kripalani, "Commentary: India: Paying Lip Service to Corporate Disclosure," *Business Week Online* (international edition), July 24, 2000.

14. "Grupo Carso, S.A. de C.V., Company Capsule," *Hoover's Online,* hoover.com, August 1, 2000; Geri Smith and Stephanie Anderson, "Slim's New World," *Business Week,* March 6, 2000, pp. 161–70.

15. James A. Michener, *Caribbean* (New York: Fawcett Books, 1989).

16. Timothy Aeppel, "Corning's Makeover: From Casseroles to Fiber Optics," *Wall Street Journal,* July 16, 1999, p. B4.

17. "Core Competencies—They're Never Obvious," in "MPA Inights, newsletter of Michael Paris Associates, 17, no. 9, September, 2000.

18. R. Nat Natarajan, "Fruit Flies, Kitty Litter, and Supply Chains," review of Charles H. Fine, *Clockspeed: Winning Industry Control in the Age of Temporary Advantage* (Reading, Mass.: Perseus Books, 1998), in *Production and Inventory Management Journal,* fourth quarter 1999, pp. 55–56.

19. K. Doerr, T. R. Mitchell, T. D. Klastorin, and K. A. Brown, "The Impact of Material Flow Policies and Goals on Job Outcomes," *Journal of Applied Psychology* 81, no. 2 (1996): 142–152.

20. John Buzacott, "Top Management and the Operations Function," From the President's Desk, *POM Chronicle* 9, no. 3 (1999): 3–4.

21. Paul D. Ericksen, "The Extended Enterprise: Aim for Mutual Gain and Competitive Advantage," *Target,* third quarter 2000, pp. 36–41.

22. Richard J. Schonberger, *Japanese Manufacturing Techniques: Nine Hidden Lessons in Simplicity* (New York: Free Press, 1982), p. 109.

23. "Working with Intel," an Intel advisory to its contractors, http://supplier.intel.com/construction/training/working1.htm, August 18, 2000.

24. Source of information for the Nypro and Exxon Chemical examples: personal communication with company executives, 1999.

25. Norihiko Shirouzu, "Honda Bucks Industry Wisdom, Aiming to Be Small and Efficient," *Wall Street Journal,* July 9, 1999, p. A12.

26. Much of the content of this box draws from Joel Millman's "The Outlook" column, "This Trade Deficit Was Made in the U.S.A.," *Wall Street Journal,* August 7, 2000, p. A1.

27. Charles Handy labels it "multidomestic" and points out its similarity to the federalist concept in politics: a large political entity made up of multiple small elements: *Beyond Certainty: The Changing Worlds of Organizations* (Boston: Harvard Business School Press, 1996), pp. 33–38.

28. Jonathan Friedland and Gary McWilliams, "How a Need for Speed Turned Guadalajara into a High-Tech Hub," *Wall Street Journal,* February 2, 2000, pp. A1, A6.

29. Ibid.

Chapter 9

1. Richard J. Schonberger, *Building a Chain of Customers: Linking Business Functions to Create the World Class Company* (New York: Free Press, 1990), pp. 40–41.

2. Charles B. Handy refers to both the family businesses that "form the backbone of the Italian economy . . . like the German mittelstand," both growing "rich by doing small things well": *Beyond Certainly: The Changing Worlds of Organizations* (Cambridge, Mass.: Harvard Business School Press, 1996), p. 142.

3. Patrick Waurzyniak, "Automotive Manufacturing's Technology Revolution," *Manufacturing Engineering,* August 1999, pp. 54–64.

4. These remarks about the Beaver facility are based on personal visits to the plant in 1990 and 1996.

5. A year later, I learned that the plant still has high turnover—but several percentage points less than the 13 percent monthly rate for the other plants in its area.

6. Robert B. Aronson, "Tailoring Cells to Customer Tastes," *Manufacturing Engineering,* January 2000, pp. 80–88.

7. Charles A. O'Reilly III and Jeffrey Pfeffer, *Hidden Value: How Great Companies Achieve Extraordinary Results with Ordinary People* (Boston: Harvard Business School Press, 2000), pp. 178–180.

8. Cited in "Workers on Working," *Industry Week,* August 21, 2000, p. 113–114.

9. Charles R. Walker and Robert H. Guest, *The Man on the Assembly Line* (Cambridge, Mass.: Harvard University Press, 1952).

10. Joseph B. White and Fara Warner, "Why Labor Unions Have Grown Reluctant to Use the 'S' Word," *Wall Street Journal,* pp. A1, A8.

11. Personal visit, December 2000.

12. "What They Say About TSS," a videotape (Greenville, S.C.: Americas 21st, Inc., 1998).

13. Richard J. Schonberger, *World Class Manufacturing Casebook: Implementing JIT and TQC* (New York: Free Press, 1987), pp. 165–172.

14. Timothy Aeppel, "Mounting Pressure: Under Glare of Recall, Tire Makers Are Giving New Technology a Spin," *Wall Street Journal,* March 23, 2001, pp. A1 and A8.
15. Takahiro Fujimoto, *The Evolution of a Manufacturing System at Toyota* (New York: Oxford University Press, 1999), pp. 229–235.
16. I had known about that practice of keeping people busy on unrelated tasks by my second trip to Japan in 1984, where I saw plentiful examples of it in a Nissan assembly plant.
17. Ann Therese Palmer, "Streamlining: Miller Brewing's Eden, N.C., Brewery," in "Special Report: Web Smart 50," *Business Week E.Biz,* September 18, 2000, p. EB 64.
18. Richard J. Schonberger, *World Class Manufacturing: The Next Decade: Building Power, Strength, and Value* (New York: Free Press, 1996), pp. 157, 181–182.
19. Roy L. Harmon and Leroy D. Peterson, *Reinventing the Factory: Productivity Breakthroughs in Manufacturing Today* (New York: Free Press, 1990).

Chapter 10

1. R. Nat Natarajan, "Fruit Flies, Kitty Litter, and Supply Chains," book review of Charles H. Fine, *Clockspeed: Winning Industry Control in the Age of Temporary Advantage* (Reading, Mass.: Perseus Books, 1998).
2. Dave Nelson, Rick Mayo, and Patricia E. Moody, *Powered by Honda: Developing Excellence in the Global Enterprise* (New York: Wiley, 1998).
3. The stated reason for this complex kanban method was to "fool the ERP" system.
4. Robert W. Hall, "Long Road to Shingo Prize," *Target,* fourth quarter 2000, pp. 22–27.
5. My first visit to R. W. Lyall was on December 6, 2000.
6. James P. Womack, Daniel T. Jones, and Daniel Roos, *The Machine That Changed the World* (New York: Rawson Associates, 1991).
7. William Kimberley, "Building the X-Type Infrastructure," *Automotive Manufacturing and Production,* April, 2001, pp. 26–29.
8. In the same vein, a common viewpoint has it that if each company has the same strategy, there is no advantage; Gary Hamel even sees it as mutual disadvantage ("Strategy convergence is hell on margins," Hamel, "Edison's Curse," *Fortune,* March 5, 2001, pp. 175–176); this ignores wide differences in ability to execute strategy.
9. Marvin B. Lieberman and Rajeev Dhawan, "Assessing the Resource Base of U.S. and Japanese Auto Producers: A Stochastic Frontier Production Function Approach," unpublished paper, UCLA, August 4, 1999.
10. B. Johnson and K. Thompson, "Can Cellular Manufacturing and ERP Live Together in Peace?," *Proceedings, The Best of North America: Third Annual Becoming Lean Conference,* Productivity, Inc., Chicago, November 4–5, 1998, pp. 115–127.

11. Cited in R. D. Ireland and M. A. Hitt, "Achieving and Maintaining Strategic Competitiveness in the 21st Century: The Role of Strategic Leadership," *Academy of Management Executive* 13, no. 1 (1999): 43–57.

12. James B. Swartz, *The Hunters and the Hunted: A Non-Linear Solution for Reengineering the Workplace* (Portland: Productivity Press, 1994), p. 27.

13. Steven Spear and H. Kent Bowen, "Decoding the DNA of the Toyota Production System," *Harvard Business Review* (September–October, 1999): 97–106.

14. Takahiro Fujimoto, *The Evolution of a Manufacturing System at Toyota* (New York: Oxford University Press, 1999).

15. William F. Roth and Marjorie Potts, pp. 63–66. The authors cite and analyze, using a systems approach framework, eight common top-down missteps leading to failure to generate empowerment.

Chapter 11

1. Gary S. Vasilash, "Standardized Lean," *Automotive Manufacturing & Production*, February 2000, pp. 52–54.

2. Taiichi Ohno, *Toyota Production System: Beyond Large-Scale Production* (Portland, Ore.: Productivity Press, 1988); Shigeo Shingo, *Toyota Production System from Industrial Engineering Viewpoint* (Tokyo: Japan Management Association, 1981); Yasuhiro Monden, *Toyota Production System* (Norcross, Ga.: Industrial Engineering and Management Press, 1983); Kiyoshi Suzaki, *The New Manufacturing Challenge: Techniques for Continuous Improvement* (New York: Free Press, 1987).

3. Robert W. Hall, *Zero Inventories* (Burr Ridge, Ill.: Dow-Jones Irwin, 1983); Roy L. Harmon and LeRoy D. Peterson, *Reinventing the Factory: Productivity Breakthroughs in Manufacturing Today* (New York: Free Press, 1990); Richard J. Schonberger, *Japanese Manufacturing Techniques: Nine Hidden Lessons in Simplicity* (New York: Free Press, 1982).

4. A few examples: John Costanza, *Just-in-Time for Manufacturing Excellence: The Guide for Survival in World Class Manufacturing* (1987); Edward J. Hay, *The Just-in-Time Breakthrough: Implementing the New Manufacturing Basics* (New York: Wiley, 1988); Richard Lubben, *Just-in-Time Manufacturing* (New York: McGraw-Hill, 1988); Kenneth A. Wantuck, *Just-in-Time for America: A Common Sense Production Strategy* (Southfield, Mich.: KWI Media, 1989).

5. Examples: Shigeo Shingo, *A Revolution in Manufacturing: The SMED System* (Portland, Ore.: Productivity Press, 1985); Michel Greif, *The Visual Factory: Building Participation Through Shared Information* (Portland, Ore.: Productivity Press, 1989); A. Ansari and B. Modarress, *Just in Time Purchasing* (New York: Free Press, 1990); Gwendolyn D. Galsworth, *Visual Systems: Harnessing the Power of a Visual Workplace* (New York: Amacom, 1997).

6. James P. Womack, D. T. Jones, and D. Roos, *The Machine That Changed the World* (New York: R. A. Rawson Associates, 1990).

7. John H. Sheridan, "Growing with Lean," *Industry Week,* October 2, 2000, pp. 32–38.

8. These quotes and paraphrasing come from Peter Burrows, "Apple: Yes, Steve, You Fixed It. Congrats! Now What's Act Two?" *Business Week,* July 31, 2000, pp. 102–113.

9. Katrina Booker, "I Built This Company; I Can Save It," *Fortune,* April 30, 2001, pp. 94–102.

10. Vanessa R. France with Robert Green, "Kaizen at Fleetwood," *Quality Digest,* March 2000, pp. 24–28.

11. John Teresko, "Toyota's New Challenge," *Industry Week,* January 15, 2001, pp. 71–74.

12. Masaaki Imai, *Kaizen: The Key to Japan's Competitive Success* (New York: McGraw-Hill, 1986).

13. Anthony C. Laraia, Patricia E. Moody, and Robert W. Hall, *The Kaizen Blitz: Accelerating Breakthroughs in Productivity and Performance* (New York: Wiley, 1999).

14. Nancy Chase, "Six Sigma Black Belts Stamp Out Tough Quality Problems," *Quality Online,* August 1999; www.qualitymag.com/articles/1999/aug99/0899f3.html.

15. T. Murphy, "Close Enough to Perfect," *Ward's Auto World* 34, no. 8 (August 1998); cited in Kim M. Henderson and James R. Evans, "Successful Implementation of Six Sigma: Benchmarking General Electric Company," *Benchmarking—An International Journal* 7, no. 4 (2000): 260–281.

16. Kim M. Henderson and James R. Evans, "Successful Implementation of Six Sigma: Benchmarking General Electric Company," *Benchmarking—An International Journal* 7, no. 4 (2000): 260–281.

17. Pierre Theriault, *Work Simplification: An Analyst's Handbook* (Norcross, Ga.: Institute of Industrial Engineers, 1996); also, Allan H. Mogensen, Rosario Rausa, and Jim Deynes (eds.), *Mogy—An Autobiography: Father of Work Simplification* (Idea Associates, 1990).

18. Lea A. P. Tonkin, "Waste-Zapping Ways at ESCO Corporation, Portland, OR," *Target,* first quarter 2000, pp. 46–50.

Chapter 12

1. One of their publications: Geoffrey Boothroyd and Peter Dewhurst, *Product Design for Assembly* (Wakefield, R.I.: Boothroyd Dewhurst, Inc., 1987).

2. SAVE originally stood for Society of American Value Engineering.

3. See, especially, Il-Woon Kim, Shahid Ansari, Jan E. Bell, and Dan Swenson, "Target Costing: Lessons from Japan," *International Journal of Strategic Cost Management* (Autumn 1999): 3–11. This article reports on recent studies of target costing in five Japanese companies. The authors found target costing usually housed in purchasing, but drawing team members from throughout the com-

pany, commonly for seven-year stints before they return to their own departments.

4. David Rocks, "Streamlining: Dell's Second Web Revolution," in "Special Report: Web Smart 50," *Business Week E.Biz,* September 18, 2000, pp. EB 62–63.

5. Robert W. Hall, "Distributed Excellence and the Dell Model," *Target,* second quarter 2000, pp. 6–11.

6. Personal communication; also see "How Don Bibeault Uses the Old 80/20 Formula in Business Turnarounds; You Can, Too," *Bottom Line Business,* May 1998.

7. Robert W. Hall, "Long Road to Shingo Prize," *Target,* fourth quarter 2000, pp. 22–27.

8. Anthony J. D'Alessandro and Alok Baveja, "Divide and Conquer: Rohm and Haas' Response to a Changing Specialty Chemicals Market," *Interfaces* 30, no. 6 (November–December 2000): 1–16.

9. Robert W. Hall, "The Rise of Electronic Manufacturing Services," *Target,* fourth quarter 2000, pp. 8–14.

10. Takahiro Fujimoto, *The Evolution of a Manufacturing System at Toyota* (New York: Oxford University Press, 1999), pp. 129–172. Fujimoto traces the development of the black-box supplier system in the Japanese auto industry and its later growing adoption by U.S. automakers. I believe the practice was well established in the defense industry in the United States, perhaps before its development at Toyota and other Japanese automakers. (Ironically, the idea of treating suppliers as a black box has also had negative connotations in purchasing circles: treating suppliers as a black box was thought to be a failure of the buyer to get to know the suppliers.)

11. Geoffrey A. Moore, *Living on the Fault Line* (New York: HarperCollins, 2000), p. 7. While quoting from this book, I am not recommending it, because it is devoid of references. How can the reader trust what is written without information as to sources?

12. Chris Malburg refers to this partial outsourcing as "tapered integration": "Vertical Integration," *Industry Week,* December 11, 2000, p. 17.

13. Frederick H. Abernathy, John T. Dunlop, Janice Hammond, and David Weil, *A Stitch in Time: Lean Retailing and the Transformation of Manufacturing: Lessons from the Apparel and Textile Industries* (Oxford, U.K.: Oxford University Press, 1999), pp. 110–113.

14. G. W. Plossl and O. W. Wight, *Production & Inventory Control* (Englewood Cliffs, N.J.: Prentice-Hall, 1967), p. 192.

15. Stephen A. Ruffa and Michael J. Perozziello, *Breaking the Cost Barrier: A Proven Approach to Managing and Implementing Lean Manufacturing* (New York: Wiley, 2000), pp. 50–51 and 156–157.

16. Benetton had achieved its own measure of fame ten years earlier with a somewhat similar strategy that Zara has been able to improve upon. The Benetton system is briefly described in Richard J. Schonberger, *Building a Chain of Cus-*

tomers: Linking Business Functions to Create the World Class Company (New York: Free Press, 1990), p. 149.

17. Modularity is generally taken to mean modular products. A modular *process* has been described as one "that can be broken down into subprocesses that can be performed concurrently or in different sequential order": Alexander O. Brown, Hau L. Lee, and Raja Petrakian, "Xilinx Improves Its Semiconductor Supply Chain Using Product and Process Postponement," *Interfaces* 30, no. 4 (July–August 2000): 65–80.

18. Hau L. Lee, V. Padmanabhan, and S. Whang, "The Bullwhip Effect in Supply Chains," *Sloan Management Review* 38, no. 3 (1997): 93–102.

19. The cited finding is on p. 40 of Jill Jusko, "Manufacturers Measure Up," *Industry Week,* December 11, 2000, pp. 23–43. Caution: As in any survey, there is the chance in this one that those responding are the eager beavers and that the non-participants are the laggards.

20. Robert W. Hall, "Distributed Excellence and the Dell Model," *Target,* second quarter 2000, pp. 6–11.

21. Richard J. Schonberger, *World Class Manufacturing: The Next Decade: Building Power, Strength, and Value* (New York: Free Press, 1996), pp. 147–150.

22. Philip E. Quigley, "Unblocking Bottlenecks," *APICS—The Performance Advantage,* November 2000, p. 68.

23. Scott Bliven and Louis W. Joy III, "Frontline Team Building & Bottleneck Management," *APICS—The Performance Advantage,* October 1997, pp. 58–62.

24. Patricia E. Moody and Richard E. Morley, *The Technology Machine: How Manufacturing Will Work in the Year 2020* (New York: Free Press, 1999), pp. 131–134.

25. Personal plant visit, September 25, 1990.

26. Other purposes of ABM, among best-practice companies, according to survey research by the American Productivity & Quality Center's International Benchmarking Clearinghouse, include profitability analysis, cost reduction, and product costing—the latter being the most popular use: Dan Swenson, "Best Practices in Activity-Based Management," *Journal of Cost Management* (November–December 1997): 6–14.

Chapter 13

1. Cited in "Making the Case for Supply Chain Management—It's High Time to Buy In," *APICS—The Performance Advantage,* February 2001, pp. 10–11. See also Kevin Hendricks and Vinod R. Singhal, "Report on Supply Chain Glitches and Shareholder Value Destruction," unpublished, December 2000.

2. Manufacturers that tried to become e-retailers include Rubbermaid, DeVilbiss, and Levi Strauss. Pressure from the likes of Home Depot and Wal-Mart ended their experiments: Doug Bartholomew, "E-Commerce Bullies," *Industry Week,* September 4, 2000, pp. 48–52.

3. Kenneth E. Kendall, "Ecommerce: Thou Shall Not Steal," *Decision Line*, July 2000, pp. 12–14.

4. Philip Evans and Thomas S. Wurster, *Blown to Bits: How the New Economics of Information Transforms Strategy* (Boston, Mass.: Harvard Business School Press, 2000), see ch. 3, "Richness and Reach," pp. 23–38.

5. Ibid., pp. 52–54.

6. Mike France and Joann Muller, "A Site for Soreheads," *Business Week*, April 12, 1999, pp. 86–90.

7. "Time to Hate the Donuts," *Harper's*, November 1999, pp. 150–151.

8. Thomas E. Weber, "Can Your Complaints, Adroitly Repackaged, Build a Web Business?" *Wall Street Journal*, January 10, 2000, p. B1.

9. Russell L. Ackoff, *Re-creating the Corporation: A Design of Organizations for the 21st Century* (New York: Oxford University Press, 1999), pp. 148–149.

10. Frederick H. Abernathy, John T. Dunlop, Janice Hammond, and David Weil, *A Stitch in Time: Lean Retailing and the Transformation of Manufacturing: Lessons from the Apparel and Textile Industries* (Oxford, U.K.: Oxford University Press, 1999), p. 58.

11. John A. Byrne, "Management by Web," part of a cover story entitled "The 21st Century Corporation," in *Business Week*, August 28, 2000, pp. 84–96.

12. Grocers were first to implement bar coding, but for cutting cashiering costs. Years later, the department store–apparel-textile sector was the innovator in using bar coding for the much more useful purpose: synchronizing the value chain: Abernathy et. al, op cit., pp. 58–61. The same authors note that Wal-Mart was active in using daily sales data for internal synchronization in the late 1970s; its pioneering external linkage—to Procter & Gamble—began in 1987, pp. 49–51.

13. Abernathy, et al., op. cit., pp. 68–70.

14. Personal on-site visit and interview, July 1997. Also see Rhonda L. Rundle, "Doctor's Orders: Hospital Cost Cutters Push Use of Scanners to Track Inventories," *Wall Street Journal*, June 10, 1997, pp. A1 & A8.

15. "Clinton-Gore Administration Announces New Actions to Improve Patient Safety and Assure Health Care Quality: Goal to Reduce Preventable Medical Errors by 50 Percent Within Five Years" (whitehouse.gov/WH/New/html/ 20000222_1. html), February 22, 2000.

16. Jeff Hansel, "Technology Is Being Used to Fight a Shortage of Pharmacists," *Bismarck Tribune*, January 6, 2000, p. C1.

17. Sameer Kumar and Charu Chandra, "A Healthy Change," *IIE Solutions*, March 2001, pp. 28–33.

18. "History Lessons," in "Letters," *Industry Week*, October 4, 1999, p. 6.

19. "Lockheed Tour Educates on Lean Principles," *IIE Solutions*, December, 2000, p. 51.

20. Internet, consumers.gov.uk/actt/casestudies/casestu2.htm, as of December 26, 2000.

21. Darrel Vande Hoef, "Finite Forward Scheduling: Magic or Myth?" *APICS—The Performance Advantage*, October 2000, pp. 57–59.

Appendix 3

1. Russell L. Ackoff, *Re-creating the Corporation: A Design of Organizations for the 21st Century* (New York: Oxford University Press, 1999), p. 35.
2. "Best Practice Benchmarking Report: Access and Intelligence for Achieving World-Class Excellence," Chapel Hill, N.C.: Best Practices, LLC, (no date; received Janurary 2001), chapter 5, "Rewards & Recognition."

RICHARD J. SCHONBERGER, PH.D.

Richard Schonberger is president of Schonberger & Associates, Inc., providing seminars and advisory services to industrial and service organizations worldwide (since 1981, involving over three hundred clients), and affiliate professor at the University of Washington. Best known as the originator of the term and concepts of "world-class manufacturing," Richard is author of over one hundred articles and papers and the following books: *World Class Manufacturing: The Next Decade: Building Power, Strength, and Value* (1996) in seven languages, six printings—recipient of the 1998 Shingo Prize for manufacturing research; *SynchroService* (1994, with Edward M. Knod Jr.); *Building a Chain of Customers* (1990) in five languages; *World Class Manufacturing Casebook* (1987); *World Class Manufacturing: The Lessons of Simplicity Applied* (1986) in eight languages, twenty printings; *Japanese Manufacturing Techniques: Nine Hidden Lessons in Simplicity* (1982) in nine languages, twenty-five printings; and a textbook, *Operations Management: Meeting Customers' Demands,* 7th ed. (2001, with Edward M. Knod Jr.). The Schonberger video program *World Class Manufacturing,* acclaimed by *Quality Digest,* is available as a twelve-tape set.

Dr. Schonberger's career includes eight years as a practicing industrial engineer, followed by a period as a full-time university professor, during which he was appointed George Cook Distinguished Professor at the University of Nebraska. He was named 1996 Puget Sound Engineer of the Year; was inducted into the 1995 Academy of the Shingo Prize for Excellence in Manufacturing; was awarded the British Institution of Production Engineers' 1990 International Award for "Outstanding Contribution to the Advancement of Manufacturing Management"; and received the Institute of Industrial Engineers' 1988 Production and Inventory Control Award.

Schonberger is consulting editor for *Benchmarking for Quality and Technology Management* and is on the editorial boards of the *Journal of Cost Management, Journal of Operations Management, Production and Inventory Management, Journal of Quality Management, International Journal of Strategic Cost Management,* and *Target.* Currently he is directing a "World Class *by* Principles" International Benchmarking study.

177 107th Ave. N.E., #2101, Bellevue, WA 98004
Tel/fax: 425-467-1143
E-mail: sainc17@qwest.net
Web site: http://www.wcm-wcp.com